What others a

A Wind in the

D0484804

This is the most important and exciting book on the world of Islam that I have ever read!

Dr. Sasan Tavassoli
Pars Theological Centre

David Garrison's herculean research throughout the vast mélange of the Muslim world moves us to give thanks for the advance of the gospel and to pray that the Lord will so mature these movements that the world will believe the Father has truly sent his Son to be its Savior and Lord.

Dr. Don McCurry, President, Ministries to Muslims
Founder of the Zwemer Institute for Muslim Studies

The word "unprecedented" hardly begins to express the historic events now taking place in the Muslim world. Until recently, Muslims came to Christian faith one person at a time. But since 2000, Muslims have begun coming to Christ in movements. David Garrison's superb book gives hope to the next generation of Christian missionaries that their work in the harvest field will not be in vain.

Dr. Robert A. Blincoe
US Director, Frontiers

David Garrison's research in *A Wind in the House of Islam* documents God's amazing providence in fulfillment of His mission, and encourages Christians to press forward in engaging all peoples to the ends of the earth.

Dr. Jerry Rankin, President Emeritus
International Mission Board, SBC

If you have a heart for Muslims, *A Wind in the House of Islam* will inspire you! If you don't have a heart for Muslims, read this book and God will give you a heart transplant. He is moving among Muslims like never before. David Garrison, thank you for this brilliant work.

Tom Doyle
Author of *Dreams and Visions—Is Jesus Awakening the Muslim World?*

Eugene Peterson in *The Message* uniquely paraphrases Revelation 2:9; "Are your ears awake? Listen. Listen to the Wind's Words, the Spirit blowing through the churches..." David Garrison's powerful and scholarly work *A Wind in the House of Islam* is truly a masterful and timely volume destined to awaken our ears to the impact of Jesus Christ among Muslims in our generation.

Dr. Dick Eastman, International President
Every Home for Christ International

Perfect timing for *A Wind in the House of Islam*! Garrison tells the real story through first-hand interviews and researched case studies. Long-awaited and well worth it!

Dr. Michael Barnett, Dean
College of Inter-Cultural Studies
Columbia International University

This book is a must read for anyone launching into ministry among Muslims. Besides the obvious up-to-date status of Muslim movements to Christ along with compelling stories, great value is found in the historical background information that Garrison gives when describing each "room." As a former missionary to the "Indo-Malaysia Room," it reminded me of the historical roots and context of Islam in that part of the world in which Christianity is now bearing fruit.

Dr. Marvin Newell
Senior Vice President
Missio Nexus

This book should be read by all those who wish to stay current with the progress of church-planting movements in the nine main regions of the Muslim world. It is thrilling to read the stories of God's work in bringing Muslims out of darkness into the light and true faith found only in Jesus Christ.

Dr. Nabeel T. Jabbour
Professor and Author of *The Crescent Through The Eyes of The Cross*

The publication of this book marks a major turning point in mission history. Every believer should read the inspiring stories of brothers and sisters courageously and joyously coming to faith. Let's pray this is just a beginning.

Dr. Don Dent
Director, Kim School of Global Missions
Golden Gate Baptist Theological Seminary

This book is the most comprehensive analysis of Muslim movements to Christ that has ever been done. By showing the various contexts and forms of their development Garrison avoids a common practice of describing how God should work based on an inadequate sample rather than how God is working in all of its variety. May the divine Wind that is blowing through the House of Islam guide many to serve more relevantly among Muslims today as a result.

Dr. Dr. Dudley Woodberry
Dean Emeritus and Senior Professor of Islamic Studies
School of Intercultural Studies
Fuller Theological Seminary

David Garrison has done it again! *Church Planting Movements* bent many paradigms we had at the beginning of this century regarding what we could expect the Lord of the Harvest to do. And I am confident that *A Wind in the House of Islam* is going to expand vision, and elevate faith within a new generation of Christ Followers!

Jerry Trousdale
Cityteam Ministries
Author of *Miraculous Movements*

I was recently on a plane trip with my wife and saw that as a good opportunity to read *A Wind in the House of Islam*. About every fifteen minutes, over the next six hours, I leaned over, touched my wife on the arm and told her, "This is a great book. David has written a really great book."

Dr. Charles Fielding, MD
Author of *Preach and Heal*

In a world awash with contradictory and unsubstantiated claims, *A Wind in the House of Islam* is a clear voice. More than just dry numbers, Garrison, with the help of others worldwide, presents compelling testimonies from various national movements of new followers of Jesus Christ that bring joy to the heart and tears to the eyes. What God is doing today is unprecedented, and this book catches a glimpse of His great work never before seen in history. Lessons drawn from across the world will challenge each reader how to move with God's wind. You will not be disappointed.

Charles Hermelink
Cultural Ministries Coordinator
Pentecostal Assemblies of Canada

A Wind in the House of Islam

A wind in the house of Islam

How God is drawing Muslims
around the world
to faith in Jesus Christ

David Garrison

WIGTake
What's It Gonna Take? Resources

WIGTake Resources
P.O. Box 1884, Monument, CO 80132
www.churchplantingmovements.com/bookstore
Product Distribution: NoHutch@wigtake.org

© 2014 by WIGTake Resources

All rights reserved. No part of this publication may be reproduced in any form without the prior written permission of the author, except in the case of brief quotations for review or critical articles.

First printing, January 2014
Second printing, April 2014
Third printing, UK Edition, March 2015
Fourth printing, May 2015
Fifth printing, June 2016

Hardcover ISBN: 978-1-939124-04-3
Paperback ISBN: 978-1-939124-03-6

1. Missions. 2. Islam. 3. Evangelism.
Garrison, David, 1957 –

Unless indicated otherwise, all Scripture quotations in this publication are from the HOLY BIBLE, NEW INTERNATIONAL VERSION ® NIV ® Copyright © 1973, 1978, 1984 by International Bible Society. All rights reserved.

Scripture quotations from the King James Version are taken from *The Holy Bible, King James Version*. New York: American Bible Society, 1999.

Printed by Bookmasters
Cover Design by Mike Mirabella
Interior Design by Megan Chadwick
Copy Editors: Melody Raines, Carla Evans, Seneca Garrison
Maps created by Jim Courson
Author photo by Hal Lohmeyer Photography
Website design by Zippersnap.com www.WindintheHouse.org

Garrison, David
    A Wind in the House of Islam

contents

dedication

To Cyd,
who loved her Lord and the Muslim people
more than life itself.

For Cyd to live was Christ and to die was gain.

acknowledgments

It has been said, "If you want to go quickly, go alone. If you want to go far, go with others." My prayer is that this book will go far. Judging from its many collaborators and contributors, it just might have a chance. This book would not have been possible without the help of many, many gracious collaborators around the world. For security purposes, several of these individuals cannot be named; others are cited only with partial abbreviations. I will be forever grateful to those individuals who took the time to point me in the right direction, help me to see what God was doing, and corrected me when I misunderstood. As always, the errors in the book are mine. Acknowledgments do not constitute endorsements. Whatever is of value in the book is by the grace of God, and intended for the benefit of his kingdom around the world. I offer here my thanks to:

The International Mission Board, SBC

> Judith Bernicchi, John Brady, Jim Courson, Tom Elliff, Gordon Fort, Wilson and Natalie Geisler, Jim Haney, Scott Holste, Chuck Lawless, Steve McCord, Clyde Meador, Mike Mirabella, Minh Ha Nguyen, Scott Peterson, Joy Shoop, Jim Slack

Field Facilitators, by region

West Africa: Tim and Charlotte C., Duane F., Jim Haney, Shodankeh Johnson, Kris R., Jerry Trousdale, David Watson

North Africa: Matt B., Trevor B., George and Sheryl G., M.K., Dr. F.S., Dennis C., Hamid and Za. R.

Arab World: John B., Trey G., Chris M., Donald C., Tom and JoAnn D., Paul C.

East Africa: Steve S., Bruce W., Aychi, Shimeles, Jeff P., Steve S., John B., Tim and Charlotte C., John Becker, Joe D., James L., Chuck C., Alan F., B.J., Grant L., Jerry T., David W., Ben W.

Turkestan: Ali, Wes F., Steven G., Kolya, Bill S., Jim T.

Persian World: Andy B., Mark B., Gasem, Jon G., Kambez, Sarah K., Sepideh, David P., Scott P., Hormoz S., Jim S., Sasan T., David Y., Sam Y.

Western South Asia: J. and D. Br., Jon D., Hank, Herbert H., Kevin H., Todd L., Don McCurry, Jim T., Eric W.

Eastern South Asia: Dave C., Kevin G., Gary and Barbara H., Kevin H., Michael J., Todd L., Dwight M., Timothy M., Andrew N., Shannon, Stacy, Phil P., George T.

Indo-Malaysia: Don D., Todd E., Mike S., Steve S., R.W., Von W.

Advisors and Consultants

John Becker, John Brady, Curtis Sergeant, Don Dent, B. G., Todd Johnson, Bill Smith, Dudley Woodberry

Encouragers, Sounding Boards, Collaborators and Enablers

Don Aaker, Bruce Ashford, Mike and Cindy Barnett, John Becker, Megan Chadwick. Bill and Karma Duggin, Carla Evans, Paul Filidis, Bob Garrett, Steve and Nelly Greisen, Max Hatfield, Nora Hutchins, Chuck Lawless, Martin E. Marty, Jon Matas, Jay Muller, Rick and Kim Peters , Melody Raines, Herschel York

Family, who never stopped sacrificing, encouraging and supporting

> Sonia, Amanda, Marcus, Seneca, Jeremiah and Liz, Etheleen, Vernon and Patsy, Vickie and Garth, Linda and Tom, and Jeff who was always my greatest prayer warrior until his death in March 2013 ~ missed every day.

The wind blows wherever it pleases. You hear its sound,
but you cannot tell where it comes from or where it is going.
So it is with everyone born of the Spirit. John 3:8

PART 1:
the hinges of history

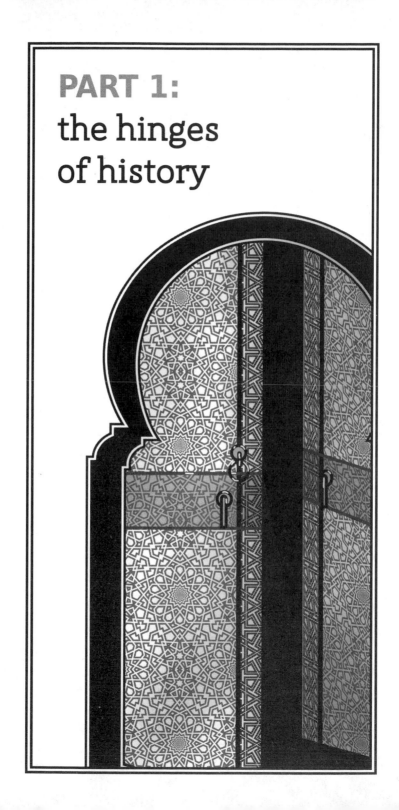

something is happening

 A WIND IS blowing through the House of Islam. The House of Islam, *Dar al-Islam* in Arabic, is the name Muslims give to an invisible religious empire that stretches from West Africa to the Indonesian archipelago, encompassing 49 nations and 1.6 billion Muslims.[1] Dwarfing the size of any previous earthly kingdom, Islam directs the spiritual affairs of nearly a quarter of the world's population. But something is happening today that is challenging the hold that Islam exercises over its adherents. Muslim movements to Jesus Christ are taking place in numbers we've never before seen.

For the sake of clarity and consistency, let's define a movement of Muslims to Christ to be at least 100 new church starts or 1,000 baptisms that occur over a two-decade period. Today, in more than 70 separate locations in 29 nations, new movements of Muslim-background followers of Christ are taking place. Each of these movements has crossed the threshold of at least 100 new church starts or 1,000 baptized believers, all of whom have come to Christ over the past two decades. In some countries the numbers within these new movements have grown to tens of thousands.

Though the total number of new Christ followers, between two and seven million, may be a statistically small drop in the vast sea of Islam, they are not insignificant. Not limited to a remote corner of the Muslim world, these new communities of faith are widespread, from West Africa's Sahel to the teeming islands of Indonesia—and everywhere in between.

The price these converts pay for their conversion has not diminished with the arrival of modern times. Qur'anic prescriptions remain unflinching: *"if they turn renegades, seize them and slay them wherever ye find them"* (Qur'an 4:89b). And these religious renegades are paying an incalculable price for their spiritual migration to Christ. Yet they continue to come. What began as a few scattered expressions of dissent is now growing more substantial. Historically unprecedented numbers of Muslim men and women are wading against the current of their societies to follow Jesus Christ. And it is only beginning.

To grasp the weight of this phenomenon, one must view it in light of the nearly fourteen-century backdrop of Islamic expansion and interaction with Christian populations. Within one century of the Prophet Muhammad's death in the year 632, his Arab warriors had defeated both Byzantine and Persian superpowers that had dominated the world, directly and through their predecessors, for more than a thousand years. Along the way, these Muslim conquerors subjected millions of Christians to Islamic governance.

Islam's advance did not stop until it reached the Pacific Ocean in the 13th century and breached the walls of Constantinople in 1453. In many respects the advance of Islam, though more subdued, continues to this day. But, following the example of its founder, the Christian faith does not die easily. Though conquered by Islamic armies, Christian populations lingered for centuries before persistent pressures and incentives to conversion eventually took their toll, relegating the Christian ancestry of millions to a distant memory.

The purpose of this review, though, is not the well-documented advance of Islam, but rather Christianity's re-emergence within the Muslim world. The Christian resurrection has been a long time coming.

Muslim Movements to Christ Through History

Though there were doubtless individual conversions among Muslims here and there over the years, the first three and a half centuries of Muslim-Christian interaction saw no community movements of Muslims toward the gospel. Only in the 10th century, nearly 350 years after the death of Muhammad, do we find the first historical evidence of any communities of Muslims converting to Christianity.

In the waning years of the Abbasid Caliphate, centered in modern-day Iraq, growing numbers of Arab and Seljuk emirs wrested themselves from Baghdad's control and forged their own lesser dynasties. In the year 972 and again in 975, the Byzantine emperor John Tzimisces seized territory on his southern border along with several cities in Syria and Palestine. It was during that window between rulers, that 12,000 Arab Muslim men, along with their wives and children, sought baptism from Byzantine Orthodox priests. The reason they gave for abandoning Islam was "the financial exactions of their Moslem rulers." The tax-relief-inspired movement occurred near the ancient city of Nisibis, on what is today the Turkish border with Syria. In the turbulent centuries that followed, however, these dubious gains and much more were lost to the expanding Turkish Muslim tribes of Anatolia.[2]

John Tzimisces

Twenty-first century research-ers may rightly challenge whether these 10th century tax converts were true believers or not. They do merit mention in this historical review, though, if only to illustrate how rare it was to find any sizable conversions from Islam. Apart from this incident, no additional movements to Christ appeared in the first 500 years of Islamic advance.

Crusades, Inquisitions and Other Failures

Though the Crusades (1096-1272) can be seen as Christian Europe's imitative response to centuries of Islamic *jihad*, these military forays proved counterproductive to the advance of the gospel. Christian minorities in lands dominated by Muslim governments actually showed a marked increase in conversion to Islam during these centuries, as their patriotic loyalties came into question in the face of European armies invading under the banner of the cross.[3]

One political exception to the crusading spirit of the times took place in the Sicilian kingdom of Roger II. Roger was a French Norman conqueror who, by 1130, had consolidated control over Sicily and southern Italy. Roger forged a Norman-Arab civilization at the crossroads of Byzantine, Arab, Greek, and his own Norman culture that developed into the most prosperous in the entire Mediterranean. Resisting the

Roger II

anti-Islamic conventions of the day, Roger's inclusive social experiment flourished for nearly a century as ideas, language and trade flowed between Muslims and Christians. There is no report of how many Muslims may have converted to the Christian faith during this century, but it deserves mention here as one of the few interludes in an otherwise violent exchange between the two great religions. The experiment ended in 1224 when Roger's grandson, Frederic II, expelled all Muslims from the realm.

The 13th century saw a new impulse of Christian outreach to Muslims, particularly in Spain where Islamic control was in retreat after half a millennium of domination. Well before the completion of the Catholic *Reconquista* of the Iberian Peninsula in 1492, European Christians were pressing their faith among the Muslim populace.

In 1219 the transcendent character Francis of Assisi (1181-1226) walked across the entrenched battle lines separating Crusader and Muslim armies near Damietta, Egypt. Francis aimed to evangelize—or attain martyrdom from—the Fatimid ruler and nephew of Saladin, Sultan al-Malik al-Kamil. Though Francis achieved neither conversion nor martyrdom, his concern for Muslim souls was transmitted to the fraternal order that followed him and bore his name.

Among his early Franciscan imitators was Englishman Roger Bacon (1214-1294), who bucked the political passions of his contemporaries to advocate the evangelization rather than the subjugation of Muslims. All that was required, Bacon insisted, was that they be "taught the Catholic doctrine in their mother tongue."[4] Flemish Franciscan William of Rubruck (1220-1293) set out in 1254 to do just that. Commissioned as a missionary to the Muslim Tatars of Constantinople, William overshot his target, eventually journeying 5,000 miles to the palace of Mongke Khan in Karakorum, Mongolia. Like their founder, Francis of Assisi, and despite their noble intent, neither Roger Bacon nor William of Rubruck saw much in the way of response among Muslims.

Francis of Assisi

One exception to the generally fruitless ministry of Franciscans among the Muslims, however, was the missionary work of Conrad of Ascoli (1234-1289).[5] Born to a noble family in Italy, Conrad's piety from childhood drew him to the Franciscan order. After a brief tenure preaching in Rome, Conrad obtained permission to go to Libya where his humble lifestyle, preaching of the gospel, and purported miracles are said to have resulted in the baptism of 6,400 Libyan converts.[6] Sometime later, Conrad's childhood friend, who grew up to become Pope Nicholas IV, recalled Conrad to Europe to intervene between warring Catholic monarchs in Spain and France. Conrad never returned to North Africa, choosing instead to remain in Paris where he became a lecturer in theology.

Sharing Francis of Assisi's zeal for Muslim souls was his contemporary, the Spaniard Dominic de Guzman. St. Dominic's Dominican Order, despite dedicating itself to preaching the gospel to the Saracens (as Muslims were anachronistically called), saw little fruit among Muslims. Neither founding saint could claim a single voluntary

St. Dominic

Muslim movement of at least a thousand converts to Christ (or
to Catholicism for that matter), though they did stimulate a more
spiritual and less violent approach to Islam.

In 1240, one of Dominic's successors, Raymond of Peñafort, resigned his post as the third master general of the Dominican Order to spend his final three decades mobilizing the
Church in Spain for missions to Muslims. Raymond inaugu-
rated schools of Arabic in Barcelona and Tunis, Tunisia, and
persuaded his friend and fellow Dominican, Thomas Aquinas,

to write the *Summa Contra Gentiles* as an apol-
ogetic response to both Muslims and Jews.[7]
These resources for communicating the
Catholic faith, coupled with the breaking of
Islamic domination in Spain contributed to
the re-Christianization of Iberia in the subsequent centuries. Unfortunately, Raymond
also employed the brutal Inquisition as a
tool to force conversions and ferret out her-
esies among the Spanish Muslim and Jewish populations, throwing into question the
depth and integrity of these conversions.[8]

Raymond of
Peñafort

On the eastern side of the Mediterranean, another
Dominican, William of Tripoli (ca. 1220–1275), born and raised
in the last Crusader outpost of what is modern-day Lebanon,
purported to have "baptized over a thousand Muslims"[9] or to
have at least seen "many Muslim converts come to faith."[10]

William is a curious fellow, perhaps best known to posterity
as one of the two missionaries sent by Pope Gregory X in 1271
on an ill-fated journey with Marco and Maffeo Polo to the
Mongol court of Kublai Khan. Illness curtailed William's trip
after going only as far as Armenia in eastern Turkey.

For our purposes, though, William may be more significant
for his success in reaching Muslims of the Levant "without
benefit of arms or philosophical argument."[11] William credited
his success to his studies of Islamic culture and language.
Given that William's very presence in the Levant was the result
of a century-long military crusade into the region, history may
rightly dismiss his claims of being "without benefit of arms."It

is unclear how many Muslims actually responded to William's appeal. With the collapse of this last Latin outpost in the Middle East in 1291, less than two decades after William's death, it is clear that none of his fruit survived.

One of the most heroic missionaries to the Muslim world was the Catalonian mystic, Ramon Llull. A master of Arabic and student of Islam, Llull rejected the Crusader paradigm to make three missionary journeys to Algeria and Tunisia before finally gaining the martyrdom he desired in the Algerian coastal town of Bougeia around 1315. Llull, like his Franciscan and Dominican contemporaries, was exceptional for eschewing violence and pursuing a reasoned Arabic-language witness to Muslims. Nonetheless, like his Franciscan and Dominican contemporaries, Llull reported very few converts to the Christian faith.[12]

Though it did not take place right away, the renewed zeal for reaching Muslims was not entirely without consequence. After the 1492 reconquest of Grenada, the last Muslim stronghold in Spain, the Catholic Archbishop, Hernando de Talavera, exhorted the clergy under his authority to reach out to the Muslims in their parish. He urged them to learn Arabic and use tact and persuasion to convert Muslims, respecting their rights to retain their religion, property and laws. Partly as a result, during the decade between 1490 and 1500, "thousands of Moslems were baptized."[13] It is difficult to assess the voluntary motivation for these baptisms, though, in light of the impending Inquisition that always loomed as an incentive to conversion. By 1610, all remaining Muslims, including the *Moriscos* or crypto-Muslims of Spain, were expelled from the Iberian Peninsula.[14]

By the 16th and 17th centuries, the Protestant Reformation and Catholic Counter Reformation were churning

Ramon Llull

through Western Europe distracting attention from the collapse of Greek and Middle Eastern Christianity in the East in the face of a swelling Turkish Ottoman empire. Western Christians turned their attention overseas to colonial adventures in the

Americas, Africa and Asia, trading conflict with Muslims for easier gains among non-Muslim populations.

As the first millennium of Christian-Muslim interaction drew to a close, millions of Christians had been assimilated into the House of Islam, while scarcely a single uncoerced Muslim movement to Christ had taken place.

The Colonial Era

The 16th and 17th centuries launched the age of Western colonial expansion with Spanish and Portuguese trade and conquests in Africa, Asia and the Americas. Dutch, French and English traders raced to catch up in the 18th and 19th centuries. Though European colonization went hand-in-hand with the missionary enterprise in most of the non-Western world, the same could not be said of the colonizers' encounters with Islam.

European traders typically took one of two approaches in relation to the Muslim populations they encountered. If the ports were controlled by Muslim sultans, the Europeans conspired with local non-Muslim factions to divide and conquer to gain an advantage. If the foreign lands contained insurmountable Muslim populations, the Europeans took a more accommodating approach, suppressing missionary efforts so as not to enrage local sensibilities.

By the close of the colonial era, Catholic missions historian Joseph Schmidlin had to admit, "Taken as a whole, the Moslem world with its two hundred million worshipers of Allah, has up to the present hour held aloof from both Catholic and Protestant Christianity, despite valiant efforts of individual missionaries."[15]

Schmidlin went on to lament,

> ...the Crescent in Asia and Africa has even pressed forward to such an extent as to have become the most powerful rival of the Christian missions. Nevertheless, one must not for this reason declare that the Moslem is absolutely unsusceptible to conversion or incapable of receiving the Gospel, since Christian communities were actually formed from among them, even during the nineteenth century—at least by the Protestants in the Dutch East Indies, and in isolated cases as the result of Catholic efforts in Kabylia (Algeria)—and have continued ever since.[16]

The two exceptions that Schmidlin highlights, the Dutch East Indies (modern-day Indonesia) and Kabylia (a Berber region of Algeria), bear closer scrutiny as two rare examples of Muslim movements to Christ in the great age of Western colonial and missionary expansion.

In the centuries following their 1605 arrival in the East Indies, Dutch armies extended control over most of the independent Muslim sultanates of what would become Indonesia. As had occurred in other European conquests, the Dutch pattern of colonization avoided conflict with the Muslim populations. Of the 245 missionaries who soon arrived in Indonesia, most were sent to evangelize the outer islands where Islam had not yet become established; only a few were sent to Java, and their task was to minister to anyone except Muslims.[17]

For their part, Indonesians generally found the austere Dutch Calvinism unappealing, while Muslim nationalists pointed to its foreignness as a reason to embrace Islam and resist the West. By 1914, Abraham Kuyper, the most influential Dutch Reformed Church leader in Holland, suggested that with only 1,614 converts including women and children, perhaps it was time for the mission to exit Java due to its lack of response.[18]

Though European churchmen were mired in frustration, Eurasian and Indonesian lay evangelists were making progress as they employed a more indigenous gospel witness. A local Javanese evangelist named Radin Abas Sadrach Surapranata (c. 1835-1924) built on the approach of earlier Euro-Indonesian evangelists to greatly expand the response to the gospel. For this he is remembered by Indonesian Christians as "Sadrach: The Apostle of Java." Sadrach used the newly published Javanese Bible translation and aggressive apologetics to engage Muslim leaders in debate. He then gathered converts into contextualized, indigenous *mesjids* (communities) of Javanese Christian believers called *Kristen Jawa*, rather than extracting them into the local Dutch Christian churches.

At the time of Sadrach's death in 1924, between 10 and 20 thousand Javanese Christians could be traced to the Apostle of Java's ministry.[19] Though they represented only a fraction of the world's most populous Islamic country, these *Kristen Jawa* marked a historic breakthrough, as the first uncoerced

Muslim movement to Christ in nearly 13 centuries of Christian witness to the Muslim world.

On the other side of the *Dar al-Islam,* another experiment in ministry to Muslims was counting some success. In 1830, Algeria came under French control and was ruled as an integral part of France until its independence in 1962. Yet it was not until 1868, following a devastating famine that left many Arab and Berber orphans, that the Catholic church began actively witnessing to its Algerian Muslim citizens.

Charles Martial Lavigerie (1825-1892) arrived as the archbishop of the See of Algiers in 1868 and soon began gathering famine orphans into villages for ministry. Fearing popular unrest, the governor-general of Algeria, Marshal McMahon, forbade proselytizing Muslims. Lavigerie complied, ordering his priests to refrain from baptizing any of the non-Christians among whom they ministered.

Charles Lavigerie

In 1874, Lavigerie took an important step in removing barriers to Muslim reception of the gospel when he founded the *Société des missionnaires d'Afrique* (Society of missionaries of Africa), popularly known as the *Pères Blancs* or White Fathers, after the white Arab cassock and woolen scarf they adopted. The White Fathers learned Arabic and embraced many of the customs of the Muslim peoples among whom they served in hopes of easing the way for gospel transmission.

Nonetheless, the first baptisms did not take place until 1887, when three Kabyle Berber boys who were visiting Rome for the jubilee of Pope Leo XIII "tearfully implored baptism and received it."[20] That same year, Lavigerie allowed, for the first time, religious instruction, but only if the local community was in agreement.

The Kabyle Berbers proved to be the most responsive of North Africa's Muslim peoples, but they hardly exhibited what could be called a movement to Christ. Many Islamic, Catholic, and French obstacles stood in their path, not the least being the burden of Algerian subjection to the foreign, culturally Christian, French occupation force. As a result, as late as 1930 one could count no more than 700 baptized Catholic converts among the Kabyle.[21]

The latter decades of the 19th century saw the arrival of numerous Protestant missionaries into North Africa. Despite the heroism of the many who labored there, history records accurately and succinctly, "not many converts were won."[22]

A third movement of Muslims to Christ escaped the attention of both Catholic and Protestant missions historians. In 1892, an Ethiopian Muslim known as Shaikh Zakaryas (1845-1920), from a village northwest of Lake Tana, began having disturbing dreams that prompted him to obtain a Bible from Swedish missionaries in Asmara, in what is now Eritrea. Initially Zakaryas tried using his new biblical insights to preach Islamic reform, but fierce opposition from Islamic leaders pushed him out of the Muslim community, and in 1896, Zakaryas began his ministry as a Christian.

Zakaryas was not baptized, however, until 1910, by which time he had already led 75 influential Muslim clerics to faith. By the time of his death in 1920, Zakaryas's baptized Muslim followers numbered 7,000. In the decades following his death, these Muslim-background believers, called *Adadis Krestiyan* (New Christians) assimilated variously into the Ethiopian Orthodox and Seventh Day Adventist churches.[23]

Though missions historians hailed the 19th century as "The Great Century" of Christian expansion around the world, the century closed with only two Muslim movements to Christ, comprising at least 1,000 baptized converts, and these only occurred nearly 13 centuries after the death of the Prophet Muhammad. It was 65 years into the 20th century before the next Muslim movement to Christ appeared, and this one took place under great duress.[24]

Twentieth Century Breakthroughs

In the year 1965, Indonesia had one of the largest Communist parties in the world. In September of that year, an aborted

Communist coup triggered a bloodletting that did not stop until more than half a million Indonesians were dead. Anyone suspected of Communist or atheist leanings was imprisoned, executed or massacred.[25] Indonesia's New Order government that rose to power in the wake of the violence abolished Communism and atheism in one fell swoop, demanding that every Indonesian citizen adhere to one of the nation's five historic religions: Islam, Protestantism, Catholicism, Hinduism or Buddhism. In the scramble that followed, two million Indonesians, some of whom had come from at least a culturally Muslim background, entered the nation's Protestant and Catholic churches.[26]

Though it would be difficult to see this as a purely voluntary turning of Muslims to Christ, it did result in many individuals later receiving Christian instruction and coming to faith who might otherwise have not.

Further Muslim movements to Christ in various corners of the Muslim world did not appear until the 1980s. Young Christians in the West, invigorated by the 1970s Jesus Movement, embraced the 1980s call to frontier missions to the world's remaining unreached people groups. Near the top of every list were the world's one billion unreached Muslims.

The next movement emerged in the most unlikely of places. After the shock of the Iranian Revolution in 1979, many Iranians discovered that an Islamic state was not the panacea they had imagined. By the mid-1980s, Armenian Pentecostals in Iran were seeing growing numbers of Shi'ite Muslims turning to them to hear the gospel. By the end of the 1980s, in the face of severe government persecution, thousands of Muslims were entering into the Christian faith.[27]

The 1990s also witnessed a resurgence of Christianity among Kabyle Berbers in Algeria. As a bloody struggle between the military government and Islamists raged, eventually claiming more than 100,000 civilian lives, Berbers in Kabylia renewed their search for alternatives. They found them in late-night shortwave gospel radio broadcasts and illicitly distributed *JESUS Films*, with the result that thousands of Berbers quietly turned to the gospel while the rest of the country descended into civil war.[28]

As the decade of the 1990s unfolded, the world witnessed the fall of the Iron Curtain and the economic collapse of the Soviet Union. Millions of Turkic Muslims in Central Asia who grew up under Soviet atheism were suddenly faced with a new horizon of possibilities. American, European and Korean evangelicals seized the window of *glasnost* (openness) to bring the gospel to the Turkic peoples of Central Asia. By the end of the 20th century, evangelical Christianity could claim indigenous movements among Azerbaijani, Kyrgyz, and Kazakh populations with beachheads of believers among most of the other largest Turkic Central Asian people groups.[29]

As the Cold War thawed, many countries in the Eastern Bloc that had previously been closed to foreign Christian witness suddenly opened. In addition to their advances among lapsed Communists, missionaries reached out to Muslims and saw movements of more than 1,000 new Christ followers in the Muslim populations of Albania and Bulgaria. The decade also saw a response among Muslims of the Sahel in West Africa where years of chronic drought had fractured loyalties to traditional folk Islam.

South Asia's Bangladeshi population also proved to be fertile ground for the gospel in the 1990s. Widely viewed as a cyclone-addled, failed nation state, Bangladesh was, in fact, gaining a new national identity. A churning mass of hard-working and intellectually vibrant men and women, Bangladeshis were transitioning from their ancient Hindu loyalties to a growing Islamic identity that was conflicted by the still-raw wounds of atrocities committed by their Pakistani co-religionists in the 1971 War of Independence.[30] In the midst of this percolating Bengali cauldron, the gospel was spreading virally, prompting tens of thousands of Bangladeshi Muslims to seek out baptism as evidence of their newfound faith in *Isa al-Masih*, Jesus the Christ.

Multiplying Movements

To recap our review of the history of Muslim movements to Christ, in Islam's first 12 centuries we found no voluntary, and only a handful of coerced, conversions to the Christian religion. Not until the end of the 19th century, twelve and a half centuries after the death of Muhammad, did we find the first voluntary movements of Muslims to Christ that numbered at least 1,000 baptisms. These two movements, the Indonesian movement led by Sadrach and the Ethiopian movement by Shaikh Zakaryas, accomplished what no other Christian had seen in more than a thousand years.

These breakthroughs were followed by a pogrom-influenced conversion of some two million Indonesians into Christian churches in 1965. But then, in the final two decades of the 20th century, there was a surge of 11 additional movements. These occurred in Iran (2), Algeria, Bulgaria, Albania, West Africa, Bangladesh (2) and Central Asia (3). By the close of the 20th century, 1,368 years after the death of Muhammad, there had been a total of 13 movements of Muslim communities to faith in Jesus Christ.

It is this long history of frustration, a history that has seen tens of millions of Christians absorbed into the Muslim world that makes the current events all the more striking. In only the first 12 years of the 21st century, an additional 69 movements to Christ of at least 1,000 baptized Muslim-background believers or 100 new worshiping fellowships have appeared. These 21st-century movements are not isolated to one or two corners of the world. They are taking place throughout the House of Islam: in sub-Saharan Africa, in the Persian world, in the Arab world, in Turkestan, in South Asia and in Southeast Asia. Something is happening—something historic, something unprecedented.

A wind is blowing through the House of Islam.

Small Group Discussion ~ Discover for Yourself

1. What is happening in the history of Muslim movements to Christ?
2. Why do you think this is happening now?
3. What are some of the reasons you think these movements did not happen for 13 centuries?

hinges of
history

ON FEBRUARY 1, 1979, the Ayatollah Ruhollah Khomeini ended his 15-year exile and boarded an Air France flight for Tehran, consummating a revolutionary struggle that would rewrite Iranian history and challenge three centuries of Western domination of the Muslim world. The Iranian Revolution marked a hinge moment in the history of Islam's relations with the West, triggering a series of events that continue to the present day. History's hinges are turning points that signal momentous changes not only for the events themselves but for those that follow. Nine months after Khomeini's return to Tehran, Iranian students seized 52 American hostages, creating an international crisis that crippled the re-election hopes of a U.S. president before it ended 444 days later.

Sixteen days after the hostages were taken the next event occurred when, on November 20, fueled by messianic aspirations, Juhayman al-Otaybi declared himself the *Mahdi* (Islamic messiah) and led a band of 500 militants to seize the Grand Mosque in Mecca. The insurrection lasted only two weeks but sparked further violence from North Africa to the Philippines. Before the year was out, U.S. embassies had been burned to the ground in Tripoli, Libya, and Islamabad, Pakistan.

The Khomeini hinge hadn't finished swinging. Almost two years later, on October 6, 1981, shouting, "I killed Pharaoh!"

Egyptian army lieutenant Khalid Islambouli assassinated Egyptian president Anwar Sadat, America's closest ally in the Arab world. On April 18, 1983, a suicide bomber killed 63 people in the American embassy in Beirut. Six months later an even larger attack demolished the U.S. Marine compound in the city, killing 241 soldiers, prompting America's evacuation the following year.

A second hinge of history swung open in 1989 as the Iron Curtain crumbled, thawing 80 years of Cold War conflict between East and West. After decades of costly proxy wars in Asia, Africa, and the Americas, the game suddenly changed. Old alliances that seemed to divide the entire world into Soviet and American camps were now up for reconsideration.

The Soviet collapse triggered an unprecedented season of access to peoples and lands that had effectively been closed to outside Christian contact for nearly a century. Despite the increased contact, Muslims remained resistant to the message of Christ. New gospel initiatives to Muslims in Indonesia, India, Bangladesh, Saudi Arabia, Yemen, Iraq, Iran, Central Asian Turkestan, Algeria, the nomads and cities of West Africa's Sahel, and the Cushitic Muslims of East Africa's Red Sea Hills increased inestimably during the years that followed, but the response remained small. Muslims were tough.

The 9/11 Hinge

On September 11, 2001, as the World Trade Towers collapsed and portions of the U.S. Pentagon were engulfed in flames, world history seemed poised once again to swing wildly on some great invisible hinge. Despite the turmoil, or perhaps because of it, the years that followed proved to be years of unprecedented response to the gospel.

As the first decade of the 21st century unfolded, both rumors and evidence of Muslim movements to Christ were on the rise. In 2007, a colleague encouraged me to conduct a study of these Muslim turnings. At that time, we could count at least 25 Muslim movements to Christ that we knew of personally or had heard about through the global grapevine. We had no idea, at the time, that the number of movements was actually much larger. By the time we completed our study, six years later, we were able to identify 82 movements to Christ taking place in every corner of the Muslim world.

In 2011, a decade after the 9/11 hinge moment, a Christian foundation stepped forward with a proposal to fund a project to investigate the growing number of Muslim movements to Christ, seeking to understand what was happening and how God was at work in them. We wondered if another hinge, this one marking a new opening in the history of Muslims coming to faith in Christ, was quietly turning.

Project Description

The project took shape with the working title "Muslim Movements to Christ." In the earliest drafts of the project, we imagined conducting 12 interviews with 12 individuals (six men and six women) from 12 representative movements in 12 settings across the Muslim world. The modesty of the scope was my own concern that a more extensive survey could prove interminable. Yet the more closely we examined the subject, the more certain we became that 12 interviews in 12 locations was an artificial and inadequate framework that did not accurately fit the Muslim world or the movements emerging there. We needed to do more, to go further.

Nine Rooms

A closer examination of the Muslim world revealed a natural grouping of our subject into nine distinct geo-cultural clusters or complexes of Muslim people groups. Defined initially by geography, these clusters have been further shaped by shared history, languages, trade, conflict and thus, destiny. Following Arab Muslims' description of their world as "The House of Islam," we called these nine geo-cultural clusters "Rooms," Rooms within the House of Islam: (1) West Africa, (2) North Africa, (3) East Africa, (4) The Arab World, (5) The Persian World, (6) Turkestan, (7) Western South Asia, (8) Eastern South Asia, and (9) Indo-Malaysia.

Fortunately for our purposes, there is at least one Muslim movement to Christ in each of the nine Rooms, and multiple movements in several of them. By taking samples from one or more movements in each Room, we hoped to obtain a global insight into how God is at work in the Muslim world.

The House of Islam

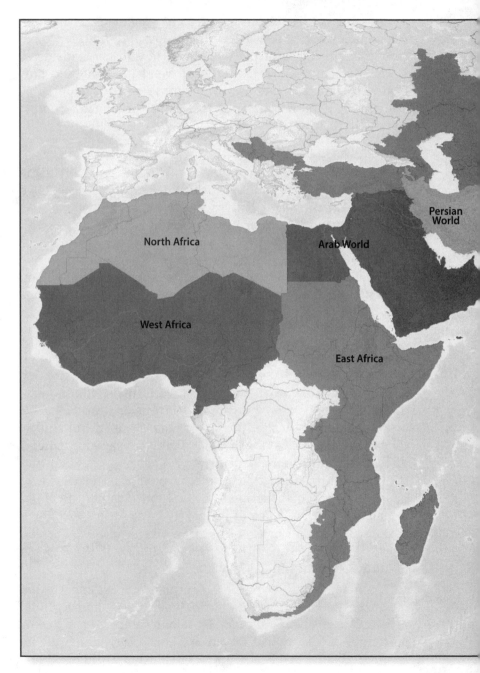

Nine Geo-Cultural Rooms

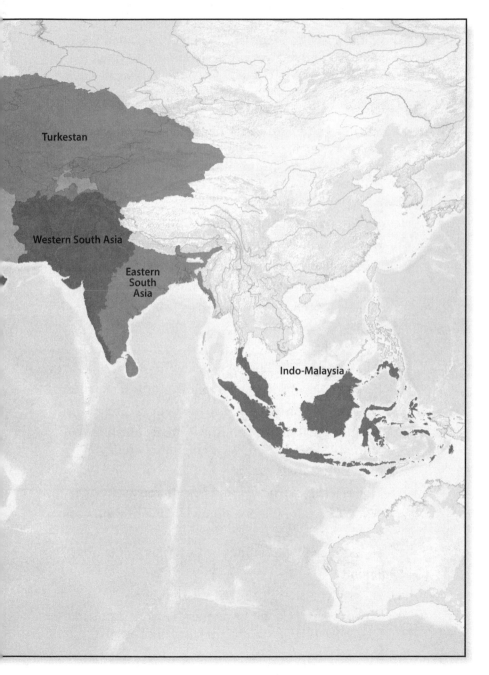

The Questionnaire

After narrowing the scope of the study to Muslim movements to Christ in each of the nine Rooms in the House of Islam, we also narrowed the survey questions. We began by asking what was the most important thing we wanted to know. One question dominated all others: *What is God using to bring Muslims to faith in Christ?* From this base question, we built concentric circles of related questions, some essential, others less so.[1]

After capturing the interviewee's basic demographic background information, such as name, ethno-linguistic people group, location, gender, age, educational level, and number of years as a follower of Christ, we moved to the heart of the inquiry. Here are the questions we asked:

1. **Before you came to faith in Christ**
    a. How active was your Muslim faith?
    b. Describe how you practiced your Muslim faith.
    c. What was your view of Christianity and Christians?
    d. What were the biggest obstacles to your turning to Christ as a believer?

2. **Turning to Christ**
    a. What led you to change your views of Jesus?
    b. How long have you been a follower of Jesus?
    c. What did God use to bring you to faith in Christ?
    d. What is God using to draw other Muslims to faith in Jesus Christ in your community today?

3. **Your life with Christ**
    a. Who is Jesus to you now, and how do you follow him?
    b. What does the Bible mean to you, and how do you use it?
    c. How do you practice church? Describe your church.

4. **Community**
    a. How do you share your faith with others?
    b. What is the role of foreigners in your faith (*do foreign funds influence this work and, if so, how*)?

   c. What individuals have been influential in your spiritual journey to Christ and with Christ?

   d. What is the role of the media (*TV, Internet, radio, JESUS Film, audio recordings, other*)?

   e. As a follower of Jesus, how do you relate to your non-Christian community?

   f. What role does persecution play in your life?

5. **Then and now**

   a. What is your view of the Qur'an and Muhammad today?

   b. Note to the interviewer: Try to deduce from your conversation how the faith of these individuals and their corresponding movements have grown, i.e. migrated toward or away from their Islamic faith. How is their faith changing?

   c. How has your life changed as a result of following Christ?

Finally:

6. **How can we pray for you?**

Change of Style

Though we retained these same questions through all of our interviews from West Africa to Indonesia, we did modify the way we gathered responses. In our first interviews, we simply clipped through the questions, inserting the answers into a data spreadsheet. Though the information we gathered was good and valid, it was only data, cold and impersonal, and that seemed grossly inadequate.

In the weeks that followed, we shifted to a conversational approach, allowing interviewees to tell their stories in their own words. After the testimony, we looked back over the questionnaire, asking the interviewee for any information that had not arisen naturally from their story. The result was a much richer, more insightful and, we believe, more accurate picture of the person being interviewed and the ways God has been at work among their people group.[2]

Through a Glass Dimly

Two and a half years, 250,000 miles, and more than 1,000 interviews later, a deeper understanding of how God is at work in the Muslim world is coming into focus. The scope of the study has gone beyond what was initially thought possible. With the assistance of numerous on-site collaborators, interviews have been collected from 45 movements in 33 Muslim people groups in 14 countries. Though not encompassing all of the movements currently unfolding, these interviews provide a broad scope to shed light on what appears to be a historic hinge moment in the spread of the gospel across the Muslim world.

Before entering the nine Rooms and listening to the stories drawn from these Muslim movements to Christ, though, one needs to have in mind some of the critical issues that surround these stories.

Small Group Discussion ~ Discover for Yourself

1. What are the key questions the author wanted to ask?
2. Is the questionnaire balanced? Why or why not?
3. After the first interview, the author changed his approach. What are the strengths and weaknesses of this changed interview style?

ten critical
issues

 IDENTIFYING CRITICAL ISSUES defines the playing field before beginning an important game or contest, ensuring consistency and mutual understanding. It's never the most exciting part of the game, but without it, all that follows would be confusing and meaningless. Locating the boundaries, clarifying disqualifying penalties, evaluating progress and success are all essential for meaning and understanding.

Numerous academics, field practitioners, researchers and Muslim-background believers themselves helped identify 10 critical issues that need to be laid bare before we examine these Muslim movements to Christ:

1. Security Concerns
2. Scope of the Project
3. Phenomenological Approach
4. View of Islam
5. Definition of Conversion
6. Definition of a Movement
7. Motivations for Conversion
8. Limitations of This Study
9. The Author's Bias
10. Desired Outcomes

Security Concerns

From the safety of America, the dangers that face converts in Muslim-majority countries seem far away. But a review of the personal testimonies and hundreds of photographed faces gathered during my travels vividly recalls those who live under very different circumstances. Were these movements occurring in the distant past, security would not be a concern. But because they are happening now, the safety of those involved is of prime importance.

An Egyptian friend named Mo, short for Mohammed, confided to me, "As a convert from Islam, my blood is no longer forbidden." Mo went on to explain, "Under Islam, no Muslim has the right to shed the blood of another Muslim. But because I have turned away from Islam, *my* blood is no longer forbidden." He continued, "A devout Muslim shopkeeper or cafe waiter wishing to implement *sharia* law has only to slip some poison into my tea or *kusherie* dish. For such obedience to Islamic law, my Muslim assassin would anticipate great rewards in the afterlife." Mo will spend the rest of his life looking over his shoulder, and cautiously stirring his tea—all for following Jesus.

The Hadith *Sahih al-Bukhari,* 9:83:17 confirms Mo's fears.

> The blood of a Muslim who confesses that none has the right to be worshiped but Allah and that I (Muhammad) am His Apostle, cannot be shed except in three cases: In retaliation for murder, for a married person who commits illegal sexual intercourse, and for the one who reverts from Islam (apostate) and leaves the Muslims.

The converts whose stories inform this study face a very real threat, and protecting them was a top priority for this project. So, none of the memorable photographs of my interviewees are included in this book, even though, in many instances those whom I interviewed urged me, "Tell my story. Tell everyone. I want them to know that Muslims are coming to faith." But having reviewed the broader implications of such disclosures, I am choosing not to be so transparent.

While every story and every quote in this book is true, places and persons' names have been altered to protect those involved. The reader should keep in mind that virtually all of the interviews were conducted in other languages that were translated by local bilingual translators, and then reproduced in intelligible English. Nonetheless, as faithfully as possible, quotations reflect the actual testimonies of those interviewed.

Even when someone gave permission to use their name, we have changed it in order to protect others who might be negatively impacted by their association with the person interviewed. Anonymization poses its own challenges, though: how does one tell stories without disclosing names and places? Whenever possible, without compromising security, accurate dates and sequences of events are provided. Since most of these events and stories are occurring at present, whenever events took place more than two decades ago, this is pointed out and generally treated as background to what is happening now.

The geographical context for these movements is critical to understanding what gave rise to them, yet naming cities, ethnic people groups, and countries could put a source in jeopardy. The solution to this dilemma became apparent as the research unfolded. The Muslim world is far from a monolith. Indonesian Muslims differ considerably from those in Nigeria, just as Chinese Uighurs differ from Yemeni Shi'ites.

Our research revealed that the world's 2,157 distinct Muslim cultures and people groups could be reasonably grouped into nine affinity clusters that cohere around shared experiences of geography, language, and history. These affinity groups have traded with each other, warred with each other, faced geographical and climatic issues together, and faced outsiders together.

By locating each movement broadly within these nine affinity clusters, we accomplished two purposes. First, we could now accurately describe the context and its impact on these movements. Second, we could protect the interviewees and their movements by "hiding" them among the millions of individuals who share their affinity group.

Scope of the Project

The enormity of the Muslim world and the growing number of movements also posed a challenge to the completion of the project. The very size of this study, movements to Christ across the Muslim world, threatened to overwhelm and sabotage the project. Though we could have limited the study to one movement and gone deep, or conducted a broad survey of individual Muslim converts unrelated to movements, these studies have already been done by other researchers.[1]

At the time of this writing, we have identified 82 voluntary Muslim movements to Christ throughout the course of history. The first two of these movements began in the 19th century; a further 11 took place in the 20th century. The focus of this book is on the 69 additional Muslim movements to Christ that have either commenced or are continuing to unfold in the 21st century. Even limiting the scope to each of the 69 contemporary movements would exact a toll in time and finances that would overwhelm the project's capacity. Fortunately, the same solution that helped resolve the security issue provides an answer to the enormity-of-scope challenge. All 69 of these contemporary movements are distributed, though not evenly, throughout the nine Rooms in the House of Islam.

Describing the context of each of the nine Rooms and then extracting interviews from one or more movements within each Room provides the best solution. In this way, we can do justice to the uniqueness of each Room and the accurate voices of each individual testimony and still obtain a global overview that allows us to compare and contrast the ways that God is at work both locally and globally in the nine Rooms: West Africa, North Africa, East Africa, the Arab World, the Persian World, Turkestan, Western South Asia, Eastern South Asia and Indo-Malaysia.

While it remains possible that the sample movements within each Room are not representative of all the movements in that particular Room, it is undeniable that they share with each of the other movements in that Room the same dynamics of geography, climate, languages, peoples and history.

To give a sense of the historical flow of these movements, we will begin with the Indo-Malaysia Room, the first Room in which movements appeared, and proceed chronologically through East Africa, North Africa and so forth, ending with the Arab Room, where the most recent movements have taken place. By surveying the movements, their contexts and their historical unfolding, we should be able to paint an accurate portrait of how God is at work in the House of Islam.

Phenomenological Approach

This study employs a phenomenological, or descriptive, approach to examining these Muslim movements to Christ. Phenomenology temporarily suspends evaluative judgments until the phenomenon has been accurately described. Once it has been described, the phenomenon can be interpreted, assessed and evaluated in light of the observer's standards and values.

As missiologist Scott Moreau has pointed out, a descriptive phenomenological approach is particularly important "when we want to appraise terrain in a new continent that we previously have not seen and thus are likely to misunderstand." Moreau goes on to explain,

> In the nineteenth century, Europeans derided travelers who came home telling of a mountain in Africa that remained snow-capped in the summer heat. Those who judged the stories as patently false could not comprehend the possibility of a Kilimanjaro—there was no space for it in their assumptions. Unless we want history to judge us as similarly quick-tongued fools, we need to take the time and energy needed to *understand* before we *pronounce*.[2]

A commitment to phenomenology requires patience, but does not preclude value judgments. We make these value judgments after first describing the phenomenon.

View of Islam

Islam is a divisive topic. It's difficult to be neutral about an all-encompassing religious system that makes absolute claims on everyone, and has been growing steadily for nearly 1400 years. Some readers of this book will categorically view Islam as false and demonic. Others may be more sympathetic, seeing it as simply a misunderstood monotheistic cousin to Christianity and Judaism. Still others may take a more secular stance and regard it as just another religious superstition.

This book is not written as a triumphalist account of Christendom's victory over the Muslim world. If anything, it should provide a sobering wake-up call to how poorly Christianity has fared in the face of Islam's growth over the past 14 centuries. After all, of the 82 movements to Christ that have occurred in our shared history, the first did not appear for nearly 13 centuries. The combined number of baptisms in all 82 movements totals no more than two to seven million, or less than one-half of one percent of the Muslim world's population, hardly a cause to gloat.

Neither is this book about proving or disproving the claims of Islam; other books have given ample attention to that subject.[3] Instead, our aim is to give voice to those who have stepped away from Islam to embrace Jesus Christ to be their only divine Savior and Lord, whose life, death, and resurrection atoned for them personally as well as for a lost and sinful humanity.

In doing so, though, these Muslim-background followers of Jesus Christ have placed themselves squarely on the border of where the claims of Christ press against the teachings of Islam. How they have responded to these contradictory demands on their allegiance goes to the heart of this study. And their response has by no means been uniform.

Keeping four interpretive frameworks in mind as we listen to the stories from these movements helps shed light on what we hear and assists in our understanding.

First is the relationship of religion and saving faith. Particularly in the case of Christianity, believing Christians must acknowledge that religion and religious identity are not the same as a personal and saving relationship with Jesus Christ. Christian history is replete with devout followers of Jesus Christ who were at odds with the predominant expression of the Christian religion in their day. In the same

way, many sincere Muslim-background followers of Christ may not fit into the predominant expressions of the Christian religion today. This is not to say that the Muslim-background follower of Christ can religiously practice both faiths, but rather that these movements may be forming new expressions of Christian faith that are distinct from the various other branches of Christianity around them.

Second, as we have already noted, the Muslim world is by no means uniform. In addition to the major divisions of Sunni, Shi'a and Sufi, and marginal traditions such as Ibadites, Ismailis, and Alawites, there are varieties of personal expression within the House of Islam. While some Muslims understand and adhere to an orthodox Islamic faith, there are those for whom Islam is simply a cultural framework into which they were born and will someday die, and in the meantime they live in this framework without ever holding any spiritual or theological commitment to it. One might call these "cultural Muslims."[4] Still other Muslims have a vibrant spirituality even though, for them, Islamic creed and doctrine mean very little. Some of these are Sufi Muslims for whom a mystical encounter with God is more important than doctrinal orthodoxy. Still others are syncretistic folk Muslims who have incorporated religious beliefs and practices from a variety of sources.[5]

In the West, we may view discrepancies between one's self-identity in these different spheres as deceptive, hypocritical, or duplicitous. They remain, nonetheless, a reality that we must keep in mind, particularly in high persecution contexts. Rather than issue a moral censure or condemnation of conflicted identities, we do well to note their possibility as we listen to the stories that are emerging from the Muslim world.

The third and most common interpretive scheme for classifying Muslim-background expressions of faith in Christ was developed in 1994 by a missionary serving in Asia who writes under the name John Travis. As Travis interacted with fellow missionaries and observed the varieties of fellowships Muslims either joined or formed when they responded to the gospel, he developed a spectrum (the C1-C6 Spectrum) that

describes six basic fellowship types. Each type of fellowship or "Christ-centered Community" ("C") along the spectrum represents a different way that Muslim-background believers relate their faith to their local culture.[6]

Travis's C-Spectrum can guide us in understanding different ways Muslim-background believers have navigated the difficulties of following Christ within a community that has little or no tolerance for converts or apostates. An abbreviated form of the spectrum as it applies to Muslim-background believers is as follows:

C1:   Followers of Christ in a traditional (often Western) style church, not using the mother tongue of the local Muslim population.

C2:   Same as C1, but the language of the local Muslim population is used.

C3:   Followers of Christ in culturally indigenous fellowships that avoid cultural forms closely associated with their Islamic past.

C4:   Followers of Christ in culturally indigenous fellowships that retain biblically permissible Islamic forms (e.g., prostrating in prayer, fasting, etc.) yet reinterpret these forms with biblical meanings. They may call themselves something other than Christians (e.g., "followers of Jesus") but do not see themselves as continuing in their previous Islamic religion.

C5:   Followers of Christ in fellowships of like-minded believers who remain within the Muslim community as witnesses, continuing to see themselves culturally, socially and officially as Muslims.

C6:   Small, often isolated groups of secret/underground/anonymous followers of Christ.

While the C-Spectrum is useful for providing a quick glimpse at varieties of Muslim-background expressions of faith and worship, its weakness is that it is static, like a snapshot photograph and people are not static. Consequently, it could lead to misunderstanding.

Just as missionaries move back and forth between the language and culture of the Christian world from which they

come and into the language and culture of the Muslim world they are seeking to reach, so too do Muslim-background believers move along a continuum. This is particularly true when these Muslim-background followers of Christ continue to live in the high-persecution context of their Muslim family and friends and seek to communicate with them their faith in Jesus Christ. In the course of this survey, you will meet followers of Christ from a Muslim background who admittedly move up and down the scale over time for a variety of reasons. Before making a judgment as to the validity of such mobility, the reader is invited to hear the stories first and then make evaluations afterwards. This leads to the fourth interpretive lens for understanding Islam and the Muslim-background believers who have shared their stories with us.

The fourth interpretive lens through which to view Muslims was put forth in David Greenlee's insightful collection of articles in *Longing for Community: Church, Ummah, or Somewhere in Between.*[7] Contributors Jens Barnett and Tim Green observed that persons moving between cultures and religions, such as Muslims coming to faith in Christ, often spend their lives juggling disparate identities and worldviews, not unlike "third-culture kids," a term first given to missionary children raised overseas who never completely fit into either the culture of their parents or the international culture in which they were raised.[8]

In the same way, some Muslim-background followers of Christ speak of a *horizontal identity* in which they relate to and share the cultural values in which they were raised, balanced against a *vertical identity* based upon their faith in the person and work of Jesus Christ.[9] Without endorsing any of these interpretive frameworks, we have, nonetheless, kept them in mind as we listened to the stories that emerged from these movements.

Definition of Conversion

When they learned of these movements, Christian colleagues often asked, "Are these genuine believers?" The question goes to the heart of this project. What do we mean when we speak of Muslims converting to faith in Christ?

Ultimately, God alone knows the heart of an individual, and we must resist the temptation to usurp this divine prerogative. We must limit ourselves to what interviewees claim for themselves and the evidence demonstrated by their lives.

Changing religion, at least in the Christian faith, has never been the point of true conversion, though it often follows true conversion and has historically been associated with true conversion. In fact, changing religion can often be the result of ulterior motives, as we saw in the historical review of Muslim movements to Christ in chapter one. The central issue as we examine Muslim conversions is that of a transformed life through a new relationship with God through the person of Jesus Christ as revealed in the New Testament.

Both the Old Testament Hebrew word *shub* and its New Testament equivalent *metanoia* speak of a change in direction or change of one's mind that leads to "the process of transformation which occurs as an individual (or group) turns to Christ in humble surrender, encountering him by the power of God."[10]

So true conversion results in a life transformation that occurs through the power of God when one turns from Islam or any other life orientation toward Christ. This new life is the very image portrayed in the baptismal experience of being "buried with him through baptism into death in order that, just as Christ was raised from the dead through the glory of the Father, we too may live a new life" (Romans 6:4).

Baptism for Christians and Muslims alike is a powerful symbol of true conversion. Muslims do not go lightly into baptismal waters. They know what it represents: death to an old life and resurrection to a new life. This is why our interviews have been limited to those who have been baptized as a visible expression of their faith, an act designed to separate Islam's many "Jesus fans" from Jesus followers.

It is important to clarify that when we speak of conversion to Christ as Savior and Lord, we are speaking of the Christ revealed in the New Testament, not the sketchy allusions to Christ offered in the Qur'an and Hadith. Though most Muslim-background believers do have an exalted view of Jesus stemming from the Qur'an, and some have even found the Qur'anic depiction of Christ to be so winsome as to compel their own conversion from Islam, the Qur'anic presentation is neither normative nor sufficient for defining a follower of Jesus Christ.

Definition a Movement

This is a study of movements. It is not merely a collection of individual conversion stories. Each interview was chosen to gain insights into why and how individual Muslims were coming to faith in Christ, but also, and importantly, why and how a growing community of believers were turning from Islam to faith in Christ. Thus, when a poignant testimony of an individual Muslim conversion was heard, it was not incorporated into this study unless it was part of a larger movement.

While there are many definitions and dimensions to the term *movement*, the most important thing for our purpose is that we are consistent in our use of the term.

Movements are corporate in nature and possess their own internal momentum. The corporate expression, for this study, is limited to turnings of at least 1,000 baptized believers over the past one or two decades or 100 new church starts over the same time frame within a given people group or ethnic Muslim community.[11] By adhering to this quantitative threshold, we will always be comparing apples to apples and oranges to oranges.

With regard to internal momentum, though movements typically begin with some measure of outside stimulus, at some point they become driven indigenously and so become independent of those original, foreign forces.

Finally, we should point out that movements have an inherently transitive nature, that is, they move toward something. For our purposes we are looking at movements to Jesus Christ as revealed in the New Testament.

Motivations for Conversion

A critical issue underlying the wave of new movements of Muslims to Christ is *What are the motivations of those who profess*

to be coming to faith in Christ? The answer might be as simple
as a sincere response to the appeal of the gospel. If this is
the case, then why now? Why so little response for nearly 14
centuries and such a large influx over the past few decades?

As we have already seen in our overview of Muslim movements through the centuries, communities can be coerced or
enticed into a change in religious affiliation. Inquisitions,
fear of violence, and other motivations have all had a role to
play in the complicated history of Muslim-Christian interaction.

In the course of this survey, we watched for ancillary
motivations that may have contributed to an individual's or
community's conversion. Ancillary motivations do not mean
the conversion is invalid, as most decisions for Christ are
influenced by a host of contributing factors. Exploring these
factors, though, can enlighten us to the complex variables that
have produced these movements. Along the way, we draw on
the insights of local experts to help us better understand and
interpret what we see and hear.

As we scrutinize motivations for conversion, we must
temper our judgments; mixed motives are nothing new to
the history of Christianity, nor are they limited to Muslim
movements to Christ. Even the first disciples, James and John,
revealed mixed motives for following Jesus when they said to
him, "Teacher, we want you to do for us whatever we ask," and
then proceeded to request prominent seats at his right and left
hand when his kingdom was revealed (Mark 10:35).

Limitations of This Study

As this project was taking shape, a respected demographer of
Islamic population growth gave this advice: do not over claim
what you can know. So let me offer some disclaimers.

Though we have attempted to collect surveys as broadly
and representatively as possible, the surveys were not evenly
distributed. Some movements in sub-Saharan Africa allowed
us to interview hundreds of Muslim-background believers,
while in parts of Western South Asia and the Arab world we
struggled to gather even a dozen interviews.

In the same manner, we sought to gather samplings
that were as random or as representative as possible, but it

would be a gross exaggeration to describe the results as 100 percent accurate portrayals of the movements from which they were extracted.

Most of the nine Rooms in the House of Islam are effectively closed and do not lend themselves to the kind of investigation that would eliminate doubts and guarantee a foolproof understanding of what is taking place. To obtain as clear a picture as possible, we attempted to gather perspectives from a variety of vantage points.

For example, as we examined each of the nine Rooms, the reports from Muslim converts themselves provided one vantage point; assessments by local Christians and missionaries on the ground gave another perspective; published dissertations offered additional insights; secular reports on economics, demographics, geography, and history provided a further picture. In this way, the interviews of Muslim-background believers that made up the heart of this study were framed and explained by the broader context to provide optimal understanding.

Taken together, these multiple views into each Room should present an accurate description and credible explanation of what is happening. But this approach also requires one to isolate anomalies and outliers that don't seem to fit the composite picture that is emerging. These anomalies can then be either dismissed or set aside for further investigation at a later time.

The more vantage points and varying perspectives we can obtain, the more accurately we can reconstruct the reality hidden within the still veiled Room. The results are mixed, but hopefully will provide a point of departure and advance for subsequent studies that can go deeper and provide better clarity.

One of the most frequently asked questions about these movements is *How large are they?* The easiest and most accurate answer is we don't know.

Though we have established a clear floor of 1,000 baptized believers or 100 churches for defining each movement, numbers beneath which no movement will be considered, we are less confident in guessing the ceiling of these movements. The cumulative number of converts to Christ in these movements seems to range somewhere between two and seven million, but even this generous range requires some qualifying comment.

Many of these movements are occurring in some of the most hostile places on earth, in countries like Somalia and Afghanistan, and along fault lines between Muslim and Christian populations such as in Nigeria and Ethiopia. In each of these places, access is limited and surveys are dangerous. For the time being, estimates of size will remain only estimates based upon as many perspectives as possible, but with no pretense of precision.

The Author's Bias

As an evangelical Christian, I come to this study with biases. I submit my own faith and practice to the authority of the Bible and the unique and exclusive salvation claims of Jesus Christ as revealed in the Bible. But as a phenomenologist, I have attempted to hold my personal convictions at bay until I accurately described the phenomenon in question.

I am also a long-time student of Islam, but I do not profess to be an expert. The more I learn, the more I can see how much I do not yet know. I have lived among Muslims in India as well as in Egypt and Tunisia, and have studied Arabic for three years.

I am both a friend and foe of Islam. I recognize its destructive elements, but find these in every human undertaking. I also recognize the good in Islam and admire many of the contributions that Islamic civilization has given to the world. Most of all, though, I have a deep love for Muslims. Muslim friends I have made through the years are among the most hospitable, generous and gracious people I have ever known. I sincerely desire God's very best for them. And that is why this study is so important to me, because it addresses what I believe to be God's very best for Muslims.

With my personal biases disclosed, I hope the reader will judge this work as an accurate witness to what I have seen and heard. I am well aware and deeply humbled by the access I have been given to lives and stories that few outsiders will ever experience. I do not take this access lightly and have endeavored to set aside biases, my own and others', to accurately and honestly report how God is at work in the Muslim world.

Desired Outcomes

Taking a phenomenological approach does not mean there are no goals for this study. No one undertakes such a lengthy project without having some outcomes in mind. Here are my goals for this project and for this book:

1. To accurately describe these movements.
2. To learn the ways God is at work across the Muslim world so that we can better participate in these movements.
3. To encourage those Muslims who are coming to faith in Christ by helping them to see how God is drawing Muslims to Christ across the Muslim world.
4. To challenge Christians everywhere not to fear and hate Muslims, but to engage them with the gospel of Jesus Christ.

Now, with these critical issues in mind, let's enter the House of Islam.

Small Group Discussion ~ Discover for Yourself

1. Why is it important to establish critical issues up front?
2. What is the author's bias? How does this relate to his "phenomenological approach?"
3. How does the author define a movement?
4. What are some of the ulterior motives in movements to watch out for?
5. How does the author define conversion? Do you agree or disagree?

PART 2:
the house
of Islam

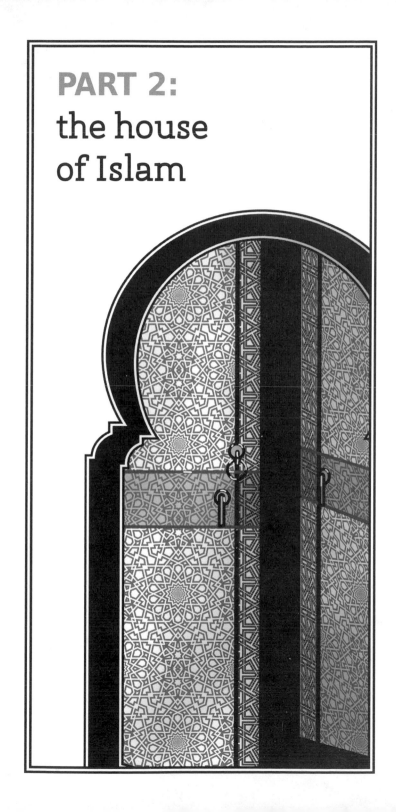

the Indo-Malaysia room

The isles, and the inhabitants thereof....
Let them give glory unto the Lord,
and declare his praise in the islands.

Isaiah 42:10, 12, KJV

 IN 1870, BY the grace of God, Indonesian evangelist Sadrach Surapranata (c. 1835-1924) witnessed what no Christian had seen in the 1,238 years since the death of the Prophet Muhammad. Through Sadrach's ministry thousands of devout Javanese Muslims turned away from Islam and sought baptism as followers of Jesus Christ. By 1873, Sadrach had already led more than 2,500 Javanese Muslims to faith, more than had been reached in the entire 268-year history of the *Indische Kerk* (the Indonesian Church) and the hundreds of Dutch missionaries who had labored with them.[1]

Sadrach's movement was not only the first Muslim movement to Christ in the Indo-Malaysia Room, it was the first voluntary movement of Muslims to Christ in history. The centuries-old contest between Christianity and Islam had not seen a single voluntary movement to Christ, despite tens of millions of Christians converting to Islam since the death of the Prophet Muhammad in 632.

What was different about Sadrach? How did this first-generation convert from Islam turn the tide in a 12-century drought of Christian outreach to Muslims?

Though Sadrach's ministry concluded nearly 100 years ago, it holds far too many lessons to ignore. In it were many of the key themes that would characterize the dozens of Muslim movements to Christ that followed.

Unique as it was, Sadrach's ministry did not emerge from a vacuum. Raised a Muslim peasant boy under the watchful administration of the Dutch East Indies colonial authorities, Sadrach was like countless other boys growing up on the crowded island of Java. After graduating from Qur'anic primary and secondary schools, Sadrach discovered that his former

guru or spiritual teacher, Pak Kurmen, had converted to Christianity after losing a debate with an Indonesian Christian evangelist named Tunggul Wulung. Over the next several years, Sadrach followed Pak Kurmen, apprenticing himself to Tunggul Wulung and learning about his new faith. In 1867, at the age of 32, Sadrach was baptized into the Dutch Calvinist Indische Kerk. Despite his affection for and loyalty to the Indonesian Church, Sadrach

Sadrach of Java

learned from his mentors Wulung and Kurmen that he needn't reject his local Javanese culture. In this, he was at variance with both the Dutch colonial church culture and the Arabizing Muslim culture.[2]

Sadrach's bending to the local culture, though, had its limitations. When his mentor Wulung took a second wife, and his guru Kurmen began using opium, Sadrach broke with the men and sought another teacher. He found his mentor in a Euro-Indonesian woman named Christina (C.P.) Petronella who had been leading Bible studies for Indonesians in her home for some time.[3] Three years later, Sadrach launched out on his own, using the public debate style of evangelism he had learned from Tunggul Wulung. The approach was not without risk. Sometimes the debates would last for days, and the loser was bound by integrity to convert to his opponent's position, along with his disciples. Sadrach proved to be particularly gifted in laying out the case for Christ and soon won many gurus and their disciples to the cause of Christ.

Though Sadrach's movement grew independently of the Dutch Indische Kerk, Sadrach still relied on the church's ordained clergy to baptize his converts — at least for the first ten years of his ministry. Increasingly, though, Sadrach's approach to evangelism and church formation distanced him from the Dutch missionary community and earned him no shortage of friction from them.

The chief difference was Sadrach's determination to retain, yet transform for Christian purposes, as many Javanese customs as possible. Sadrach called his disciples *Kristen Jawa* (Javanese Christians) and their churches *mesjids*, the same term (meaning 'gathering') used by Muslims for their mosques. Sadrach's Kristen Jawa sanctuaries, which his community built without foreign assistance, looked more like the village mosque than the Dutch *kerk*, except that Sadrach's mesjids employed a three-tiered roof to symbolize the Holy Trinity. Unlike the Indische Kerk buildings, Kristen Jawa buildings had no cross on top, choosing instead a pre-Islamic Javanese symbol that Sadrach's community used to communicate "the power of God's Gospel to pierce even the most obstinate of human hearts."[4]

Sadrach's Trinity Mesjid

Kristen Jawa church leaders wore traditional Javanese clothing, unlike the black robes donned by the Dutch Reformed clerics. They were called by their parishioners *imams* (another Muslim term literally meaning "the one in front"). Men and women sat separately in the meetings, and the women often covered their heads.

Sadrach also adapted the Muslim creed, the *shahada* ("There is no God but Allah and Muhammad is His Prophet"), to fit the Christian faith. He replaced the words "...and Muhammad is His Prophet" with "...and *Jesus Kristus* (Jesus Christ) is the *Roh Allah* (Spirit of God)."[5] Sadrach's choice of wording in his new creed was revealing. He employed the common Javanese and Arabic name for God, *Allah*, but rather than using the Qur'anic

Isa al-Masih for Jesus Christ, Sadrach chose the term he found in the newly translated Javanese Bible: Jesus Kristus. He defined Jesus in his Creed as the Spirit of God, using words derived from Arabic (*Roh Allah*) that he believed to be congenial to both Christians and the Muslims he was trying to reach.[6]

In short, Sadrach's mode of church and gospel expression was harmonious enough with Javanese folk Muslim culture to be acceptable to those he was seeking to win, yet different enough to spark the ire of the Dutch Calvinist community around him. And spark it did.

Almost from the beginning, Sadrach and his ministry came under fire from both the missionary and traditional Indische Kerk communities. Many of the charges stemmed from Dutch misunderstandings of Javanese language and culture, while other criticisms arose from fabrications that Indonesians, who were jealous of his ministry, spread to the Dutch missionaries to undermine it. Still other conflicts resulted from Sadrach's conscious decision to take a different approach from that of the Reformed and missionary traditions that preceded him.

By 1883, Sadrach's ministry had drawn thousands of Indonesian Muslims to his Kristen Jawa, provoking further alarm in the traditional church leadership. In an attempt to reel in Sadrach's work, Indische Kerk minister, Petrus Heyting, appealed to colonial authorities. Heyting reported some of the wild charges he had heard from Sadrach's jealous rivals. Heyting accused Sadrach of "displaying the stigmata (marks of crucifixion on his hands and feet); rendering himself invisible, only to reappear four days later; allowing himself to be called spiritual lord; pretending to have divine wisdom; allowing his disciples to kiss his hand and feet; retaining weapons in his home and encouraging his followers to do the same."[7] The last charge was aimed at portraying Sadrach and his community as a threat to the colonial order. However, after initially arresting Sadrach, the colonial government's investigation could find no basis in the charges and dismissed them.

A Multilayered Cake

When the global circumnavigator, Ferdinand Magellan, crossed the Pacific in 1521, he encountered a lush ring of 24,000 volca-

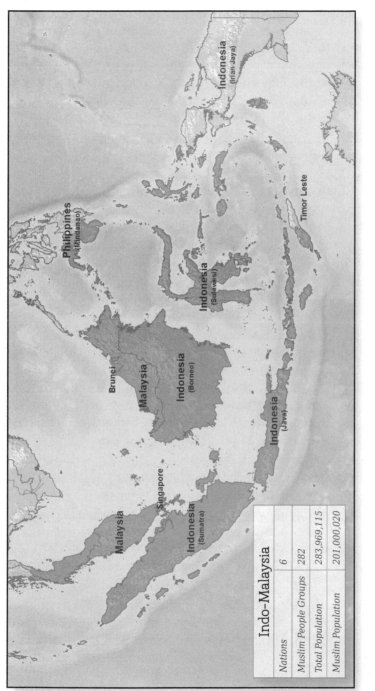

Indo-Malaysia

Indo-Malaysia	
Nations	6
Muslim People Groups	282
Total Population	283,969,115
Muslim Population	201,000,020

nic islands guarding the great continent of Asia. The conquistadors and monks who followed Magellan named the northern islands for King Philip II of Spain and began the Christianization of what would become the third largest Catholic country in the world. Quickly eclipsing the Portuguese outpost of Timor, the Philippines would serve as Spain's bastion of trade in the Pacific for the next 300 years.

Islam had a 250-year head start in the region, beginning with the establishment of a Muslim trading sultanate on the Sumatra side of the Malacca straits in 1267. By the time the Spanish and Portuguese arrived, the muezzin's call to prayer was already sounding in several key cities of what would become Indonesia, Singapore and Malaysia. Over the next few centuries an ideological contest that could rival the 20th-century Cold War would unfold between the two great religions, as Catholicism pressed southward from the Philippines while Islam spread rapidly into the Malay peninsula and Indonesian archipelago.

Today more than 90 percent of the Philippines' 97 million citizens profess some form of Christianity. A beachhead of Muslims in the south is a reminder of the vast sea of Islam dominating the surrounding nations of Indonesia and Malaysia. Malaysia's 28 million citizens are ethnically and religiously divided between Muslim Malays, Hindu Tamils, Chinese Folk Religionists and Christians scattered among the rural tribals and urban Chinese.

Though Indonesia is the largest Muslim country in the world, its religious and ethnic identity is much more complex than its government census figures imply. Indonesians describe their country as a multilayered cake, representing the different religions, cultures and races that have successively settled their land. The oldest layers were Animists, followed by Hindus and Buddhists before the arrival of Islam and, later still, Christianity.

The advance guard of Islam was a mystical folk Islam that blended easily with the Animistic Hinduism and Buddhism that preceded it. On the heels of this mystical Islam, though, were Qur'anic teachers and imams who established madrasas

(Islamic schools) to firm up the faith of the believers. By the 21st century, Islam claimed more than 192 million adherents in Indonesia, 78 percent of the nation's population of 248 million. Even devout Muslims in the country, though, acknowledge the persistence of those earlier layers — Animism, Hinduism and Buddhism — still seeping into the now dominant Muslim layer and flavoring the Indonesian worldview.

Not until the Portuguese arrival in 1522 did Christianity begin to establish a presence in the East Indies. Franciscans, Dominicans and Jesuits soon followed, including Francis Xavier who spent nearly a year there in 1546. By the end of the 16th century, Catholic missionaries had established 18 mission outposts in Indonesia with 25,000 baptized congregants. Nearly all of these converts, though, were from the non-Muslim population of Animists.[8]

Dutch Treatment

The Dutch East India Company was formed in March 1602, in anticipation of exploiting the lucrative East Indies spice trade. Three years later, Dutch Admiral Matelieff overran Portuguese positions in Indonesia, and the Netherlands secured a monopoly on East Indies trade. That same year, Matelieff ordered the conversion of Indonesia's Roman Catholics to Dutch Reformed Christianity.

The Dutch trading company was steeped in religious commitment. They opened their meetings with prayer, Bible reading and a commitment to "protect the sacred ministry, and . . . remove and prevent all idolatry and false worship."[9] However, when evangelizing efforts by Dutch missionaries stirred opposition from local Muslim communities, the colonial authorities sent the missionaries

Dutch East India Symbol

to less volatile peoples and islands — generally farther to the east — and signed accords with local sultans prohibiting missionaries from converting Muslims.

By 1771, the Dutch East Indies Company had employed 254 Dutch men and 800 women as missionaries directed primarily to the non-Muslim peoples of the East Indies. Though these missionaries saw more than 80,000 conversions, they were almost exclusively from non-Muslim Animist and Chinese traditional religionist backgrounds.[10]

Islam, for its part, took advantage of the Dutch in Indonesia and the English incursions into Malaysia to fuel anti-colonial and anti-foreign sentiment among the populous, thus gathering converts into the Islamic fold.

Meanwhile, in the West, as separation of church and state gained popularity, Dutch missionaries bound for Indonesia gained increasing freedom from their colonial governors. By the end of the 18th century, newly independent Dutch missions organizations began directing their attention to the Muslim majorities they had formerly avoided. Rather than building bridges to these local Muslims, however, these strict Calvinists took a hardline approach to the local culture, demanding that converts make a complete break with their Islamic and Javanese past.

Nature of the Great Turning

After Sadrach's pioneering movement (1870-1924), the Indo-Malaysia Room experienced two more waves of Muslims coming to faith in Christ. One took place after an aborted Communist coup in Indonesia in 1965. The other is happening today.

President Sukarno

A freedom fighter in the struggle for Indonesian independence, Kusno Sosrodihardjo Sukarno (1901-1970), collaborated with Japanese occupation forces during World War II to wrest control of the country from the Dutch. Sukarno emerged after the war as the president of the new nation of Indonesia. Over the next decade, Sukarno attempted to create a "guided democracy," a common post-war euphemism that sought to balance the fledgling state on the three conflicted pillars of military-backed nationalism, religion and Communism. Sukarno's edifice crumbled, however, when an aborted Communist coup in 1965 prompted Indonesia's first two pillars — in the form of the army and political Islam — to destroy the third pillar, Communism.

In 1965, Communists were threatening not only to win the war in Vietnam but to roll across Southeast Asia as well. Indonesia had one of the largest Communist parties in the world with more than 800,000 members, and it enjoyed growing support from President Sukarno. All of that changed on September 30, 1965, when Communist militants killed six army generals in an attempted coup d'état. One of the remaining generals, Major General Suharto, took charge of the embattled military and launched a counterattack against the insurgent Communist plotters. General Suharto seized power, arrested President Sukarno and placed the country under martial law.

Over the next two years the military conspired with vigilante bands of Muslim youth in a door-to-door campaign throughout the country, extracting and executing known and alleged Communists. Before the purge was over, at least 500,000, and as many as one million, Indonesians had been murdered. Tens of thousands of bodies clogged the rivers and waterways of central and eastern Java, their rotting corpses with evidence of throats slit, bullet holes in their head or heads completely decapitated. On the island of Bali, known more for Hinduism than Communism, 80,000 persons were killed, five percent of the island's population, in a slaughter that included the settling of old scores and ethnic purges against Chinese that had little or nothing to do with Communism.[11]

President Suharto

To ensure the elimination of any lingering Communism, General Suharto, who became acting president in 1967,

required every Indonesian to identify with one of the nation's
five authorized religions: Islam, Catholicism, Protestantism,
Hinduism or Buddhism. What followed no one could have
anticipated. Over the next five years, more than two million
Indonesians joined the recognized Protestant and Catholic
Christian churches. Though the chaos of the time made it
difficult to claim precision on these numbers, Frank Cooley, a
leading historian of Christianity in Indonesia, estimated that
during the years of the great turning, roughly 1965-1971,
Protestants baptized 1,870,512 new believers while Catholics
baptized a further 938,786.[12] This may constitute the largest
turning of Muslims to Christianity in history, but as with
everything in Indonesia, not all is as it seems. Who turned and
why? In retrospect, there were three groups that joined the
churches.

1. **Communists and Communist sympathizers.** Many of
   those who survived the Communist purges had only
   marginal religious identity, if any at all. Even those
   who did have a religious background were sometimes
   branded as Communists due to their support of such
   leftist concerns as land reform and peasants' rights.
   Scanning the horizon of religious options, they found
   Christianity to be the most congenial faith available
   to them.

2. **Ethnic Chinese.** It is conspicuous that Chinese
   traditional religion, a syncretistic blend of Taoism,
   Confucianism and Animism which had been in the
   country for centuries, failed to make the list of five
   legitimate Indonesian religions. Indonesians, like
   many other Southeast Asian peoples, had a tenuous
   relationship with the tight-knit Chinese families that had
   grown wealthy through their prosperous international
   business and trading networks. So when the assault on
   suspected Communists erupted, many Chinese were
   swept up in the slaughter. Many of these embattled
   Chinese sought refuge by converting to Christianity.

   In 1967, local Dayak peoples on the Indonesian
   island of West Kalimantan took advantage of Suharto's
   Communist eradication program to ethnically cleanse

the economically dominant Chinese from their island. In the process, 2,000-5,000 Chinese were killed, while a further 1,500 Chinese children died while interred in refugee camps.[13]

3. **Muslim conversions.** The third and largest group that flowed into the churches were Muslims, but many of them did not come from the orthodox Muslim community. In his 1960 study, *The Religion of Java,* anthropologist Clifford Geertz distinguished two types of Islam in Indonesia: *abangan,* which was mystical folk Islam, and *santri,* a more orthodox or Qur'anic Islam. Another way to describe this would be cultural Muslims and doctrinal Muslims.[14]

In 1965, the government's Muslim-dominated Department of Religion sought to bolster the official size of the Muslim population as they counted 89 percent of Indonesia's population to be Muslim, rising to 91 percent in 1970. In doing this, the Department of Religion had reclassified as Muslims the 47 percent of Java's population who actually practiced Javanese traditional religion called *Agama Jawa,* a sort of mystical Animism. Were these Agama Jawa really Muslims? Or perhaps it is more accurate to ask, *How Muslim were these newly reclassified Muslims?* We get a clue from a 1955 referendum that would have implemented *sharia* law, making Indonesia an Islamic state. The country's five Islamic parties could garner no more than 43 percent of the nation's popular vote to support such an initiative. This has led independent demographers to question how Muslim Indonesia truly was.[15]

Those who were the most Islamic, the *santri* or orthodox Muslims, were the ones who conspired most closely with the military to purge the thousands of real and suspected Communists. For them it was a religious service, an act of jihad. The remaining *abangan* or mystical folk Muslims, steeped in Javanese traditions of harmony and tolerance, were appalled by the slaughter. These abangan folk Muslims responded to the carnage by converting in droves to Christianity. It was as if they were saying, "If this is Islam, then I must be a Christian."

When Avery Willis surveyed 500 Javanese Muslim converts to Christianity in 1976, they replied that, after Spiritual Need

(52%), the twin factors of Government (25.2%) and Protection (23.2%) were the greatest influences prompting their conversion to Christianity.[16]

As we will see in many subsequent Rooms in the House of Islam, one of the greatest recurring motivations for Muslims coming to Christ is a rejection of the militant expression of Islam itself.

Today's Movements

Of the three most populous countries in the Indo-Malaysia Room, Malaysia remains the country where draconian restrictions continue to prevent Malays from turning from Islam to any other faith. Even the Philippines, where Islamic insurgents have long plagued the stability of Mindanao and neighboring islands, has seen significant numbers of Muslims come to faith in Christ over the past two decades.

Ordinary Christianity

In the decades that followed Sadrach's death in 1924, many churches in Indonesia benefited from his contextualizing model. Those churches best able to synthesize the local culture with biblical mandates for evangelism were the ones best positioned to receive and assimilate the enormous turning that followed the anti-Communist purges.[17]

Over the years there has also been a steady influx of Muslim converts into Indonesian churches through what missionary Roger Dixon has termed "The Major Model of Muslim Ministry." A less flashy, more pedestrian mode of outreach and conversion, Dixon contends that it is through normal Indonesian church life that conversion has taken place in the country for decades.[18]

A striking characteristic of this Major Model was what Dixon called the "unintentional evangelism" that Indonesian Muslims experienced in their day-to-day interaction with Indonesian Christians, as opposed to deliberate strategies of outreach to convert them. When these Indonesian Muslims were stressed by unpalatable aspects of their Islamic religion such as legalism, violence or Arabization, evangelization from "the natural and open initiative of lay (Christians)" provided Muslims with an alternative sanctuary.[19]

By 2002, Dixon was attributing to the Major Model unofficial estimates of over 12 million Javanese Muslims who had converted to Protestant Christianity, mostly through informal evangelism by ordinary Christians without deliberate efforts to spread it.[20] However, the second edition of the *World Christian Encyclopedia* — which has never been accused of undercounting Christian numbers — could account for no more than 2.82 million Christians on Java, only two percent of the total Javanese population, many of whom would have come from non-Muslim backgrounds and nearly half of whom were Roman Catholic.[21]

Churches and missionaries who were impatient with unintentional approaches that had failed to reach 98 percent of the Javanese population began testing more aggressive, intentional means. In 2011, Pastor Petrus Agung of the 12,000-member Gospel of the Kingdom of God Church (*Gereja JKI Injil Kerajaan Allah*) in Semarang, Central Java, offered on his website: "Let us teach you how your city can have a Muslim revival!" The site went on to declare: "God gives us great favor with the Muslim people in Indonesia. Last Sunday on October 28, we baptized about 3,000 people and in October we baptized more than 3,800 people." Though Pastor Agung did not state that all of those baptized were Muslims, the implication was threatening enough to local Muslim sensibilities that the church's website posting was removed soon afterwards.[22]

Intentional Approaches

Others, while taking a more cautious approach than Pastor Agung have, nonetheless, been very intentional in their Muslim outreach, ranging from the highly contextualized "Insider" model to methods such as "Any-3," an evangelistic outreach to Muslims that has seen more than ten thousand Muslims come to faith over the past five years.

Insiders have followed Sadrach's lead in trying to remove as many cultural barriers to the gospel as possible by presenting it in a manner that is non-offensive to Muslims. And like Sadrach before them, these Insiders have caught the ire of the Christian community for their efforts. It is not the purpose of this book to weigh all of the pros and cons of this issue, but rather to acknowledge its existence as a part of the mixture that is present in the Indo-Malaysia Room.

Any-3, Mike Shipman's outreach tool that stands for Anyone, Anywhere, Any Time, is less contextualized and so less controversial with the Christian community, though still quite intentional and effective in reaching Muslims.[23] Any-3 equips a Christian to lead a Muslim friend through an intentional gospel-sharing relationship. Any-3 evangelists then follow up interested Muslim-background seekers with a season of interactive Bible studies that use Old Testament prophet stories that have been effective in deepening a Muslim-background believer's understanding of the necessity of Christ's atoning salvation.

Any-3 by Mike Shipman

Any-3's clear five-step evangelism and the weekly follow-up meetings not only nurtured and discipled new believers, but also trained and challenged them to immediately share their faith with family and friends. This has resulted in more than 800 reproducing churches and church starts among several different Muslim people groups in the Indo-Malaysia Room.

Any-3 is only one of many ways that Christians are sharing their faith with Muslims in the Indo-Malaysia Room. A Western Christian who has spent 20 years in the region commented, "In March 2011, looking back on two decades of working with Muslims, we were a little surprised to see that our teams now have 353 small believer groups." To maintain their progress, he and his network of Muslim-focused witnesses have established a Leaders' Learning Community where they practice "ruthless evaluation" and thus learn from one another the ways that God is at work. "In 2005," he said, "we had only one Muslim people group that had reached a third generation of reproduction. By 2010, we had 12 to 14 teams that were seeing third generation reproduction (i.e. churches that had reproduced themselves three times) in eight different Muslim people groups. One Muslim outreach team has gotten to 25 new believers groups, while another has reached 137 groups."

Another Christian witness serving God in a different part of the Indo-Malaysia Room reported, "We have spent the last several weeks doing a new assessment, particularly of the status of groups and baptized believers connected with weekly meetings." By the end of September 2011, this network was reporting 80 new churches, 87 second-generation churches (i.e., churches planted by other churches), 84 third-generation churches, 45 fourth-generation churches and nine fifth-generation churches, for a total of 305 churches, and a further 255 beginning groups of Muslim-background believers. The total number of Muslim-background believers who had been baptized in this stream had risen to more than 3,000.

Beyond the Traditional Churches

Of the Muslim-background believers who were interviewed, each of them reflected an intentional witness from someone to draw them to faith in Christ. A 40-year-old man from a strong Muslim background reported that an evangelist from a Muslim background visited him eight times in one month, showing him 97 verses in the Qur'an that supported the uniqueness of Isa al-Masih, before he was finally persuaded and came to faith. Asked what it was that convinced him to follow Christ, the man cited the Qur'an 3:47, 19:7-19 and 21:91, all of which convinced him that *Isa al-Masih* (Jesus Christ) was the Spirit of God and the only one who has ever lived who has been perfect and holy since birth. He concluded, "Since Isa is the only one who is holy, that's the reason I finally believed in Him." Once he became persuaded of Christ's identity he submitted himself to the full and complete revelation of Christ in the Bible.

A 53-year-old leader of a house church network came to Christ from an *abangan*, cultural Muslim, background. Before becoming a believer, he had always believed that Christians were *kafir* (heathen) and that Islam was the only true religion. When asked what caused him to change his views and embrace Isa as his Savior and Lord, he replied: "For the first time, someone told me about Isa. I had only to compare Isa with what I formerly believed."

For many, it was a realization that Christ alone was God's way of salvation. A 39-year-old woman from a strong Islamic background said, "I realized that with my own works and efforts I couldn't reach heaven. There was only one way, that is believe in Isa as the one and only way to heaven."

As a part of their discipleship, these Muslim-background believers were challenged and trained to share their new faith with others in their community. Asked how they shared their faith with Muslims in their community, a 50-year-old house church leader gave what was a typical response: "I get to know them first, to see whether they are a fanatic or not." After asking about how they practice their religious faith, "I ask them, 'Why do you do this?' Typically, they do not know." The informant went on to explain, "Early in the conversation, I don't speak about Isa's divinity . . . . I tell them how the prophets told of how the Messiah would come and save us. I explain that we are all sinners. I also tell them that Isa can give us new life." This approach, following Any-3's five-step pathway, has seen many Muslims respond to an offer to pray for salvation with both affirmation and appreciation.

Though some of these Muslim-background converts may not have begun their pilgrimage to Christ with a full understanding of Christ's divinity, they soon arrived there. A 42-year-old Muslim man who had studied Islam for 11 years before becoming a follower of Christ four years ago, had formerly believed that "Christians worshiped three gods" and "were kafir." Today he says without equivocation, "Isa is the foremost in this world and in the next. Only Isa knows the Judgment Day. Isa raised from the dead, so He can raise us up once we've died. He's the living God and the forgiver of my sins." Asked what changed his views of Isa, he spoke of the direct involvement of Jesus in his life: "The doctor told me I was going to die, but Isa did a miracle for me, so that energy was given to me to bring others to faith."

Each of the persons interviewed experienced persecution for their newfound faith, ranging from ostracism, to threats, to physical violence. "As a follower of Christ," a former Islamic teacher said, "I have been shunned. My children have been shunned as well. I suffer emotional abuse, but not physical abuse." A 42-year-old mother from a devout Muslim community received threats from both her family and her community. "My electricity was cut off," she said. "We didn't receive financial help from our family anymore."

Knowing that many of these believers had come from strong Islamic backgrounds, we wanted to see how much their theological understandings had shifted from Islamic to Christian. An unexpected response occurred again and again, as these Muslim-background followers redirected the question away from doctrine and toward holiness and life transformation.

When asked, "How is your faith changing? Have you moved away from Islamic beliefs and practices? Have you grown in your allegiance to Christ?" a 61-year-old man from a nominal Muslim background said, "Formerly I was easily angered, often lied, and drank alcohol. Now I'm patient, honest and don't drink anymore." A woman from a strong Muslim background replied, "Now I'm more patient and humble. I used to be an angry person, but not anymore." Another woman from a strong Muslim background answered, "My faith continues to deepen, and I'm growing closer to Isa.... I always try to obey the Word." A third woman said, "I'm more patient in facing difficulties and am better at resolving conflict, rather than becoming angry. Formerly, I didn't pray at all, but now I pray often to Isa."

Concerns about any lingering Islamic doctrines were dispelled in response to the question, "What is your view of the Qur'an and Muhammad today?" A 50-year-old house church leader said, "Muhammad led many people astray." A 53-year old man replied, "The Qur'an is confusing and has many references from the Bible. Muhammad is just a normal person. But I do sometimes use the accurate verses in the Qur'an to witness or teach others."

In the Indo-Malaysia Room, God is at work both through the traditional churches as well as deep within Muslim communities themselves. Thousands of Muslims are coming to faith and remaining immersed within their Muslim villages and communities. There they continue to intentionally spread the news to family and friends that Jesus and Jesus alone can offer them assurance of salvation.

Except a Grain of Wheat

In a time and place where life expectancy rarely stretched past

60, Sadrach Radin Surapranata may have lived into his 90s. Biographers estimate that the number of converts beyond the immediate scope of his parish may well have numbered 10,000 to 20,000.[24] The 86 Kristen Jawa churches with 7,552 baptized Muslim-background believers regarded Sadrach not only as the leader of their flock, but also as God's chosen "Apostle of Java."

Prior to his death in 1924, Sadrach designated his adopted son, Yotham Martareja, to inherit the mantle of leadership over the network of churches. Eight years later, Yotham did what Sadrach would not; he negotiated with the Dutch Calvinist Indische Kerk to integrate his followers into their denomination.[25] Thus ended a chapter in a bold and unique experiment in indigenous missions that led to history's first voluntary movement of Muslims to Christ. But the emergence of new Muslim movements to Christ around the world was just beginning.

Small Group Discussion ~ Discover for Yourself

1. What impressions do you take away from this chapter?
2. How is God at work in the Indo-Malaysia Room?
3. Why do you think Sadrach was able to succeed when more than 200 years of Catholic and Protestant missionaries before him did not?
4. What is God using today to multiply Muslim-back-ground believers in the Indo-Malaysia Room?

the
East Africa
room

Cush will submit herself to God.
Psalm 68:31b

 SHEIKH HAKIM WAS a slender man in his mid-30s with a neatly trimmed beard, intense lively eyes, wearing a bright purple shirt beneath the ubiquitous second-hand suit. Hakim was one of nine sheikhs who had walked for several miles from their villages in the Horn of Africa to join me for breakfast in a crossroads cafe and to tell me their stories.

"How did you become a follower of Jesus?" I asked.

Hakim replied, "My father came from the Boro Mountain Muslims who are known for their zealous faith. Islam in (this East African country) began in the Boro Mountains.

"When I was born, my father took a vow, 'My son will only study the Qur'an and never work for me.' So from the age of two until I was 18, I only studied the Qur'an." Hakim is a *hafez*, meaning he has memorized the Qur'an.

As Muslims, Hakim and his fellow Muslims once believed Jesus was only a prophet for Israel. "If someone told us that Jesus was the Son of God," Hakim said, "that would be very hard for us to hear. The Qur'an says, 'If you say that Jesus is God, you become *kafir* (pagan).' So if someone said that Jesus was God, we would kill him. When I was a Muslim, I burned churches for Islam.

"I accepted the gospel because it came to me in my own way of understanding. At the time, I was the overseer of four mosques and was training 300 Islamic teachers. One day, a local African evangelist gave me an *Injil* (a New Testament) in Arabic. Before this happened, I thought that all Injils were corrupt and lost, but this was in Arabic. I believed Arabic to be the language of God, so it could not be corrupted.

"First, this evangelist shared with me a teaching that both Muslims and Christians share: that Jesus is coming again, and those who do not believe in him, he will destroy with his breath. This was the same teaching as the Qur'an teaches, so I was confused. I prayed to Allah, *You know my heart. If there's something I must do, show me*.

"That night Isa came to me in a dream. In my dream I could see someone trying to repair the speaker at the top of the mosque's minaret. And then I looked at the base of the minaret and saw a man there chopping it down with an ax. Then, as I looked closer, I saw that the man was me!

"Four times I had this dream.

"The next morning, I went and found the evangelist who had given me the Injil and asked him what this meant. He smiled and explained to me, 'You are going to win many sheikhs to the Lord.' So immediately I became a follower of Jesus. And immediately I met with great persecution."

Though Hakim did not say it, some of the other sheikhs told me that, as a result of his conversion to Christ, Sheikh Hakim lost his job, his farm, and nearly his life. His own father hurled a spear at his apostate son, piercing his back and nearly killing him. Today, Hakim moves from town to town because there are always those who are trying to kill him.

Hakim smiled and pointed to three of the other sheikhs seated around the breakfast table. "These were my first converts: Sheikh Abu Salam, Sheikh Hafez and Sheikh Mehmed."

He continued, "I was able to accept the gospel because it was given to me in Arabic. Even though Arabic was not my heart language, as a sheikh I knew it well and considered it holy. Over the next seven months, we saw 74 sheikhs from our people group come to faith in Jesus. Right now there are more than 400 sheikhs who have come to the Lord."

Incredulous, I asked, "How many of these sheikhs have been baptized?"

Hakim responded immediately, "More than 300 so far." Later, I was shown a photograph of 75 sheikhs dressed in white, standing in line before one of the region's beautiful lakes, awaiting baptism.

A Region of Rifts

The East Africa Room in the House of Islam includes all or parts of 19 nations, from Sudan in the north to South Africa in the south. In this Room are 298 Muslim people groups with a combined population of more than 357 million persons.

The Great Rift Valley cuts through East Africa and serves as a metaphor for ancient separations between tribes and peoples that began deep in the region's pre-history. In the great "Scramble for Africa" of the 19th and 20th centuries, European colonizers exploited these ethnic rifts to gain control of the region from north to south.[1] The Portuguese, who arrived first in the region, retained control of Mozambique. The British won the lion's share, ruling Sudan, Uganda, Kenya, British Somaliland, and South Africa, which they wrested from the Dutch in 1814. The Germans possessed Tanzania, Burundi and Rwanda. France secured a protectorate over Djibouti. Italy struggled to subdue Ethiopia, eventually carving out Italian Eritrea in the north and Italian Somaliland on the coast. By the end of the colonial era, the strategic coastal territory of the Horn of Africa was divided between Italian, British and French spheres of influence before descending into a chaotic civil war in the late 20th century that has yet to be resolved.

Long before Europeans made their colonial imprint on the African continent, indigenous Africans were busy with their own colonization. Nilotic peoples from Sudan's Nile River valley competed with robust tribes of migrating Bantu peoples believed to have originated in West African Cameroon before spreading across the continent. Occasionally the two African races clashed. In 1994 Bantu Hutus, claiming a fear of their Nilotic neighbors in Rwanda, killed 800,000 Nilotic Tutsis in just 100 days.

More often, though, the two lived in a commercial symbiosis, each benefiting from the other's strengths. The real victims of the African indigenous colonization were the aboriginal Pygmies, Khoisan, and San peoples, sometimes referred to

as the Bushmen tribes who preceded both Nilotic and Bantu peoples. These original inhabitants were scattered through every corner of Africa before Bantu and Nilotic colonization left them marginal and endangered, living in jungles and deserts too inhospitable for other races.

Another pre-European race were the Amharic-speaking Semitic peoples of ancient Abyssinia. These Orthodox Christians found refuge from invading Cushitic Muslims who pressed inland from their coastal strongholds. From the Ethiopian highlands, these historic Christian tribes jousted for centuries with neighboring Cushitic Muslims such as the Afar, the Oromo, and Somalis who dominated the lowland plains of the Horn of Africa.

Khoisan Tribesman

The Afar, Oromo, and Somali make up a fourth ethnolinguistic family of peoples in East Africa. These Cushites, whose name is derived from biblical Noah's grandson, Cush (Genesis 10:6), occupy much of the Horn of Africa: Somalia, eastern Ethiopia, and the Red Sea Hills of Sudan.

Swahili is the trade language of the southeastern half of East Africa and widely spoken in Kenya, Tanzania, Uganda, Burundi, Rwanda, and Mozambique. Swahili is a Bantu language filled with Arabic words borrowed from the Muslim Arabs with whom they traded. The language name itself, Swahili, is adapted from the Arabic word *Saheli* meaning coastal.

It was with these Swahili-speaking coastal Bantu peoples and the Cushitic Somalis on the Horn of Africa that the Arabs enjoyed an 800-year monopoly on East Africa's rich trade in spices, ivory, gold, and slaves, a trade that would be taken over by the Portuguese when they arrived in the late 15th century. Arab trade flowed through a string of cities from Suakin (Sudan), Massawa (Eritrea), and Mombasa (Kenya) in

East Africa

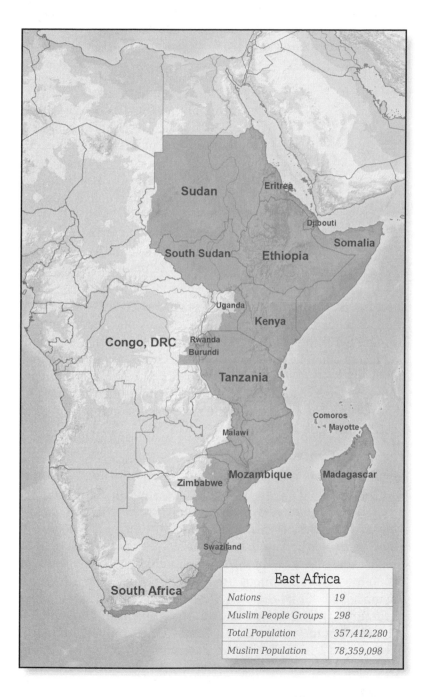

East Africa	
Nations	19
Muslim People Groups	298
Total Population	357,412,280
Muslim Population	78,359,098

the north to Kilwa (Tanzania) and Sofala (Mozambique) in the south. Most important, though, was the Sultanate of Mogadishu that maintained a trading empire on the Horn of Africa from the 10th to 16th centuries.

Ivory Traders

Arrival of the West

In 1497, determined to break the Muslim monopoly on the East Indies spice trade, Portugal's Vasco da Gama sailed around the Cape of Good Hope, reaching the East Africa coast in 1498. Thus began a long history of European adventurism and eventual colonization of the African continent. Europeans who followed him achieved their aim, supplanting the Muslim control of the Indian Ocean that had existed for eight centuries.

When the Portuguese established "Fort Jesus" in 1593 in the Muslim town of Mombasa, in what is today Kenya, they were making a symbolic statement: Europe has arrived; it has arrived to do trade; it has arrived with military backing; and it has come in the name of Jesus. Over the centuries that followed, a succession of European powers—Portuguese, Dutch, French, German, Italian and British—each took their share of the Indian Ocean trade routes while colonizing all of Eastern Africa.

The Great Contest

Muslims officially mark the beginning of their calendar with Muhammad's *hijra* or flight to Medina in the year 622, when the Prophet's own Qurayshi tribe drove him out of Mecca. However, the first Muslim hijra actually occurred eight years earlier, and it was to Africa, not Medina, that these Muslims fled. In 614, Muhammad sent a group of his followers as refugees to Ethiopia where the Christian Aksumite king Ella-Sahama (*Ashama* in Arabic) gave them sanctuary. Had Sahama known that this fugitive band of Muslims would lead to a 14-century-long contest, he might have turned them over to the pursuing Qurayshi delegation that sought their extradition.

Today, most of that ancient Aksumite empire that included southern Arabia, western Yemen, Somalia, Djibouti, eastern Ethiopia, and coastal Eritrea is Muslim. Islam is also a majority religion in Sudan and the island nations of Mayotte and Comoros.

Fort Jesus

For eight centuries, Arab merchants carried on a brisk trade with Eastern Africa in ivory and slaves until the arrival of the Portuguese. For the next four hundred years, Europeans—Portuguese, French, Germans, Italians, and British—ruled the Indian Ocean and dominated the East African region.

During this season of European hegemony, Christianity flourished. At the dawn of the 20th century, Christians numbered about six million adherents. A century later there were nearly 177 million Christians well established throughout the region.[2] Nearly all of the Christian growth, though, was from the non-Muslim Tribal religionists in the region. Christians generally treated Muslims as either trading partners or enemies, but not promising prospects for conversion.

Islam also grew in the region in the 20th century from 6.8 million in 1900 to nearly 78 million in the year 2000.[3] While much of this growth was the result of lower infant mortality rates, the Muslim *dawa* (missionary outreach) was also very active in the region.

The Current Contest

A Muslim convert to Christianity, who now works with churches in the Horn of Africa to spread the gospel among Muslims, related his previous life as a *da'i*—a Muslim missionary to Christians.

"My Muslim name was Sheikh Mahmud. I served in the Islamic Front and Liberation Organization. For three years I was a *mujahid* (Muslim warrior). I trained for nine months in a military training camp in a town just across the border.[4]

"Mujahedeen had come to this town from all over the world, especially from Pakistan. Al-Qaeda also has a base in the town. I was taught how to mobilize the youth to be *da'i* (Muslim missionaries, doers of *dawa*), and how to get the Christians' strategic plans for Islam. We focused on the largest ethnic group in this country because they make up 75 percent of the nation's population. After the mujahid training, we became more *Salafi* (fundamentalist Muslims).

"The training I received in the mujahid camp taught us three dawa strategies for reaching Christians:

1. Win them with money and material enticements.

2. Encourage Muslim girls to marry Christians. She can say, 'If you marry me, I'll become a Christian.' But after the marriage, she will simply inform him that she is remaining a Muslim. After two days, she has a legal right to half of all his possessions. If this does not work, she can put a curse on him (which generally entails poisoning him).

3. Or, we may tell the Christian, 'If you convert to Islam, we will get you a job in Saudi Arabia or the Emirates, but first you have to convert to Islam.'

"We received tactical training as well. We practiced home-to-home outreach. We learned how to research and profile the behavior of the Christians in our community: their habits and lifestyle, strengths and weaknesses. If we couldn't convert him, we would buy his home and move him out. In this way, we would take this country, neighborhood by neighborhood, town by town."

Roving interviews throughout East Africa revealed that Islam itself was in ferment in the region. Muslims in rural villages complained of the sorcery, curses, and magic that plagued their syncretistic Muslim religion.

A Muslim-background believer named Issa from a strong Muslim people group told us of a controversy brewing in his home village as fundamentalist Salafi Muslim reformers challenged the more nominal folk Islam practiced by the majority. The Salafi reformers railed against the community for celebrating the birthday of the Prophet Muhammad. "This is not justifiable from the Qur'an," the Salafis protested. "Then the Salafis said something that surprised me," Issa said. "The Salafis insisted that the Qur'an places Isa al-Masih (Jesus) above Muhammad!" Though these Salafis were in no way professing faith in Jesus or attesting to his divinity, we found it interesting that their strict adherence to the Qur'an had elevated the status of Jesus in their understanding.

We later learned that in other Muslim villages, the issue has gone beyond an internal dispute. Muslim comparisons of Jesus to Muhammad in the Qur'an have led them to investigate what Jesus says about himself in the New Testament.

Insights into the Movements

There are now many movements of Muslims to Christ in Eastern Africa with numbers in the tens of thousands. Each movement, and indeed each individual story is unique, but some patterns are evident.

Among rural Muslims, Islam is grossly infused with African Tribal Religion; practices of witchcraft, fear of evil spirits, curses, and disease bind the population to the control of local *imams* (mosque leaders) whose functions in the community are not much different from the witch doctors who preceded them. In Jesus Christ, these syncretistic Muslims are finding a power that can free them from their previous bondage and dependence on the imam.

An imam named Salah was beloved in his Muslim community before announcing he was no longer interested in practicing the "black magic" that had been in his family for generations. Though his local Muslim community pleaded with him to remain, he renounced his past and began leading a small group of Christian believers.

The gospel is also making powerful inroads within more orthodox Muslim communities. One of the large predominantly Muslim people groups has seen tens of thousands of Muslims turn to faith in Christ. The leaders of these converts are referred to as imams and sheikhs, like Hakim whom we met in the beginning of this chapter. These Christ-following imams and sheikhs are now guiding entire communities to follow Isa al-Masih in baptism.

On Christmas Day 2011, I set out early from my hotel in an East African city for a two-hour drive into the mountains to a rustic lodge located on a beautiful alpine lake. Awaiting me were 20 leaders from an influential Muslim people group who had come to receive further training in their newfound Christian faith. Yusuf, a self-supporting African businessman from an Orthodox evangelical background, had adopted the Muslims in this region as his mission field and led many of their leaders to faith. A key to his effectiveness, he said, was "learning how to communicate in a way that was not culturally offensive to Muslims."

"I used to try to make them Christian," Yusuf said. "Now I try to help them come to the Lord without the religious blanket."

Sitting on the floor with these Muslim-background followers of Christ, I learned they had never before spoken with a Western Christian. One by one they shared the story of how they had come to see that Isa al-Masih was the only way to a right relationship with Allah.

"How many of you have been baptized?" I asked. Nineteen of the twenty hands went up.

"How are you able to do this without persecution?" I asked.

"There is persecution," they replied, and pointed to Sheikh Abu Salam, a man in his 30s armed with an Arabic-language New Testament. "Since I began teaching about Isa," Abu Salam said, "I was chased from the mosque. Now I am fighting my case in the court. I am defending myself as a Muslim follower of Isa al-Masih. I have told the court, 'This is my mosque! Why should I leave it? I have a right to worship here.'"

Abu Salam's courage was not lost on me. The courts in this country had recently determined that Muslims were free to implement *sharia* (Islamic law) in their own communities. This meant that, by choosing to remain in the mosque, Sheikh Abu Salam risked a death sentence for the crime of apostasy.

Another sheikh named Hussein, a balding man in his 40s, said, "We continue to go to the mosque, but our community does not know that we come to trainings like this. If they knew it, there would be trouble."

"Why do you not just leave the mosque and become Christians?" I asked, "What is the benefit of being in the mosque?"

Several voices answered quickly, "To reach others! If we create another faith community outside the mosque, there will be a gap between us and the lost. Instead, we insert Jesus into all of our Muslim practices."

A middle-aged Muslim woman, one of three women in the group, spoke up, "Jesus came as a human to save humans, even though he is God. If God had wanted to save hyenas, he would have become like a hyena. We want to save Muslims and so this compels us to go into the mosque. And so our brothers and sisters risk themselves to go into the mosque to win others."

A sheikh named Hussein spoke up, "We don't worry much about Muhammad. Our burden is for those who are not yet in the kingdom of God. With the help of the Holy Spirit, we have been born again."

Another sheikh said, "Muhammad didn't say, 'I'm a Prophet.' He said, 'Unless something comes on me, I can't say anything. The people—not the Qur'an—said Muhammad is a Prophet. Today, we can read the Qur'an and better understand who the Prophet Muhammad is and is not."

Sheikh Bilal added, "The translation of the Qur'an is changing everything. Before, it was only in Arabic, which no one understood. It didn't matter if I blessed my people or cursed them in Arabic, they would just say, 'Amen!'" This prompted laughter from several.

"Today," Bilal continued, "knowledge is growing. I've graduated more than 200 students from my *madrasa* (Islamic school). When we compare Muhammad and Isa, we see a big gap. There is no comparison. We are troubled by the way other Muslim sheikhs are keeping our people in the dark. Now that we know the truth, we want to take it to our people. I tell you honestly, I feel ashamed at what I did in the past, and so I don't even want to be called a sheikh any more."

Another man said, "In the Qur'an it says, 'If you are confused, ask the people of the previous books.'" It also says, "If

you don't accept the previous books (i.e. the Old and New Testaments), then the fire of hell is waiting for you." And, "Mohammed said, 'I have accepted all the books without separation.'"

Afterwards, I asked Yusuf, the Christian businessman, to
help me understand how he had led these Muslim leaders to
know Jesus.

"We use a discovery approach," Yusuf said. "From this,
they can see that the Qur'an clearly says that if you follow
Muhammad, you'll never get to heaven."

Yusuf explained his discovery approach. On the first day, we
invite these Muslim sheikhs and imams to form small groups
of four, and we ask them this question, 'Who is Muhammad?'
They spend the better part of the day using the Qur'an to
discuss and debate who Muhammad is. At the end of the day,
the groups return and report 'Muhammad is not fit to be a
prophet of God.'"

I was stunned. "How is this possible?"

Yusuf immediately opened an 8-by-5-inch notebook filled
with Qur'an and Hadith references that the sheikhs and imams
used to point out the sins and shortcomings of Muhammad:

Qur'an 46:9	"I am no new thing among the messengers, nor know I what will be done with me or with you. . . .I am but a plain warner."
Qur'an 41:43	"Nothing is said to you that was not said to the messengers before you."
Qur'an 47:19	"So know (O Muhammad), that there is no deity except Allah and ask for the forgiveness of your sin. . . ."
Qur'an 6:50	"Say (O Muhammad), 'I don't say that I know the unseen or that with me are the treasures of Allah. . . . I but follow what is revealed unto me. Are the blind and those who see equal? Take thought!'"

One of the sheikhs listening in on my conversation with
Yusuf inserted, "Muhammad is the most blind of all."

Qur'an 34:24	"We or you are right or in plain error."
Qur'an 57:27	"We gave to them Isa and the Injil."[5]

Yusuf continued, "The sheikhs also pointed to shortcomings in Muhammad's personal life. Though Islam allows up to four wives for a man (Qur'an 4:3), when Muhammad was struck by the beauty of his adopted son Zayd's wife, Zaynab, the Prophet received a new revelation allowing him to marry not

Opened Qur'an

only a fifth wife, but the wife of his own adopted son, something regarded as taboo in the Qur'an (Qur'an 4:23).

Yusuf concluded, "In the Qur'an Muhammad only claims to be a warner. The Qur'an says that those who read the Qur'an are filled with pride, but those who read the Injil are humble."

I stopped Yusuf, to let his words sink in, but he could have continued with pages of additional Qur'anic citations.

"What else are you teaching them?" I asked.

He said, "Their second question is, 'Who is Jesus?'" Yusuf followed the same practice, putting the sheikhs into groups of four and letting them discover for themselves who Jesus is. "They begin with the Qur'an," he said, "but then they turn to the New Testament."

"And their conclusion?" I asked.

"Jesus is the Son of God, the only way of salvation."

How God is Bringing Them to Faith

As the stories above illustrate, God is using dissatisfaction within the Muslim community itself to draw Muslims to faith in Christ. While it is true that many of these stories of conversion begin with the Qur'an before moving to the Injil, this is not the only way Muslims are coming to faith.

One of the largest movements, with numbers exceeding 30,000 baptized believers, began with the intentional outreach to Muslims by an indigenous church, the Gospel for All Nations Church in the capital city.

God began stirring in the hearts of a husband-and-wife pastor team at the Gospel for All Nations Church about the need to reach out to Muslims. They did not know how to begin, so they asked the chief of a Muslim village how they could be a blessing to his people. The chief's response was pragmatic. He asked them to start clean water projects, schools and clinics in the village. The church did as he requested, but coupled these ministries with open-air evangelistic meetings.

Sheikh Rumi attended some of those first open-air meetings seven years ago. He recalled:

"I had studied the Qur'an at school since I was a child. But in my school experience, they didn't teach us; they just beat us. Teaching was done with force, not with love. I wanted a secular education, but my father, who was a sheikh, said no.

"When my oldest sister became very sick, I went with her to three different hospitals. The Lord used this hard time to teach me. I saw Christians in the hospital praying for the sick. I studied them carefully, like doing research.

"Though the Christians prayed for one another, no one (no sheikhs) came to pray for sick Muslims. I realized that an evil spirit was oppressing my sister, and I had no god close to me that I could pray to.

"When my sister died, I decided to study the Qur'an well. I wanted to read it in the local language so I could get the meaning.

"Meanwhile, a Christian came to witness to me. He said he'd give me a Bible, but I said, 'Don't talk to me.'

"I realized there were contradictions in the Qur'an, and I had many questions. So I went to a *Dawa*, a Muslim missionary conference, in town. One of the *da'i* (Muslim missionaries) was preaching about contradictions in the Bible, so I gave him my list of 21 questions about the Qur'an. He refused to answer. Instead, he said I was spoiled, and threw me out of the conference. This filled me with despair.

"I still had notes on the 'biblical contradictions' they had given me at the conference, so I took my notes, along with a Bible, and climbed a mountain to reflect.

"By the time I came down from the mountain, I was filled with joy. I sought out a meeting that was being led by the Gospel for All Nations Church. That afternoon, while the preacher was preaching, a big wind came up, pulling down the tent. Then rain began to soak the audience.

"The woman preacher, who with her husband was co-founder of the church, stood up and prayed out loud, 'Lord, we want to worship, let the rain come back in the evening.'

"In my mind I said, 'God if you listen to her prayer, I'll believe in you, even though I don't know Jesus. Otherwise, I'll know what she is teaching is false.'

"The wind stopped right away, and the rain stopped in a 100-meter circle around the tent.

The Nature of the Movements

There are many ways Muslims are coming to faith in Christ in East Africa: dreams, answered prayers, dissatisfaction with Islam, changed lives. Many of the churches in the region are vibrant and are now shedding their fear of outreach to Muslims. Particularly war and famine have battered the Muslim communities, Christians have been there to offer an alternative to Islam. Village Muslims who, generations ago, embraced Islam as another means to manipulate the ever-present threat of spirits and demons, are finding in Christ a power greater than the fears that beset them.

East Africans have a long history of following their leaders, whether those leaders are tribal chiefs, village witch doctors or Muslim imams. Important decisions are rarely made individually, but as a community. So it is not surprising that the movements that are taking place in the region often begin with sheikhs and imams. These are the leaders to whom the people look for guidance, and it is they who are guiding their followers to Christ.

Islam provided East Africans with a powerful tool for rallying resistance to Western colonial powers. The absence of Western colonizers has given the gospel a new hearing, particularly when it comes from local witnesses. It is much more difficult in the 21st century for Muslim *jihadis* to incite an anti-Christian mob when the voice of the witness is the sheikh himself.

How They Are Living Out Their Faith

A 28-year-old Muslim who came to faith in Christ one and a half years ago reflected a widely held sentiment: "I love to pray. I like that my prayers to God as a follower of Christ are not guided, as Muslim prayers are, but rather are expressed as a true conversation with God. I can tell him what is on my heart."

The stories of East African Muslims who come to faith in Christ reveal that they are on a journey. A recent doctoral dissertation that examined a large Muslim people group with more than 10,000 baptized followers of Christ illustrates this journey.[6] Though they began as Muslims, their discovery of Christ has slowly and inexorably led them to marginalize the role of Muhammad and the Qur'an. Over time, they have immersed themselves more and more deeply in the New Testament, while setting their Qur'an on the shelf.

We Need the Gospel

Elias was an East African missionary living in the crowded Somali refugee quarter of a large city in the Horn of Africa. As Elias prepared his dinner alone, after a long day of ministering to refugees, he was startled at the knock on his door by a 65-year old Somali sheikh named Abdul-Ahad. The sheikh had come from the war-torn city of Mogadishu, Somalia. Elias was nervous, wondering if this would be the night that *Al-Shabaab* (Somali militants) chose to extract their revenge on yet another Christian.

When Elias opened his door, the sheikh abruptly demanded, "Yes or No. Jesus' blood paid for the sins of everyone in the world?"

Elias replied, "Yes."

The sheikh responded adamantly, "You're lying!" Then he hesitated before saying, "The blood of Jesus cannot forgive my sins."

He told Elias of the violence he had committed in Mogadishu. The old sheikh began to tremble and weep. "I need relief from that," he said.

Elias told him, "If you and I agree tonight, then God will forgive you."

The old sheikh prayed with Elias, and Abdul-Ahad was saved that night.

Before he left, Abdul-Ahad turned to Elias, grasped his arm, and said to him, "When you look at me on the street, you see my Muslim hat and my beard, and you are afraid of me. And, to tell you the truth, that is why we dress this way, to make you afraid of us. But you need to know—you need to know that inside we are empty. Don't be afraid of us. We need the gospel."

Small Group Discussion ~ Discover for Yourself

1. What impressions do you take away from this chapter?
2. How is God at work in the East Africa Room?
3. How is God using "the discovery approach?"
4. What are your impressions of the story of Elias and Abdul-Ahad?

the North Africa room

He tends his flock like a shepherd:
He gathers the lambs in his arms.

Isaiah 40:11

 TWO DECADES AGO, in the remote mountains of North Africa, in one of the most turbulent and repressive corners of the *Dar al-Islam*, a movement of Muslims to Christ began to surface. Today the movement numbers in the tens of thousands and marks the first indigenous turning of Muslims to Christ in the 14-century history of Islam in North Africa.

He Already Has Me

I sat with Rafiq in his studio, a cramped apartment in a mixed-use commercial high rise, packed with recording and mixing equipment. Rafiq is a spirited 35-year-old Berber whose dark eyes danced as he told the story of how his life had been transformed.

"It was 2001, and I was working in Paris as a musician, writing music for an international film and music company."[1]

Rafiq was one of the millions of North Africans who had migrated to France following his country's independence in the 1960s.[2] "Though I was born in North Africa, I grew up a European. Though my family was ethnically Berber, I was French in every way. Like most Frenchmen, I had never been religious. I was Muslim in name, but an atheist in practice.

"I had a wife, Nora, back in North Africa. I would send her money when I could, and return to visit every year or so. But for me, I was consumed with my life in France. Music was my life and my gift. Though I never had formal training, I could play many instruments and would use these to play the songs I had written.

"After several of my songs were published, my bosses at the entertainment company encouraged me to do more. 'You should write a musical,' they suggested. I was thinking about this as I left their office. As I walked down the street, the rain began to pour. Lost in thought, I stepped into a doorway and lit a cigarette. After a moment, I turned around and saw that I was in the entryway to a Catholic Church.

"I stepped inside, the first time I'd ever entered a church. Near the front there were candles that you could purchase and light as a prayer. I noticed that the longer candles cost more than the shorter ones, and this struck me as funny. I joked to the priest, 'Can you loan me some money to buy a prayer?' The priest smiled and handed me a candle. 'It is free,' he said.

"I looked up at the large statue of Jesus crucified suspended from the ceiling. On the wall beside it, I saw another image of Jesus, this one with him holding a lamb. Under it were the words, *The good shepherd lays down his life for the sheep.*

"I began to think, 'What kind of person was this who would lay down his life for others?'

Good Shepherd

"Then I said to myself, 'Ah! This would make a great subject for a musical!'

"So I asked the priest for the Scriptures that told the story of Jesus. He offered me a large Catholic Bible. 'No, no,' I said, 'I just want the part about Jesus.' So he gave me the four gospels.

"I took them home and read them over and over. I began to have dreams filled with Jesus and music. The music and the scenes began to pour out of my imagination. In one month I wrote the entire life of Jesus, a two-and-a-half-hour musical from Gabriel's announcement to the Virgin Mary to the resurrection and ascension of Christ to heaven.

"I used a synthesizer, starting with the violin score, and then added each orchestral instrument. I envisioned the scenes one by one and wrote out the lyrics. I called my musical 'Nazareth,'" Rafiq said. "The more I gave myself to this life of Jesus, the more he changed me. My friends in the music business warned me, 'Be careful!' they said, 'Do not lose yourself in this person of Jesus.' I told them, 'It is too late. He already has me.'

"I took the musical to my bosses at the entertainment company. Though this was very unusual, they sat and listened for the entire two and a half hours as I played the musical for them. After I finished they said, 'Well, Jesus is very marketable. Let's do this.' We began discussing who would be cast for the various parts: Jesus, Mary, Judas, Satan. . . .

"Later that same year, Mel Gibson's *The Passion of the Christ* was released to global attention, but within the Jewish entertainment community, the movie seemed anti Semitic. Immediately, a chill went over any movies or music with a Jesus theme. My boss called me into his office and told me they would not produce my musical. Not long afterwards, I was fired.

"My musical said nothing about the Jews," Rafiq said, shaking his head.

Then he looked up at me and smiled, "But it no longer mattered to me. Jesus had become my life. I stopped smoking and drinking. I no longer wanted to spend time in the bars or partying. Instead, I wanted to return to North Africa to tell Nora and my family about the one who had come into my life.

"When I got home, I recruited my wife Nora, who is an artist, to make storyboards of the life of Jesus for the musical. It was while creating these storyboards that Nora was touched by the beauty of Jesus."

Nora interrupted, "But it was after Jesus answered my prayers, prayers for Rafiq's sister to be healed, that I knew he was real." Trembling, with tears in her eyes, Nora continued, "I said to God, 'Either reveal yourself to me or take me out of here.' And God revealed himself." Wiping away tears, she said, "Whenever the questions come, I say, 'How can I doubt or question what he has done in my life?'"

Rafiq played for me the opening song of his musical, *le Messie de Dieu* (God's Messiah), and unfolded the scene for me with passionate descriptions of Mary alone on a darkened stage when the angel Gabriel appears to her and tells her that she will give birth to the Messiah. "How can this be," she asked, "since I have never been with a man?" The voice of the woman singing the part of Mary was angelic. "That is my wife," Rafiq said, "that is Nora who is singing." The music was spellbinding. The thought that such beautiful music and its composer were in exile here in this remote corner of Africa grieved me, until Rafiq changed my perspective.

Wrapping his arm around his lovely expectant wife, touching the cheek of his lively three-year-old, Rafiq said, "And now I am serving the Lord here in North Africa. I compose and produce music in French, Arabic and Berber all to the glory of God."

The Maghreb

Muslims call the six nations of North Africa—Mauritania, Western Sahara, Morocco, Algeria, Tunisia and Libya—*the Maghreb*, meaning "the west" or "the place of the sunset." The Maghreb has a population of just under 90 million, 88.9 million of whom are Muslims.

MUSLIMS IN THE MAGHREB

Algeria (37 million, 99% Muslim, 1% Jewish & Christian)

Libya (5.6 million, 99% Muslim)

Mauritania (3.3 million, 100% Muslim)

Morocco (32 million, 99% Muslim)

Tunisia (10.5 million, 98% Muslim; 1% Christian; 1% Jewish)

Western Sahara (.5 million, 100% Muslim)

North Africans describe their ethnicity as a mélange, a fascinating blend of centuries of human history that has washed across their shores. Today many North African governments are reviving an Arabization process that began in the 8th century, and was renewed with invasions by *beni Hillal* and *beni Yamin* Bedouin tribes in the 12th century, before being interrupted by three centuries of Turkish and European colonization.

Despite the predominance of Arabic language and culture, DNA analysis reveals that today's Algerian population is still predominantly Berber (50%) followed by Arab (30%) with scores of other competing ethnicities.[3] Even before the Arab invasions, the aboriginal Berber tribes had already witnessed centuries of Phoenician, Greek, Roman, Germanic Vandal, Bantu and Nilotic infusions.

Following the Spanish *Reconquista* of the Iberian Peninsula in 1492 and expulsion of the last *Moriscos* (converts from Islam who were suspected of still being Muslims) from the European mainland in 1610, embittered Muslim refugees returned to North Africa to wage a centuries-long cold war against Christian Europe. Even today, street signs in Tunis and Algiers such as *Sharia Andalusia* and *Tariq Toledo* still bear witness to lost, but not forgotten, dominions across the sea.

Between 1530 and 1815, Ottoman corsairs, or Barbary Coast pirates as they were known to the West, captured hundreds of Western ships, and made countless raids on European coastal towns from Italy to Iceland filling forced labor compounds and harems in Tripoli, Tunis, Oran and Algiers with more than a million Christian slaves.[4] Americans have little collective memory of this today, but these same pirate actions prompted two of America's earliest foreign wars, the First and Second Barbary Wars (1801-05 and 1815), and served as the primary catalysts for the creation of both the U.S. Navy and the U.S. Marines.[5]

In its westernmost boundaries, on the streets of Nouakchott, Mauritania, one still hears *Hassaniya* Arabic, originally spoken by Bedouin tribes in Yemen more than 4,000 miles to the east. In the teeming port city of Algiers, one still encounters green-eyed or blond-haired Algerian descendants of pirated Europeans from days gone by. Tripoli's Arab population is seasoned with Berber, Jewish and sub-Saharan Africans, remnants of a once thriving slave industry that transported captives 2,000 miles across the Sahara from Omdurman, Sudan, to the Mediterranean.

A main street in downtown Tunis proudly bears the name *Kheir ed-Din bin Pasha* Boulevard, named for the admiral of the Ottoman Navy, infamous in the West as Barbarossa (1474-1518), or Red Beard the Pirate. Kheir ed-Din was the son of a Greek Orthodox widow and a Muslim Turk from the frontier island of Lesbos. Both Kheir ed-Din and his brother, Aruj, bore the name Barbarossa and together terrorized European trade in the Mediterranean for decades.

A favorite question I asked of North Africans as I traveled across the Maghreb was *Ailatik min ay balid, min al-asl*? "What country did your family come from in the beginning?" The question would stir proud recollections: "from Yemen," "from Jordan," "from Turkey," "from Africa," "from the Berbers," "from Israel." Together, these images painted a picture of what a truly global phenomenon the House of Islam was and is, and how successful Islam has been at assimilating all who crossed its path.

Throughout its Islamic history, North Africa has been a cultural and political battlefield between Islam and the West. Scarcely a generation has passed in nearly 14 centuries without some skirmish or all-out war between the Islamic governments imposed there in the 8th century and the various European powers that have sought to subdue and, if possible, supplant them. This interminable stalemate between the nations of North Africa and the West continues to shape the intense ethos within these Maghrebi nations today.

From Pirates to the Present

In 1830 France brought to an end the era of Ottoman pirates in North Africa, launching a program of colonization in Algeria that would eventually lead to French "protectorates" over Morocco, Tunisia and Mauritania. The Italian conquest of Libya

in 1911 brought the rest of the
Maghreb under European control
until liberation and nationhood in
the 1950s and 60s. The bloodiest
of the independence movements
was the Algerian Revolution that
lasted from 1945 to 1962 claiming
more than 700,000 Algerian and
26,500 French lives.[6]

Barbarossa

Independence movements in
each Maghrebi state coalesced
around nativist sentiments and Islamic jihad, a potent formula for
ousting Europeans, but less con-
ducive to subsequent governance. In an effort to unify their
country and purge it of colonial residue, Algeria's National
Liberation Front government (FLN) imported teachers of Arabic and Islam to assist the Arabization process. Looking back
today, many Algerians point to this importation of Arabic and
Islamic teachers as the seed that bore fruit in the radical Islamic conflicts that appeared in the decade of the 1990s.

Following economic turmoil in the 1980s, Algerians voted
in December 1991 to replace the National Liberation Front
that had governed the country for more than two decades.
Rather than relinquish power to their opponents, the FLN
canceled run-off elections. The clashes that followed prompted
a military coup d'état. Failed negotiations led to a civil war
that marked the decade of the 1990s as the "dark decade,"
resulting in perhaps 100,000 civilian and military deaths.[7]
Atrocities committed by the army and the opposition GIA
(Armed Islamic Group) and its urban counterpart, the FIS
(Islamic Salvation Front), washed the country in blood, with
both sides professing Allah's mandate for their actions. The
spectacle of Algerian men, women, and children, along with
Catholic monks and nuns with throats slashed, the massacres
of entire villages left many North Africans yearning for a
different path.

A Movement Rises

There was a window in North African history between the close of the Algerian War of Independence in 1962 and the beginning of its internal war with Islamists in 1992 when gospel light from the outside world was able to enter. I sat with Mahmoud, a 62-year-old leader of Muslim-background Christians in his country. Few persons had contributed more to the birth of the movement among his people.

"It was 1968," he said. "The Vietnam War was at its peak. Across Europe as well as the U.S., students were in revolt. I was a troubled 17-year-old Berber living in the housing projects of Lyon, France. A young Berber teenager named Yusuf befriended me, often speaking of God and Jesus. 'I want to learn more about my own culture, more about Islam,' I told him. Yusuf said, 'Go and buy a Qur'an in French and read it for yourself.'

"I did this, and over the weeks that followed, I asked Yusuf many questions. Yusuf always had thoughtful answers, and never dismissed my questions. It was in those days that I first asked the question *What is this evil that is in me?* Yusuf patiently responded, 'If you want to know God, ask him to reveal himself to you.'

"During that week, I prayed, *God, if you exist, I want to know you.* Instantly, I was filled with a new joy I had never felt before. The next day Yusuf said to me, 'You don't have to say anything. I can see what has happened.'"

Mahmoud recalled, "Yusuf put me in touch with God, and from there, God began to change me." I asked Mahmoud if repentance had been an initial part of his conversion process. "Not in the beginning," he said, "but repentance is a lifelong process, not a one-time thing."

Around this time, a Swiss evangelical from Geneva named Eldon Bleu had a vision to minister to North Africans in France. Eldon's vision led him to Lyon in 1969 where he started a Youth Center in one of the old military barracks in the city.

"I was so thirsty for God," Mahmoud said, "that I plunged into this ministry and into a church that was birthed in the Youth Center. I stayed with this church for seven years before

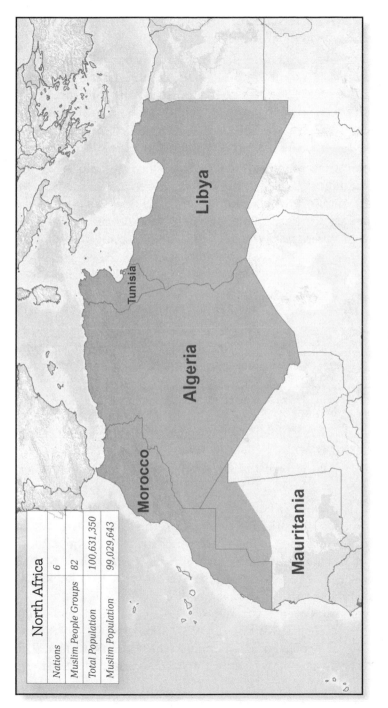

North Africa

North Africa	
Nations	6
Muslim People Groups	82
Total Population	100,631,350
Muslim Population	99,029,643

moving to a Brethren Church in Lyon. I preferred the shared leadership style of the Brethren Church."

Soon these young Berber believers formed a Berber-background mission organization called ACEB, *L'Association Chretienne d'Expression Berbere*, dedicated to Berber-language Bible translation, *JESUS Film* production and radio programming.[8] In the years that followed, Berber-language media played an invaluable role in the response to the gospel in North Africa.

Operation Mobilization's *Love Europe* campaign in the 1980s and 1990s spread the gospel widely among the North African immigrant population in France. Many of these immigrants were disillusioned youth, fleeing the civil unrest that was endemic in their homeland. Port distributions of

Berber Mélange

thousands of *JESUS Films* and New Testaments in the Berber language fueled the movement and spread the gospel into coastal cities across North Africa.

During that same window of openness in North Africa, an American Baptist missionary named Bob Cane secured a rare visa and began an outreach in North Africa to university students. Khalid, now a physician in the Berber interior, was a medical student in 1980 when he heard other classmates talking about *Bonne Nouvelle* (Good News).

"At the time," Khalid said, "I was only a pseudo-Muslim with no religious practices. I asked Ahmed, a fellow student and friend of mine, 'What is this good news?' He gave me a copy of the Gospel of John and told me to read it. I was so impressed by the person of Jesus that I went to a bookstore and bought a copy of the whole Bible in French and read it from cover to cover. My friend took note of this and invited me to attend the *Bonne Nouvelle* Church. "Soon afterwards," Khalid said, "I read a gospel tract and prayed the 'Sinner's Prayer.' The next day I awakened with a joy that I could not deny."

Dr. Khalid's story was multiplied many times over in the 1980s, even after Bob Cane was expelled and the *Bonne Nouvelle* Church was temporarily closed. One of the ministries that issued from the young believers in the *Bonne Nouvelle* Church was a youth soccer camp in the Berber mountains. It was there that they met a 21-year-old athlete named Reddah. Reddah's father had been a *mujahid* (freedom fighter) who was killed a month before Reddah was born. Reddah's young mother tried to console her child with the words, "Son, it was Allah who took your father." For Reddah, though, the words were torturous. If this was Allah's doing, then he would oppose this Allah in any way he could.

"During Ramadan (the month of fasting), I ate and drank," Reddah said. "In the *madrasa* (religious school) I provoked my teacher by asking, 'Why must I pray in Arabic? Can I not pray in my Berber language?' At that time I hated Allah and Arabic and all things related to Islam.

"In the summer of 1981, a soccer team made up of Arabs and Berbers came to my village and joined our soccer tournament. They didn't curse or drink like many of the other teams. Instead, they prayed together and read a book as they sat together in their camp at night.

"One morning, as our team prepared for a semi-final match, I woke up with a high fever and could not move. The game was that afternoon, but I could not play. It was July 6th, and very hot. But I wrapped myself in a blanket and went to watch the match. One of the Christians came over to me and asked me what was wrong. I told him I had a fever and could not play. He said, 'Come to our camp, we have some medicine.' When I reached their camp, one of them asked, 'Do you want the medicine, or would you like for me to pray for you?' I thought to myself I can always ask for the medicine later, but this will be another chance to prove that God does not exist. So I said, 'Pray for me.'

"They prayed in French. One of them opened a Bible, and read a passage about where Jesus had healed Simon Peter's mother-in-law. He ordered the fever to leave my body.

"I immediately felt something go out of me. Normally, even when the fever goes down, we are still tired. But it was as if I had not even been sick. I didn't even say thank you. I just ran straight to the coach and said I'm ready to play. I played the rest of the game.

"After the match I thought about what had happened. My friends were already calling me a hypocrite and accusing me of faking my sickness. I tried to explain but they did not want to listen. I insisted and explained what had happened: 'I think their God is real; He is not like ours.' From that moment, I began asking myself serious questions.

"Each evening we would sit with the Christians and learn from them. They taught us how to read the Bible and pray. In the days that followed, God allowed us to see many miracles and answers to prayer. Over the next week, 40 of us gave our lives to Christ. Three years later I was baptized in the *Bonne Nouvelle* Church. Since 2000, I have been working full time with the development of churches here in the Berber Mountains."

In January 2013, a year after my meeting with Reddah, I sat with a group of 12 men who were leaders in the Berber churches of their community. These believers exhibited a fearlessness that belied the hostile conditions around them. I began by assuring them that I would not publish the photos I had taken of them or use their real names in my writing.

They laughed, "Why not? We don't care if you tell everyone that we are followers of Jesus! You can use our photos and put it on *al-Hayat* ("The Life," the Arabic-language satellite TV channel)!"

I asked if they all felt this way, and they all said, "Yes!"

The men exuded a joy characteristic of virtually all of the Berbers I interviewed. Instead of dwelling on their difficulties, these men emphasized the role that the living Christ had played among their people. In all of the worst years of the civil war, they said, not a single Christian—Berber or Arab—was killed. A remarkable claim that no one disputed, even though the Berber region had seen some of the worst atrocities.

What is God Using to Bring Muslims to Faith?

These Berber church leaders, all converts from Islam, recalled a legacy that had produced some of Christendom's most famous Church Fathers: Cyprian, Tertullian, Augustine. I asked the church leaders the question *What is God using today to bring Muslims to Christ?* They told me:

> We were Christians; we are just coming back to the house. There are lots of hypotheses. Persons preached the gospel. We were tired of terrorists. Maybe now people have more of an open mind and are seeking out the truth. The man who carried Jesus' cross was a Libyan Berber, and now it is up to us to follow him. The Berbers have always been marginalized. Berbers are not afraid of taboos and trying something different. We Mountain Berbers are more open than persons in other parts of the country, even more open than other Berbers.

St. Augustine

The interviews that followed brought additional insights to this core question. Most of the Berber Muslim-background believers had come to faith during the 1990s, the decade filled with Muslim violence against fellow Muslims. They saw in the way of Jesus a stark contrast to that of Muhammad. Radio broadcasts, the first satellite TV programming, and the *JESUS Film* (the life of Jesus) in the Berber language played a powerful role in penetrating the homes of Muslims who had been sheltered from alternatives for centuries. Resentment of the government's Arabization program and the forced suppression of their own culture opened many to a Savior who spoke their own language. Though the Scripture in their Berber language is still a little strange to them since there is little other literature in their own language, they read it with great delight and teach it to their children.

While the local-language presentation of the gospel through media was beneficial, two other elements weighed heavier in this movement that produced several thousand believers. The first was personal witness. Again and again, converts spoke of someone—a family member, a casual friend, an intentional witness—who took the time to share a testimony and the gospel of Jesus Christ. The courage exhibited in this personal evangelism was all the more remarkable in a season when French Catholic missionaries and thousands of ordinary citizens were having their throats slashed by Islamic extremists.

The second critical element that God used in fostering such a widespread turning to Christ was answered prayers. The first steps in this movement were not doctrinal persuasion or repentance from known sins, though both of these came later. The launch of the movement came after hearing a testimony of Christ followed by a personal encounter with Jesus Christ. Some of these encounters began with dreams, others through answered prayers and healings, but all of them involved a vital meeting with the living, transforming power of Jesus Christ.

Prayer and Fasting

Reddah was widely recognized as one who had been with the movement from the beginning. Following his conversion on the soccer fields in 1981 and baptism in 1984, he spent some time in Bible school in France in the mid-1980s.

"Our fledgling church began to take shape in 1989-90," he said. "In 1990 we organized another camp outing and invited believers from all the other villages. We had prayer, Bible study and worship scheduled for a week."

"When we finished, the Lord said, 'Now that your week is over, my week can start.' We had no more provisions, though, so the Lord said, 'Now you will enter into a fast.' We did a seven-day fast, drinking only water. It was a miracle for us because we'd never done anything like that before. During this time, God told us what to pray for. It was like we really experienced Pentecost. There were deliverances, healings, revelations from God.

"We did a chain of fasting and prayer so that someone was praying and fasting at all times. In 1991, we arranged another campout. It was just before the beginning of terrorism. We invited other Christians from different villages for teaching, prayer, etc.

"It was then and there that God told us that our country was going to go through difficult times with lots of bloodshed. He said, 'Do not be afraid, for I will protect you.' Our country entered into years of terror and bloodshed that cost the lives of 100,000 citizens. It was during those years that there was a great explosion of growth in the churches. We had freedom, because the government was occupied with the terrorists. Throughout this time, no local Christians— Mountain Berber or Arab—were killed.

"There are many stories of Christians, even in the military, who were miraculously spared from death, when thousands died all around them. One fellow read the passage 'A thousand may fall at your side, and ten thousand at your right hand, but it will not come near you' (Psalm 91:7). That day, in an ambush, all of his battalion were killed except him. His superiors interrogated him with great suspicion, and then kicked him out of the army."

Reddah's story was echoed wherever I went. Traveling through the villages of the Berber mountains, visiting homes and churches of the believers, I often noticed the framed pictures of Jesus depicted as the Good Shepherd. Written beneath these images were the same words that Rafiq had seen in the Catholic sanctuary in Paris: *The good shepherd lays down his life for the sheep.* Only this time they were written in Berber. A Berber woman named Zeinab explained to me, "The shepherd means so much to us because we are a people who have sheep. We know how the shepherd must love the sheep and hold the sheep close to his heart."

These Berbers were no longer sheep without a shepherd. They had found their Shepherd and were attuned to His voice.

If You Build It, They Will Come

As the movement took root in the 1990s, emerging Christian leaders in North Africa gathered congregations too large to meet in homes and living rooms. Whenever possible, they secured an apartment or dedicated building and began conducting worship services that mirrored those they had witnessed among Evangelicals in France. This became one of the few movements inside the *Dar al-Islam* that is building-centered and professional-pastor led. A 2002 study identified 80 churches in the movement, many of them still hidden from official sanction.[9] In 2013, the numbers had not increased by much. Land was costly and buildings, though attractive to the believers, invited attack from militants.

Several of the church leaders testified to a ministry of following up on respondents to satellite television and radio broadcasts. There was less of the bold soccer-camp outreach of the 1980s and less evidence of laypersons trained and ready "to give a reason for the hope that was within them" (1 Peter 3:15).

The ethos was shifting from an out-of-control movement to a more institution-based work. If one could secure a building, purchase a plot of land and erect a structure, he could be assured of drawing a community of believers. These churches, centrally located in crossroad towns, served as beacons that would draw isolated believers from the mountains like moths to a torch. It was as if believers were scattered throughout the mountain villages through the Berber region, just waiting for a venue to congregate. "If you build it, they will come."

The 2002 study revealed a pattern that continues to the present: " . . . as various individuals and families within this particular people group heard about the vital Christian worship going on in that somewhat central church site, they were drawn to it and into it. When Muslim-background believers came to town from the rugged countryside for supplies, heard and then observed this vibrant church in worship, they were attracted to it."[10] This attractional, church-building model of gospel advance was the predominant pattern among the Berber believers in 2002 and continues to be today, in a movement whose zenith may have passed.

Buildings are hard to come by in the remote mountains of North Africa, so foreigners are invited to provide the necessary resources to erect facilities. However, even with these buildings, the study conducted in 2002 further revealed that the "total attendance on a given worship day has not increased by the hundreds of people as its membership should have, when counting up all the baptisms."[11] The same was true a decade later. If one counts attendance in the courageous church congregations meeting each week, the numbers fall far short of the numbers of those who have responded to the gospel message they have encountered through broadcast media, dreams and personal witness to Christ.

Meanwhile, the government's Arabization process continues. Latifa, a young mother, explained, "It is difficult to raise Christian children in a Muslim society. I, like most, studied Arabic in school from age six to 18. My children are being indoctrinated in the school system. Not just Arabization, but also Islamization. To pass the baccalaureate, they must memorize long Qur'anic passages." Latifa's concerns echo in homes across the Berber movement, raising questions as to its future.

They Belong to Me

As I concluded my time with the musical prodigy, Rafiq, and his wife Nora, I wondered how someone so gifted could remain hidden in a Berber province in North Africa. Surely Paris or New York would offer him a much greater prospect for the future.

I asked Rafiq about this.

"Last year,' Rafiq said, 'I did become sad. I wondered if I should continue doing what I was doing. So I prayed to God that he would teach me.

"Soon afterwards, I began having dreams in which an old man spoke to me and taught me.

"In one dream, I saw a beautiful meadow with sheep and a stream. I heard the voice of the old man say to me, 'What do you see?'

"'I see a meadow and a stream,' I said, 'and sheep grazing in the meadow.'

"Next, I saw a little shepherd boy sitting on the hillside playing a flute.

"The old man in my dream said, 'What else do you see?'

"'I see a little shepherd boy.'

"'And what is he doing?' the old man asked.

"'He is playing a flute,' I said.

"'And why is he playing a flute?'

"'He is playing it,' I said, 'so the sheep will know that they belong to him.'

"The old man said gently, 'You are that shepherd boy. And that is why you must continue your music, so the sheep will know that they belong to him.'

"'I awoke weeping,' Rafiq said, 'and I knew that I had my answer."

Small Group Discussion ~ Discover for Yourself

1. What impressions do you take away from this chapter?

2. How is God at work in the North Africa Room?

3. What role did Muslim-on-Muslim violence play in this Room?

4. See how many different ways you can identify that God is drawing North Africans to Christ.

the Eastern South Asia room

Those who sow in tears
will reap with songs of joy.

Psalm 126:5

 THERE MAY WELL be dozens of Muslim movements to Christ in Eastern South Asia today. In a one-month stretch, working with colleagues on the ground, we gathered more than 300 interviews from seven movements, and could have doubled this number.

The movements are far from uniform. Some issue into multiplying house churches, often called *Isa Jamaats* or Jesus Groups, while others dissolve invisibly back into Muslim communities where they have come to be known as Insider or C5 Movements.[1] This Western designation is one they do not ascribe to themselves, and yet they acknowledge a desire to remain within their Muslim community while reorienting their life around a personal relationship with Jesus Christ as Savior and Lord. Their leaders say these Insiders number in the tens or perhaps hundreds of thousands. At this point in time, it is impossible to know.

Surveys done as early as 2002 indicated tens of thousands of less deeply contextualized C4 believers as well. These followers of Christ typically call themselves *Isai Muslims* (Muslims who belong to Jesus), but in contrast to C5 Insiders, the C4 believers have taken a more open Christian identity while still retaining ties to their Muslim communities.

What we do know now is that some of the earliest ripples of these movements began when an elderly Norwegian missionary invested time in the confused 17-year-old son of a Bengali imam.

"It was 1969," began Thomas Mori, "and I was 17 years old. My father was an imam, and we were direct descendants of the Central Asians who came from Afghanistan bringing Islam to Bengal. So I am part Mongol!" he said proudly.

"I used to ask questions of my teachers in the *madrasa*, questions that they could not answer, and it would make them so angry. Just to ridicule me, one of them took to calling me 'a Christian.' Rebellious youth that I was, I thought to myself, *Maybe he's right. Maybe I am a Christian.* However, I had no idea what this meant. But I knew that there was a missionary in my town. He was an old Norwegian man with a long white beard that made him look a little like Santa Claus.

"This missionary had labored for 30 years in India without a single convert before moving to my town in East Pakistan in 1962. When I met him seven years later, he still had not seen any converts to Christ.

"The Norwegian patiently answered all my questions, teaching me from the Bible who Jesus is, what Jesus had done for us, and how I could become a follower of him. Soon after, I gave my life to Christ.

"When I returned home and told my father, he would not even let me collect any clothes. He disowned me immediately, and expelled me from my home and family.

"I made my way to Dhaka (the capital city). But I had nothing. For a time I fed myself by pulling a rickshaw through the streets. Then, in 1971, the War of Liberation struck, turning everything in our country upside down.

"After the Liberation War, I found a job doing relief work with the secular Danish Relief Mission. Because of my work with the Danish relief team, for many, many months while I was with them I drank no water; we drank only beer, wine and whiskey.

"Then, in 1972 I met a Baptist missionary named B.T. Rucker. B.T. changed my life more than anyone else. B.T. found me living on the streets after the Liberation. Instead

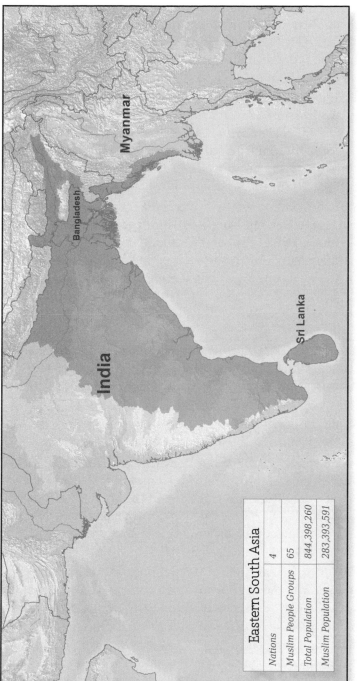

Eastern South Asia

Eastern South Asia	
Nations	4
Muslim People Groups	65
Total Population	844,398,260
Muslim Population	283,393,591

of judging me for my lifestyle, B.T. invited me to have a Bible study with him. He discipled me for nine months as we worked together through a Theological Education by Extension (TEE) course that B.T. provided. After we completed the course, B.T. pressed a local Baptist church to baptize me.

"Later, B.T. challenged me to return to my people and evangelize them. So I went back to the northern part of the country and joined up with the Presbyterians. I started a Bible study every morning at 6:00 a.m. I just taught them what Rucker had taught me.

"In those days, most of the Christians in our Presbyterian church were from a tribal background. I was different from them; I was a Bengali from a Muslim background. The tribal people had a saying, 'If you are walking down a path and come across a Bengali (i.e., Muslim) and a poisonous snake, first kill the Bengali.' It was we Bengalis who had pushed the tribal people off their land and taken over their country, so I could understand their resentment toward us, even though we were now brothers.

"In 1976 one of the American Presbyterian missionaries came to me with a problem. 'There are six young men who have come here from the village,' he said. 'They are all Muslims and they want to know how to be saved.'

"'You understand Muslims,' he said. 'Come and talk with these young men and see if they are earnest or not.'

"So I spent two or three hours with them. It was clear to me that they had Jesus in their hearts. They had received some Christian literature from one of the traveling Operation Mobilization teams.[2] These young Muslim men had read the literature, believed on Jesus, and had invited him into their hearts.

"Up to this point, as a Muslim-background believer, my experience with the church had been quite negative. Christians wanted Muslims to come to faith, but they didn't want to fellowship with them.

"So I told the young Muslim men, 'I can see that Jesus is in your heart. Go back home, but don't become Christians.[3]

Your parents will know very soon, because your life will be changed. When they ask you, you can tell them about Jesus.'

"After the young men left, I reported to the missionary what had happened. He was very upset, because he thought I had lost my chance. But one month later, one of the six Muslims came back with 15 elders from his community. He said, 'All of these men want to be followers of Jesus too.'

"The next month, they came back with 16 or 17 more people. This pattern continued for the next eight years. Hundreds came just to do Bible study with me."

Land of Rivers

Snowfall on the Himalayas descends 20,000 feet through more than 800 river channels of Eastern South Asia before flowing into the mangrove swamps of the Sundarbans, and emptying its silty cargo into the Bay of Bengal. The Sundarbans are like the Florida Everglades of greater Bengal, only five times larger.[4] Bangladesh and West Bengal make up the heart of Eastern South Asia, but the region also encompasses much of the Indian subcontinent and stretches eastward into Myanmar's Rakhine western border state.

The rich soil deposited by these rivers sustains one of the most densely populated regions on earth. Imagine nearly half the U.S. population, 150 million persons, packed into a country a little smaller than Iowa, and you have Bangladesh. Though this delta land has blessed its inhabitants, it also extracts its toll as millions of subsistence farmers live and die under the perennial threat of seaborne cyclones that conspire with flooded rivers to wash them from the planet.

In November 1970, the deadliest cyclone in human history struck the region, killing more than 500,000 Bengalis. Again in April 1991, a cyclone that was equivalent to a Category 5 hurricane struck the eastern city of Chittagong claiming another 150,000 lives, while leaving 10 million persons homeless.

A Crowded Room

Bengalis make up the cultural and demographic core of Eastern South Asia. The Bengali language is the eastern-most extension of the far-flung Indo-European language family whose speakers also include the Latin-based languages of Europe and the Americas. With 230 million speakers, Bengali (or Bangla) is the sixth most widely spoken language in the world.

Radiating out from this Bengali center are fellow Indo-Aryan Assamese and Oriya speakers in neighboring India, followed by myriad tribal languages before reaching the great South Indian Dravidian languages in Andhra Pradesh and Tamil Nadu. To the east of Bangladesh, the region includes the Rohingya and Arakanese Muslims of Rakhine State in western Myanmar.

Megacities Kolkata, India (14.1 million), and Dhaka, Bangladesh (12.8 million), act as black holes drawing into their orbits an endless stream of laborers from the 122,000 villages of West Bengal and Bangladesh.[5]

The Cobbler's Legacy

When the English cobbler William Carey landed in Calcutta in 1793, he had no inkling that he was launching the modern Protestant missionary movement. Six years after first settling

in Calcutta, Carey's little band moved up the Hooghly River to the Danish port town of Serampore. Before his death in 1834, Carey translated all or portions of the Bible into 44 languages, but his starting point was Bengali. Carey's *Bengali Bible* spawned a Bengali literary renaissance eventually resulting in Rabindranath Tagore's Nobel Prize in literature a century later.

William Carey

Though the modern Protestant missionary movement began in Eastern South Asia, the first missionaries avoided Muslims, instead directing their outreach to more responsive tribal Animists, low-caste Hindus and Buddhists. The immediate and often violent resistance of Muslims to Christian missions was an effective deterrent, preventing missionaries from engaging them for decades.

As a result, the church that emerged in the region was from a largely Hindu and Animist background, and quite different from the Muslim majority around them. Christians used a different name for God, held different dietary practices, and generally maintained a different worldview from that of their Bengali Muslim neighbors.

The 1971 Liberation War tore East and West Pakistan apart with the great majority of the casualties occurring in the East, in what is now Bangladesh. Though the war lasted only nine months, it claimed thousands, and perhaps hundreds of thousands, of Bangladeshi military and civilian lives. In the closing months of the war, the Pakistani army rounded up Bengali intellectuals, physicians, professors, writers, and engineers and ordered their execution. Before they left the country, Pakistani soldiers had also raped thousands of Bengali women.[6]

It is significant that it was Muslims who committed these atrocities against their fellow Muslims. Though the U.S. and Soviet superpowers participated behind the scenes in what they viewed as a proxy war, this was fundamentally a Muslim-on-Muslim conflict.[7]

Cyclones, civil war, population explosion, and religious ferment created the backdrop for the Muslim movements to Christ that emerged in the decades that followed.

Eastern South Asian Islam

By 1900 the land of Bengal that Carey found somewhat equally divided between Hindus and Muslims had grown to 65 percent Muslim. The August 1947 partition of British South Asia into India and Pakistan accelerated the process of Islamization, as millions of Bengali Muslims fled India's West Bengal state to find sanctuary in the newly created nation of East Pakistan (now Bangladesh). By 2010 Bangladesh would claim more than 90 percent of their population as Muslim.[8]

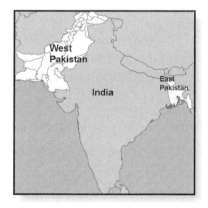

West & East Pakistan, 1947-1971

Contributing to the post-partition Islamization of Bangladesh has been the *Tablighi Jamaat*, a non-political grassroots movement of Islamic devotees that began gathering annually in 1966 for three days of prayer and Qur'anic study. Afterwards, thousands of *tablighis* fan out across the countryside

exhorting villagers to rededicate themselves to the faith. Today, the congregation claims to rival the annual pilgrimage to Mecca as one of the largest Muslim gatherings in the world.[9]

Tablighi Jamaat

Despite the predominance of mainstream Sunni Islam, a pre-Islamic, Hindu-Animistic worldview persists, even within Islam. Sufism, a mystical Islam emphasizing personal experience and oneness with Allah, provides a natural bridge between Hindu-Animistic spirituality and Sunni orthodoxy. Though popular among the people, Sufis are often persecuted by educated *mawlanas* (Islamic teachers) as syncretistic heretics.

Nature of the Movement

Some have speculated that the viral nature of the deeply contextualized C5 Insider movements in the region has caused them to grow much more rapidly than the more pedestrian C4 movements. At the same time, the virtual invisibility of these groups—to outsiders—has led others to doubt their existence at all. We found that, though the size of the movements cannot be confirmed nor their rate of growth, their existence is undeniable. Additionally, we encountered the less deeply contextualized C4 movements in many corners of the region. As a result, we were able to tap into a range of these movements, gathering hundreds of interviews, to learn how God is at work in them.

A 2011 survey of 204 Muslim-background believers who would be more closely described as C4, revealed that, before coming to Christ, most of these believers came from a strong Muslim background, and held a very negative view of Christianity.[10] In fact, only one out of 204 surveyed expressed a positive view of Christians prior to becoming a follower of Christ. These Isai Muslims revealed that the biggest obstacle they faced in coming to Christ was their own Muslim family and community.

When asked what God had used to change their views of Jesus, 168 of the 204 mentioned the salvation they had found in Jesus Christ. Most of them cited specific biblical passages such as Romans 8:1 ("Therefore, there is now no condemnation for those who are in Christ Jesus"); Acts 4:12 ("Salvation is found in no one else, for there is no other name under heaven given to men by which we must be saved"); and John 14:6 ("Jesus answered, 'I am the way and the truth and the life. No one comes to the Father except through me'").

In multiple testimonies, these Muslim-background believers referenced three recurring themes that influenced their conversion: (1) the Word of God, (2) the Holy Spirit, and (3) faithful witnesses. However, when asked how they are seeing God draw other Muslims to faith in Christ, they often pointed to Qur'anic passages they use to create a bridge into the Bi-

A Crowded Room

ble or into a conversation about Jesus.[11] Several referenced the *JESUS Film*. Many others testified to dreams and miraculous answers to prayers.

Like their Insider counterparts, the C4 movement churches have generally kept their distance from the non-Muslim-background churches. Despite their shared core beliefs with Christians from non-Muslim backgrounds, there remain strong cultural differences between the two.[12] This cultural separation has led some foreign and local Christians to wonder if the movements truly exist or are a fabrication.

The Musulmani Bible

Critical to the emergence of both the C4 and C5 movements of Muslims to Christ was the publication of the *Musulmani Bengali Common Language Bible*, a Bible in the colloquial language of Bengali Muslims. To understand its importance, one must return to the pioneering translation work of William Carey.

When William Carey published his Bengali Bible in 1809, most Bengalis were either Hindus or Muslims. Carey faced a fork in the road: he knew his choice of religious vocabulary would either incline his translation toward the Muslim population or the Hindu. Carey tilted toward the Hindu population, choosing the Sanskrit-based *Ishwar* to translate the word *God* rather than *Allah* or *Khoda*, names that were used by the Muslims.[13]

For the next 170 years, Carey's translation choice helped to convince Muslims that Christians worshiped some other god, likely one from a Hindu background. When translators produced the earliest gospel portions of the contextualized Musulmani translation in the 1970s, they employed the word *Khoda* for God. Khoda was an Urdu-language loan word that was commonly used by both Muslims and Christians in East and West Pakistan.

After the brutal War of Liberation with West Pakistan, Bangladeshis distanced themselves from Urdu and used the name Allah for God. Consequently, when the complete *Musulmani Bengali Common Language Bible* was published in 2000, the term translators chose for God was Allah.

Though Christians in the West typically associate the name Allah with Islam, it was, in fact, Christian in origin. Arab Muslims borrowed the name from Arab Christians who had been praying to Allah for centuries before Muhammad was born. Today, millions of Arab, Hausa, Malay and Bengali Christians continue to pray to God by the name "Allah." What distinguishes Christians from Muslims is not the name they use for God, but their theological understanding of God. Christians derive their understanding from the Bible, while Muslims glean theirs from the Qur'an.

A more controversial issue arose when other Bible translators went beyond vocabulary matters to address the divine family terms used in the Bible. Though Muslims are offended by references to God as Father or Jesus as Son, most Christians see these as non-negotiable aspects of the biblical revelation of God. The Musulmani Bengali Bible, like most Muslim idiom translations, adopts the language of Muslims, but does not shy away from the family names attributed to God the Father and Jesus the Son.

More Insights into the Movement

Today, there appear to be three types of Protestant Christianity within Eastern South Asia. The oldest stream, tracing back to Carey's Bible translation decisions, is comprised primarily of non-Muslim Tribal, low-caste Hindu, and Animist background believers. This stream has greatly advantaged the poor and the dispossessed of South Asian society, of whom there are many, but has shown little effectiveness in reaching Muslims.

On the other end of the Christian spectrum, and quite removed from the traditional Hindu- and Tribal-background churches, are Insider (C5) streams of Muslims coming to faith in Christ. Insiders reject Christian identity while retaining an intimate relationship with Jesus Christ, as they understand him from the New Testament. Insider movements remain cloaked to outside assessment, in part, because many of their adherents are indistinguishable to most outsiders from the Muslims around them. These Insiders range from full-time evangelists and teachers of the gospel to invisible participants within the Muslim mosque. Nonetheless, their testimonies appear to indicate a genuine conversion experience resulting from a personal encounter with Christ—the Christ as revealed in the Bible. They see Christ as their indispensable Savior and, in their testimonies at least, as their Lord. As to Christ's divinity, though, many Insiders seem willing to hedge their position depending upon who is asking them. In our interviews, we heard answers ranging from clear confessions that "Isa is Allah" to "I'm not too sure."

In between these polarities are multiplying movements of communities that missiologists would describe as C4 believers, i.e., Christ followers who retain biblically permissible cultural and religious forms, clearly seeing themselves as no longer a part of the Muslim faith, though seeking to remain within the Muslim community. These C4 believers are not assimilated into the Hindu- and Tribal-background churches, but neither have they dissolved invisibly back into the mosques. Though they do remain within the Muslim communities, they often face persecution because of their steadfast assertion that they are *Isai Muslims*, meaning they are followers of Jesus (literally, Muslims who belong to Jesus).

Both the C4 Isai Muslims and the less visible Insider believers avoid using the name Christian to describe themselves, and neither has much interaction with the churches whose members come from tribal and Hindu backgrounds. Let's now peel back the layers and see if we can better understand how God is at work in these two Muslim-background streams.

How God Is At Work

In an inner-city Muslim slum, a community radiates out from the modest home and study of a 68-year-old Sufi sage who provides them with his blessing and spiritual direction. Jafar is revered not only among the slum dwellers who surround him, but among his peers across South Asia as well. Jafar is a scholar, the published author of 22 books on Islam. Five years ago, Jafar had a profound experience with Jesus Christ and was baptized. His decision to follow Christ came after several months of studying a New Testament with Baptist and YWAM (Youth With A Mission) missionaries. Jafar's 23rd book was a commentary on the Qur'an, based on the teachings of the *Kitab al-Moqadis*, the Bible.[14]

Jafar's testimony was that in *Isa Ruhullah* (Jesus the Spirit of God) he had found what his heart had always longed for. Rather than leave his community, though, and join the Christians, Jafar determined to remain with his Muslim flock, and infuse Isa into all that he did, pointing as many as would listen to the object of his heart's yearnings.

Jafar said, "I now have 100,000 Isai brothers in this state. They work in secret. I've seen them, though, and I've been with them." When I asked Jafar how many of these 100,000 have been baptized like him, he replied, "Only about 1,000."

I asked Jafar, "Why are Muslims turning to Isa?" He answered, "Inside man there is a void. Everyone is now saying Isa is my *Pir* (spiritual guru). Isa fits into their hunger for spirituality."

I decided to press the question further with Jafar, "Some say Jesus is God. What do you say?" Jafar took a long pause and then said, "If you do not take Isa, you are in the unfortunate wrong path in life. If you do not go on the path of Jesus, it is the wrong path. If someone does not say that Jesus is the way, I correct them."

I noted Jafar's avoidance of a direct answer, but knew too, that he had lived under a *fatwa*, a death sentence, from Islamic hardliners who rightly interpreted his teachings as heretically Christian.

Some critics have depicted Insider movements as the creation and impositions of Western missionaries on naive Muslim-background believers. The testimonies of several Indian and Bengali Insider pioneers in South Asia argue to the contrary. It is true that a handful of Western missionaries have encouraged some of the Insider leaders, providing them with counsel and support, both missiologically and materially, but this occurred only after the movements had already taken root and begun to grow. In their fundamental opposition to what they perceive to be Christendom and the West, these Insider Movements have little tolerance for foreign control or even influence from the West.

Older denominations whose leadership posts were already occupied by Tribal- and Hindu-background churchmen held little attraction to the majority of the grassroots awakening of Muslims that was taking place outside the range of their churches. At the same time, a number of the Western missions were learning to tailor their outreach to the Muslim majorities around them. By the mid-1970s, Australian Baptists and International Christian Fellowship (now SIM) missionaries were both beginning to see response to new initiatives aimed at Muslims. Without the faithful witness of the old Norwegian missionary or the Baptist missionary, B.T. Rucker, a young Thomas Mori might never have found his faith. Likewise many of the Insiders interviewed attested to receiving Christian literature from OM traveling teams, or an act of Christian kindness from a World Vision development worker. Others described encounters with American, New Zealand, and

British Baptists who were instrumental in conveying to them the gospel.

Inside and Outside

A consistent theme in the testimonies of both C4 and the more deeply contextualized Insider believers was the discovery that apart from Isa there was no salvation, yet in submission to Isa there was a deep and unshakable assurance of salvation. Indigenous praise songs, such as *At the Feet of Jesus*, reflected this personal relationship with Christ:

> At the end of a dark night I came to the feet of Isa.
>
> I found forgiveness of my sins at the side of the cross.
>
> Isa came and lovingly wiped the tears flowing from my eyes,
>
> At the point of death I found hope, I, who was totally hopeless.
>
> For sinners like you and me, He gave his life on the cross.
>
> That glad news we will proclaim in our land of Bangladesh.

These Muslim-background Christ followers knew full well that their new faith put them at odds with the Islamic community and their own Muslim identity, but they were not anxious to engage either of these threats until absolutely necessary. Leaving their families and villages to go and join a Tribal-background Christian church was not an appealing prospect.

As to the identity of Jesus, he was universally viewed as Savior and Lord. Yet when asked about Christ's divinity, some of the more deeply Insider believers conveyed a nuanced response. I put the question to Bhutto, a 37-year-old farmer who had mortgaged his own land to support his ministry of evangelism and church planting, "Do you believe Jesus is God?" His initial response was revealing, "I do not have a concrete decision about this. I'm still studying it. The church is saying, 'Jesus is God.' But I got the teaching from the gospel of Mark and other books that Jesus is not saying that, 'I myself am God.'"

When he saw my surprised response, Bhutto leaned forward to explain to me, "I believe 100 percent that Jesus is God, but I cannot tell this to the Muslims. If I say this, then the Muslims will open torture upon us. I am following Jesus' example.

When the demons saw his miracles, they said, 'You are the Son of God.' Jesus said to them, 'Be quiet.' This is a great teaching for us, i.e., when Jesus said, 'Be quiet. It is not the time to teach that I am the Son of God.'"[15]

Another Insider, Mehmet Khaleed, expressed a similar response when asked, "Who is Jesus?" He replied, "He is my Lord, my Savior. Even when I am in darkness he is my light. He provided me the right answer when I was confused. Many times when I fail, he is my only Redeemer. He helps me to learn more and more and gives me a passion for Muslims."

I pressed a little further, "Is Jesus God?"

Mehmet replied, "He has everything that we see in God, the same power in God. I believe this, but I don't want to say this to outside people (i.e. Muslims), because it will cause them confusion. But this is who he is in my heart. I do not tell people this because I would rather them see Jesus and understand who he is on their own."

A few weeks later, though, I sat with a dozen Insider imams and *mawlanas* (the South Asian term for an Islamic leader or religious teacher) who were also evangelists and planters of Isa jamaats in their communities. Across from me, a burly bearded mawlana named Salwar sat clothed in white with an embroidered prayer cap perched above his calloused forehead (earned from years of prostrated prayers with his head rubbing the carpet before him) and piercing black eyes. I had the distinct impression that he had never sat so close to a foreigner in his life. I asked him, "Who is Jesus?" He looked at me as if I were daft and replied with a single word, "Allah." No further explanation was offered or requested.

I took a different angle, "Tell me about the Qur'an and Bible."

Mehmet paused thoughtfully and said, "There are so many differences. The most important thing is, the resurrection of Christ."

I continued, "When the Qur'an and Bible disagree, which do you hold as the authority?"

Mehmet replied, "Since Jesus is the Beloved of Allah, whenever there is disagreement, we fall back to Jesus."

Westerners mistakenly suspect that Muslim-background believers wrestle with the loyalty demands of Christ and Muhammad, but this was rarely the case. For the Muslim-background believers I interviewed, Muhammad was not a rival to Christ. They knew that Muhammad never claimed deity or status as a savior; he faded into irrelevance once a Muslim accepted that Jesus was, in fact, Allah's provision for salvation.

This may, in part, explain why Muslim followers of Christ, particularly those who would be viewed as Insiders, found little need to attack Muhammad. I rarely heard a disparaging word uttered against Muhammad. Instead, he was often described as "a disciple of Allah," "a prophet of Allah," "one of God's children," and the like. The worst I heard was a simple admission that "he is a sinner in need of salvation." Attacking Muhammad had no value for these Muslim-background Insiders who were more interested in winning their friends and family than making a bone of contention out of the ultimately insignificant person of Muhammad.

How do you share your faith?
Most of those interviewed began their witness by developing a friendship. They then used Qur'anic passages to bridge their friend into a conversation that ultimately revealed the necessity of Jesus for salvation. From the Qur'an they highlighted the unique virgin birth of Jesus, His holiness, His miraculous power and His divinely ordained death and ascension to heaven. These progressive steps sometimes took place in one meeting, but were more typically stretched over a lengthy period of time. Once it was certain the person was genuinely interested in Isa, the Insider offered an *Injil*, a New Testament.

Western Christians, particularly those who have emphasized the radical dissonance between Islam and Christianity, would be surprised, as I was, to learn that many South Asian Muslims, who went on to become whole-hearted followers of Jesus Christ, came to an *initial* faith in Jesus Christ through the Qur'an. Granted, their initial understanding of Jesus was limited and doubtless would not pass a theological quiz, but it was sufficient to drive them to the living Christ who saved them and guided them to the Bible, from which their faith has gained clarity and understanding.

One such example came from an Insider pioneer named Amid Hasan. Amid said, "I suppose the most influential person in my coming to faith in Christ was a Spanish ship captain named Captain Fernandez." Amid Hasan is a 55-year-old father of four with one granddaughter. Amid has the firm handshake of a man who serves as the political leader in the state's powerful nationalist party. He comes from a devout Sunni family, and his father served as an elected member of the national government. Yet for the past 11 years, Amid has been a follower of Jesus Christ, all because of the question he was asked by Captain Fernandez.

It was 1987 and I was serving in the Merchant Marines, but unlike the other sailors I never put in overtime. One day, Captain Fernandez asked me, 'Why do you only work eight hours a day and spend the other 16 hours reading that book? What is that book that you are always reading?'

I explained to him that it was my Qur'an. He said, 'Come and read some to me.' I read to him and he said, 'That is nice. What does it mean?'

I looked up and said, 'I do not know.' Though I knew how to read Arabic, I really didn't understand it.

Fernandez laughed, 'What? You are reading all day, and you do not know what it means? That is the stupidest thing I've ever heard.'

I was angry, but over time, I wondered if he was right.

When I returned home later that year, I bought a copy of the Qur'an in the Bangla language. The first thing I noticed was that there were many stories in the Qur'an that were at variance with what I had heard from the *mawlanas*, the Islamic teachers in the mosque. I searched the Qur'an to understand more about Muhammad, but instead, I found Isa, and this disturbed me.

I asked Amid to explain.

"In the Qur'an," he said, "I found no titles of honor for Muhammad, but 23 honorable titles that Allah gave to Isa. I saw
that Muhammad is not with Allah now, but Isa is in heaven with
Allah now. Muhammad is not coming again, but Isa is coming
again. Muhammad will not be at the Last Judgment, but Isa
will be at the Last Judgment Day. Muhammad is dead, but Isa
is alive. Only four times does the Qur'an speak of Muhammad,
and yet 97 times it talks about Isa. Muhammad is not a savior,
according to the Qur'an, but Isa's very name means 'Savior.'
Muhammad is only a messenger, but Isa is called *Ruhullah*, the
Spirit of Allah."

Amid continued with his litany of comparisons for several
minutes explaining how, in every way, the Qur'an itself elevated
Isa above Muhammad.

"At stake," Amid said, "either the Qur'an is right and Isa is
Allah's Savior, or the mawlanas are right and we should follow
Muhammad." So Amid debated the mawlanas, challenging
them to obey the Qur'an and follow Isa.

"Some of them said, 'You are mad.' But others said, 'You
are right.' One of those mawlanas, an 80-year-old sheikh,
advised Amid, 'You need to search the Christian community to
find what is the life of Isa al-Masih.'"

This prompted Amid to obtain a Bible, from which he
learned more about the life and teachings of Jesus. In 2002,
Amid was baptized. But Amid had no desire to take on a new
religion. "I will not be a Christian," Amid said, "I just want to
follow Jesus."

Amid uses the same approach through which he came to
faith to spread the gospel to others. He said, "First we show
them from the Qur'an that only Isa al-Masih is the Savior, and
then we baptize them. Then we give them the Bible and we
disciple them. Over time, they move away from the Qur'an and
into the Bible, though they continue to use the Qur'an to bring
other Muslims to faith in Isa."

Amid was firmly convinced that the mawlanas had kept the
truth from the people. Hidden behind the veil of Arabic, the
truth that Isa alone was Allah's way of salvation was a secret
too important to keep to himself. As a seasoned community

organizer, Amid developed a strategy to reach all the Muslims of his state. Soon he had 63 persons ready for baptism. All of them were convinced, from the Qur'an, that Isa was God's only way of salvation. "We developed a strategy," Amid said, "to win mawlanas and spend two years training them in what the Qur'an says about Isa al-Masih, and send them back into the community to teach about Isa al-Masih."

He continued, "Our aim is that we will follow Isa al-Masih, and we will teach them that Isa al-Masih is the Savior and we will baptize them. Then we will give them the *Kitab al-Moqadis* (the Bible) and we will disciple them. On the day that they invite Isa into their life, we introduce them to Matthew 28:18-20 and say to them, 'If you want to have Isa with you all of your days to the ends of the earth, then you must be baptized.'"

Back in Bangladesh, Thomas Mori further presented the ways that Insiders in his movement were communicating the faith. "We have four negative rules," he said: "(1) Never speak against the Qur'an, (2) Never speak against Allah, (3) Never speak against the Prophet Muhammad, and (4) Never speak against the *ummah* (the Muslim community)."

Thomas continued:

> Though we never ask them to stop going to the mosque, after one or two years, 70-90 percent stop going to the mosque. Some continue at the mosque, but only on Fridays. Most of them stop doing the Ramadan fast, or only do it for a few days. Most of the believers still participate in the eid festivals, but they no longer sacrifice the sheep during the korbani festival. Likewise, they feel no need to do the Hajj to Mecca. I don't know of any followers of Isa in this country who go on the Hajj.

He continued:

> Here are the things our Isai Muslims give up: they do not believe Muhammad has anything to do with salvation; they do believe he is a prophet who brought our people from polytheism to monotheism; most of our Isai still read the Qur'an, at least a page, in their home in the morning. They want their kids to learn to read it in Arabic, even if they don't understand it. However, after two to three years the believers stop reading

it even though we don't ask them to do this. When I ask them, 'Why don't you read the Qur'an any more?' They say, 'We don't see any value in it. We don't understand it anyway.'

Mori pointed to his colleagues, "These brothers teach, 'You can read the Qur'an if you like. It's up to you.'"

A Plan to Reach Them All

Over the past decade, Amid, who came to faith through the teasing words of Captain Fernandez, has seen his network of Isai Muslims in India grow. He has organized these believers into districts and house groups. "A district leader is called the Imam," Amid explained, "and he may have several hundred *jamaats* (worshiping groups) under him. The leader of a house group we call a *Rabbur*, which means 'one who shows the way.' Then we also have itinerating teachers, called *Hiko*."

"We have now formed a madrasa just for training Isai mawlanas," Amid said. "Now we have many Isai mawlanas who can use the Qur'an to bring other Muslims to faith in Isa, and then use the Injil to disciple them."

"Now we have many Isai mawlanas. It is gaining momentum because now there are so many Isai mawlanas and many teachers of the Bible and the Qur'an.

"Among our people there are sometimes conflicts between the husbands and wives. This often happens when the wife discovers that her husband is a follower of Isa. Whenever this happens, they are required by the community to seek counseling from the mawlana. We respond by sending to them an Isai mawlana. He always listens to their complaint and then counsels her to become a follower of Isa like her husband," Amid smiled.

I asked Amid how many Muslim-background believers there were now in his state. "It is very hard to say," he replied. "In my jamaat network I know, but I do not know about the others. In my jamaats there are nearly 33,000 Muslims who have become followers of Isa."

I asked Amid how many of the 33,000 Isa followers have now been baptized. "Sixteen thousand have been baptized," he said. "We have about 3,000 Isa jamaats. We baptize twice a year during the flood season, so we are expecting another 3,000 or more baptisms next January."

Small Group Discussion ~ Discover for Yourself

1. What impressions do you take away from this chapter?
2. How is God at work in the Eastern South Asia Room?
3. Discuss Thomas's story. Do you agree or disagree with the choices he made?
4. See how many different ways you can identify that God was drawing Muslims in Eastern South Asia to Christ.

the Persian room

I will set my throne in Elam.
Jeremiah 49:38

 ON THE EVE of the 1979 Islamic Revolution in Iran, there were likely no more than 500 Muslim-background followers of Christ in a nation of 40 million mostly Shi'ite Muslims. Three decades later, hundreds of thousands of Iranian Muslims have given their lives to Jesus Christ. What happened? How is God at work in this Islamic nation? To answer these questions, we must enter the Persian Room and listen to its Muslim-background followers of Christ.

Nadia's Story

Praise music filled the night air of an Armenian sanctuary in a crowded Mediterranean city. Two floors below, in a basement Sunday school classroom, I interviewed Nadia, a 43-year-old-Iranian-widowed mother of three. Nadia has been a believer for six years, and a refugee for nine months.

"What did God use to bring you to faith in Christ?" I asked. "Tell me your story."

"From my childhood," Nadia said, "I have been very curious about Jesus. I felt that there was an empty place inside of me. Even when I watched TV shows and movies depicting Christian families praying before their meals I sensed that there was a peace within them.

"Our mullahs have always told us that foreigners were heathen and that we Muslims were righteous, but when I watched the Christians, they always seemed to be at peace, and more importantly, I knew that we were not. In our family we prayed the daily *namaz*, and we were always crying out to Allah, but inside there was nothing. I felt nothing."

It would have been hard to imagine Nadia finding peace in the life she had known. When she was 10 years old, her father signed her marriage contract, and two years later she moved in with her 20-year-old husband Sasan. Crime and drugs ravaged Nadia's family. Sasan became an opium addict soon after they married. Two of Nadia's brothers died from drug overdoses, and another was arrested, and then sentenced to death, for killing a man in a fight. Nadia's response was to sink into a depression that only deepened with each calamity. When the court sentenced one of Nadia's brothers to attend a drug rehabilitation program, he asked Nadia to go with him, hoping it would help her overcome her depression.

"In our community," Nadia said, "the mullahs taught us that if you cry more tears on earth, you will have more rewards in heaven. But it was their laws and rules that were making us cry. They said to us women, 'If even one hair hangs down from your *hijab*, you will spend eternity hanging between heaven and earth.'

"In the Narcotics Anonymous class, I learned differently. The people there were very broken, but they loved each other. They didn't look at my clothes, but showed love to me. There was no talk about imams and prophets, only about God.

"It was around that time that Jesus introduced himself to me. Reading through the literature about Narcotics Anonymous, I discovered that it was started by an American named Bill Wilson and founded on the Christian faith. I read the story of how Wilson became sober and a Christian. The Iranian government had tried to remove Jesus from the program, but they could not.[1]

"I learned that one of my cousins had become a Christian. When his family came to visit us, I asked him for a New Testament, and I read it. Inside I was in a revolution. So I prayed, *God, show me what is really true.* When I got home that night, I took out my Qur'an and prayed, *God, if this is your word, show yourself to me through this book.* But, instead, something drew me to the New Testament.

"As I read it, I felt my heart open like an old door, and I understood every verse with all my being. I set the Qur'an aside. Inside I felt very warm and very thirsty. It was like drinking cool water, and I wanted to drink it all.

"From that time on, Jesus's work started inside me. It was a strange happiness like nothing I'd ever known. I was like the Samaritan woman telling everyone about Jesus. Within a week my husband, Sasan, and three children came to faith in Christ."

Nadia's testimony is one of thousands that are bubbling up in contemporary Iran in what is certainly the greatest turning of Muslims to Christ in Iran's history, and quite possibly the largest turning of Muslims to Christ in the world today. Within Nadia's story are ten clues to the ways God is introducing Iranian Muslims to salvation in his Son: (1) Drawn to Jesus, (2) Iranian Islam, (3) Christian Witness, (4) Media Ministries, (5) Hunger for Freedom, (6) Social Turmoil, (7) Family Witness, (8) New Testaments, (9) Jesus Visitations, and (10) House Churches.

Drawn to Jesus

Nadia's comment, "From my childhood, I have been curious about Jesus," was echoed in many testimonies of Muslim-background believers in the Persian Room. A Muslim-background believer named Reza recalled a story from his primary school days as a soccer player. "My hero," he said, "was the Brazilian soccer player Pelé. I loved him. So when I scored my first goal as a seven-year-old boy, I slid across the grass on my knees like Pelé, and crossed myself as I had seen him do." The act of celebration earned Reza a stern reprimand from his Muslim school principal, but left Reza more curious than ever about what this simple act meant and why it was so dangerous.

Sara is a 28-year-old refugee from northern Iran with carefully coiffed hair, makeup, and fashionable Western clothes. She said, "I was raised a secular Muslim and never read the Qur'an apart from what was required in school. I never really believed in Islam. I was ashamed when I saw people worshiping the dead at Sufi tombs."

"How did you come to faith?" I asked.

"Before I was a Christian," she said, "I had a problem with an evil spirit attacking me with fear when I tried to sleep at night. The fear was so severe that I tried to kill myself. I cried out to God for him to save me. A younger male cousin who had become a Christian was the one who first told me about Jesus. When my cousin said, 'I am a Christian,' it made me happy, because I've always loved Jesus. After I gave my life to Jesus, he gave me a deep peace, and my night terrors ended."

Darius is a 25-year-old Muslim convert who said, "I was always drawn to the shape of the cross. Even as a Muslim, I had a T-shirt with a large cross on it and the words, 'Only for you.' I also wore a necklace and a ring with crosses. I didn't know why, but I loved Jesus."

Many Muslims in Iran are drawn to the person of Jesus, even though they know little about him. To begin to understand why, we need to look into the unique nature of Islam in the Islamic Republic of Iran.

Iranian Islam

Islam in Iran is unlike Islam in any other Room in the House of Islam. While 90 percent of the Muslim world adheres to what they regard as orthodox or Sunni Islam, Iran follows a different path. Its people are overwhelmingly Shi'ite, literally "partisans of Ali," the son-in-law and cousin of the Prophet Muhammad. Shi'ites believe that the dominant Sunni stream of Islam disregarded the Prophet's desire for his son-in-law to succeed him as leader of the faithful.

For the first 700 years of its history, though, Iran was Sunni, like most of the rest of the Muslim world. But in the 16th century, Ismail I, founder of Iran's Safavid Dynasty (1501-1736), turned the population toward Shi'ism as a Persian bulwark against both Ottoman and Arab enemies who were Sunni Muslims. Since that time Iranian Shi'ite Muslims have defined themselves in stark contrast to the rest of the Sunni Muslim world.

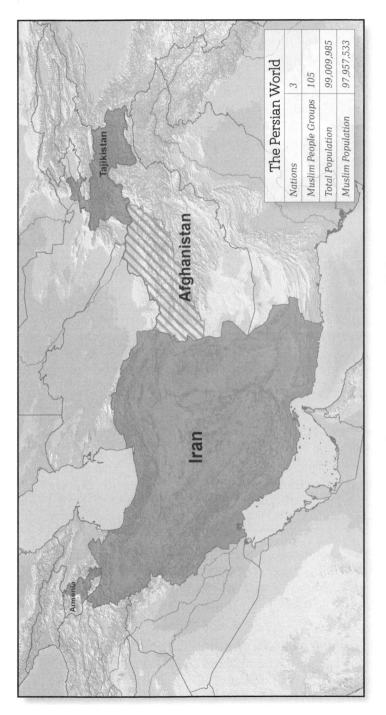

The Persian World	
Nations	3
Muslim People Groups	105
Total Population	99,009,985
Muslim Population	97,957,533

The Persian World

While Sunnis draw their authority more exclusively from the textual tradition of the Qur'an, Shi'ites are different. Though they venerate the Qur'an, they also rely on religious authorities, *ayatollahs* (literally "signs of Allah") to interpret Islam for the Shi'ite faithful. The tradition stems back to the belief that Ali, the son-in-law and cousin of the Prophet Muhammad, and Ali's son Hussein, were the rightful inheritors of the Prophet's mantle of leadership. When Hussein married a Persian woman, it further endeared Iranians to the Shi'a tradition by ensuring that all of Hussein's successors were at least biologically Persian as well.[2]

In the year 661, renegade Arab warriors called *Kharijites* (literally, "those who went out"), martyred Ali during the chaotic struggles that followed the death of the Prophet Muhammad. In the year 680, the Arab Muslim armies of Yazid I killed Ali's son Hussein near the town of Karbala, in what is now Iraq. Even though Hussein's death occurred in battle, Shi'ites view it as an act of self-sacrifice and martyrdom. Every year they mourn his martyrdom during the sacred month of Muharram.

Both Ali and, even more so Hussein, have been lionized in Shi'ite lore as righteous, suffering martyrs whose exemplary lives represent the true ideal to which all Muslims should aspire. After Hussein's death, his descendants continued to lead the small Shi'ite community for the next two centuries through a successive series of Imams. This succession culminated in the Twelfth Imam, Hujjat ibn al-Hasan al-Mahdi, who was born in the year 869. This Twelfth Imam mysteriously disappeared before any further successors could be named. According to Shi'ite doctrine, this enigmatic Twelfth Imam is the Mahdi ("the messianic guided one") who is not really dead, but is hidden. One day, they believe, he will return and usher in a new era of justice and righteousness for the faithful.

Hussein's "martyrdom" and the doctrine of an imminent return of a messianic Mahdi who will restore a righteous world order has become ingrained into the national consciousness of Shi'ite Iranians. One needn't look far to see a parallel in the

Among the many Muslim-background converts who were imprisoned by the new Islamic regime, was the Rev. Mehdi Dibaj. Dibaj had been a member of the Assemblies' Jama'at-e

Mehdi Dibaj

Rabbani Church in Tehran as a young man. In 1983, Dibaj was arrested without trial and imprisoned for 10 years, during which time he "faced physical beatings, mock executions and . . . two years of solitary confinement in a small unlit three-yard cell" where he was continually pressured to recant his faith.[11] Dibaj endured with the confession, "I am not only satisfied to be in prison for the honor of His Holy Name, but am ready to give my life for the sake of Jesus my Lord."[12] In 1993, in a secret tribunal, Dibaj was sentenced to death for converting from Islam.

When Iranian government spokesmen publicly denied the existence of the death sentence, Haik, who had learned about the sentence of execution from sources within the prison, was faced with a choice. As an Armenian, he could remain silent and avoid the wrath of the government, or he could speak out. Haik refused to turn his back on his Muslim-background brother. Instead, he went public, transmitting to the world the news of Rev. Dibaj's imminent execution as well as many other violations of religious freedom in Iran. Privately Haik remarked to a colleague, "I have placed my hand over the hole of the snake."[13] But Haik's efforts proved effective. In response to international outcry, Rev. Dibaj was released on January 16, 1994.

Three days later, on January 19, 1994, Bishop Haik was abducted from the streets of Tehran. Though the police claimed they could not find him, a laborer in a Muslim cemetery remembered burying the brutalized body of a man with a cross attached to his lapel. Ten days after he had gone missing, Haik's tortured body was exhumed from an unmarked grave in a Muslim cemetery. There were 27 stab wounds in his chest.[14]

Two thousand persons, including many Muslims, gathered at the gravesite in the frigid rain for Haik's reburial in a Christian

---

life of Jesus who, as a righteous suffering servant died for the sins of the world, is ever-present, and will return again.[3]

Further shaping the unique nature of Islam in Iran is an ancient Persian civilization that was superior in virtually every way to the Arab invaders who conquered them in the 7th century. This civilization continues to express itself through literature, philosophy, and poetry that have fostered an identity that, though Islamic, has a core that is uniquely Persian. Within this Persian Islam is a rich tradition of Sufi mysticism. Sufism has provided the nation's poets and saints with a means of transcending the legalistic restrictions that characterize Islam in many other corners of the Muslim world.[4]

All of these elements of Iranian Islam, its history, values, philosophical and mystical traditions, were challenged when Ayatollah Ruhollah Khomeini came to power in 1979. Khomeini's new Islamic government imposed a stringent vision for the country that began with a massive cleanup of all the Western remnants of Shah Reza Pahlavi's regime. Thousands of real and perceived political opponents were rounded up, sentenced, and executed by Revolutionary Tribunals.[5] Islamic vigilante groups called *Komiteh* moved throughout society imposing Islamic justice that prescribed lashing and even stoning for such crimes as pre-marital sex, adultery, homosexuality, and even alcohol consumption by repeat offenders.[6] From the age of nine, girls were forbidden to appear in public without a veil.[7]

The new Islamic regime was also extending its influence into the Christian communities. In 1983 the Ministry of Education published a new textbook for Christian catechism that reflected the Qur'an's teachings about Jesus. The following year all Christian schools were given Muslim headmasters.[8] Anglicans were among the hardest hit, as their association with Britain brought charges of being foreign agents. Likewise, the Presbyterian churches saw properties confiscated and allegations of being agents of the American

Armenian Cross

government levied against them. The ancient Assyrian and Armenian communities were generally tolerated, so long as they kept to themselves and did not evangelize Muslims.

As the Islamic Revolution tightened control over the nation, the Shi'ite ideal of the righteous leader who is martyred by an unjust yet overwhelming power, was turned upside down. It was now the Shi'ite state that was crushing its opposition, leaving shattered opponents scattered throughout society where they reprised the role of the righteous martyr.

Christian Witness

It was no coincidence that I found Nadia in an Armenian church. The ancient Armenian church played a crucial role in the current awakening in Iran. Christians from other traditions, Assyrian, Catholic, Anglican, Presbyterian, and Brethren, appeared in the stories of Muslim-background believers from Iran, but none so prominently as the Armenian-background Assemblies of God.

Armenians are the largest Christian minority in Iran today. The Persian Shah Abbas the Great relocated thousands of Armenians to Iran in the late 16th century to help construct his new Pahlavi capital in Isfahan. Afterwards, these Armenians remained and prospered. They were joined by thousands more Armenians who entered the country under less pleasant circumstances fleeing the 1915 Armenian genocide in neighboring Turkey. Turkey, at the time, was embroiled in a World War I alliance against Russian and other European Allies. Turkish concerns that the Armenian Christians in their country might collaborate with Armenians in Russia prompted a nation-wide extermination campaign that left 1.5 million Armenian men, women, and children dead. As a respected minority in Iran, Armenians were tolerated, so long as they did not proselytize the Muslim majority. All of this began to change, though, in the mid-20th century when a Holy Spirit awakening began to stir in the hearts of Armenian Christians.

An Armenian named Seth Yeghnazar (1911-1989) came to faith through the ministry of the Brethren Church in the 1930s. The 1950s found Seth yearning to experience God in a deeper measure, leading him to study the New Testament

Pentecost and outpourings of the Holy Spirit through history. After praying and fasting for 42 days, Seth had a life-changing encounter with God that he described as a baptism by fire. In January 1956, Seth and his wife Vartouhi began a prayer meeting and Bible study in their home that met every day for the next four years. In 1959, the Yeghnazars joined their Bible study to a community of like-minded believers in a rented basement in Tehran that emerged as one of the first *Jama'at-e Rabbani*, or Assembly of God churches in Iran.[9]

The spiritual awakening in the emerging Assemblies of God movement helped many Armenian Christians rise above the limitations of an ethnic faith. A major figure in this ethnic transcendence was the Armenian Haik Hovsepian Mehr (1945-1994).

Haik's father left when Haik was just a boy, and some years later, his mother remarried, to a Muslim, which was considered taboo by many in the Armenian community. Yet Haik grew to love Muslims, and took the Persian name Mehr ("kind") to demonstrate his affection for Muslim people. Haik was a renaissance man, often seen reading, playing the piano, writing music, boxing, and playing football. Seth Yeghnazar's

Haik Hovsepian Mehr

cousin, Leon Hyrapetian, led young Haik to faith in Christ, and together Leon and Seth discipled and mentored Haik.

At 22 years of age, Haik dedicated his life to Christian ministry. Fifteen years later, in 1980, Haik was called to Tehran to serve as the first national bishop of the Assemblies of God churches. Haik arrived in the capital just as the Ayatollah Khomeini began to implement Islamic *sharia* (Islamic law). While the government was content to allow ethnic Christians to practice their faith, they drew the line at Muslim evangelization. Fearless, Haik refused to yield to government pressures saying, "If we go to jail or die for our faith, we will not yield to these demands."[10]

cemetery. A tearful Mehdi Dibaj addressed the mourners, "When Jesus died on the cross, there was one man who knew for certain that Jesus had died for him. That man was Barabbas. When Brother Haik was killed, I knew that it was I who should have died, not Brother Haik."[15] Six months later Dibaj joined Brother Haik. His body was found in a Tehran park; he too had been stabbed in the heart.[16]

Rather than quench the movement, the martyrdom of the two men fueled it. In the years that followed their deaths, Iranians found heroes worth emulating in the bold examples of Hovsepian and Dibaj, brother martyrs—one from an Armenian background, the other from a Muslim.

The story of courageous Christian witness for the sake of Iranian Muslims' salvation is not limited to the Armenian or Assemblies of God community. The many testimonies emanating from Iran today are filled with bold and sacrificial witness from ancient Assyrian church members, Anglicans, Presbyterians, Roman Catholics, Brethren, Pentecostals, and others "who did not love their lives so much as to shrink from death."[17]

Media Ministries

Even as a child, Nadia had seen Christians on television, and she was influenced by their lives. After the 1979 Iranian Revolution, the government took over state television, but they could not stop the growing number of satellite television programs and video recordings that were transmitting a gospel message into the homes of Iranian Muslims.

Thousands of Iranians have come to faith today through satellite television and Internet websites that feature a growing number of evangelists from Persian Muslim backgrounds. Often heard in the testimonies of Iranian believers are references to illicitly circulated gospel videos such as the *JESUS Film* and *God is Love.*

Leila is a vivacious 34-year-old mother of three who told this story:

> I used to record the television programs of Pastor Hormoz and Pastor Kamil. They taught me how I could understand why there was sin and suffering in the world.

Pastor Hormoz' program was called *God is Love*. I think I understood what he was saying, because two years earlier I had prayed at the close of watching the *JESUS Film*.

Hormoz answered every question that I had. Each week his program came on, he was answering some question I'd been having that week. This happened for seven weeks in a row. The last time, I told my husband what my questions were before Hormoz' program came on, and then I said, "Watch this." I played the recording, and once again the program answered the very questions I had.

I subsequently recorded and watched 100 six-hour programs of Brother Hormoz. After the first two weeks of listening, I repented and invited Jesus into my life.

I was struck by how very different Leila seemed from many of the repressed Muslim women I had interviewed in other countries. She wore makeup; she dressed Western; she was eloquent and outspoken. When I asked Leila's husband about these stereotype-shattering impressions, he responded with one sentence, "We are not Arabs."

Interviews with Iranians involved in the broadcast of satellite television, radio, and Internet ministry attest to the increase in both the quantity and the breadth of the broadcasts' effect in the country. International Antioch Ministries alone estimated in 2008 that "3,000 (persons) a month are turning to Christ just through their broadcasts."[18] Added to this are multiple other media streams that are spreading the gospel, not only into the cities, but into the villages and countryside as well.

Hunger for Freedom

Nadia's lament, "it was their laws and rules that were making us cry," revealed the aspirations of a growing number of Iranians. For most Iranians the popular movement that brought Khomeini to power in 1979 was not a yearning for Islam, but a desire for freedom from the despotic rule of Shah Reza Pahlavi.

In the same vein, for many Iranians, vitriol against America was not a rejection of America's people or even her values, but was aimed at American support for the Shah. Iranians knew well the 1953 American-backed coup d'état that had removed Iran's democratically elected prime minister, Dr. Mohammed Mossadeq, and replaced him with the Western-backed Shah Reza Pahlavi.[19]

During the 2006 World Cup soccer tournament in Germany, Iranians attending the event were asked what changes they would most like to see in their country. Their answer was summed up in a single word, *Azadi* (freedom).[20]

Of Iran's population today, 64 percent were born after the 1979 Islamic Revolution, and have little affection for it.[21] While Christianity is growing rapidly in the country, so too are many other worldviews as Muslim Iranians seek a respite from the state religion. It is common to find Iranian young adults walking away from Islam and turning to atheism, secularism, hedonism, drugs, and even ancient pathways such as Zoroastrianism and Buddhism.

Hundreds of thousands of Iranians have fled the country rather than submit to the stifling regime that now rules their homeland. So many Iranians today have relatives in Los Angeles that they refer to the city as *Tehrangeles*. Well-educated Iranians are departing the country at the rate of about 150,000-180,000 per year, an estimated 25 percent of all Iranians with a post-secondary education.[22]

Despite government-backed denunciations of America as "the Great Satan," for many Iranians, America represents the very freedom for which they yearn. American journalist Scott Peterson observed, "hidden behind the mullah's mask is the most unashamedly pro-American population in the Middle East."[23] The sentiment was expressed spontaneously after the 9/11 terrorist attacks in America, when 60,000 Iranians gathered in Tehran's football stadium dressed in black to hold a candlelight vigil.[24] *Smithsonian Magazine* recently stated, "The paradox of Iran is that it just might be the most pro-American—or, perhaps, least anti-American—populace in the Muslim world."[25]

Iran's young population is hungry for freedom, and a growing number of them are finding that freedom, not in

America or in domestic political reform, but in the person of Jesus Christ.

Social Turmoil

Nadia's experience of having one brother who was executed for killing a man in a fight, along with having two other brothers and a husband who were addicted to opium are not uncommon in today's Iran. Circumstances like these are symptoms of a society under great stress. Iran today has the highest rate of opium addiction in the world. Despite claiming 85 percent of the world's seizures of opium, the country's 600-mile-long border with Afghanistan ensures a continuing flow of opium traffic.[26]

International embargoes against Iran have also taken their toll. Since sanctions were tightened in 2011, the value of the Iranian rial has plunged by 80 percent.[27] Even though the U.N.'s sanctions exempted the importation of pharmaceuticals and medical equipment, restrictions on financial transactions have made it all but impossible for these items to be paid for and imported. Thousands of Iranian patients reliant upon treatments for cancer, HIV/AIDS, and hemophilia have become the unintended victims of these sanctions.[28] Iran's economic woes have led many Iranians to conclude that the Islamic Republic is going in the wrong direction, and a new path forward is needed.

Family Witness

As Iranian Muslims discover Jesus, they are sharing the good news with their families and friends. When Nadia began her search for Jesus, she didn't have to look far. Her cousin had already become a Christian, and it was he who first gave her a New Testament.

Hamideh is a 29-year-old refugee who wears a cross necklace; she has been following Christ for eight months. She came to faith through the witness of her husband, Nabil, who had been led to faith by Iranian Christian friends from Armenian, Assyrian, and Muslim backgrounds.

"When we first talked of marriage," Hamideh said, "Nabil told me about Jesus. He had initially been drawn to Jesus because he and Jesus shared the same birthdate, December 25.

After Nabil was identified attending church while at university, he was expelled from the school."

A few years into their marriage, Hamideh was stricken with multiple sclerosis and went blind. Nabil asked God to heal her, and he did. But still Hamideh did not accept Jesus. "Soon afterward," she said, "my husband was jailed for 10 days. Then in 2011, they arrested him again. At that point we both fled the country."

It was while in exile that Hamideh's multiple sclerosis returned. This time Nabil said she should pray for healing herself. Hamideh did, and this time, when Jesus healed her, she gave her life to him. "Before this," she said, "I didn't believe in any religion, only in God. But Jesus helped me. I could see the peace in Nabil's life, and so I gave my life to Jesus too. After I came to Christ, I could see his work in my life. A week later I was baptized."

Farah is a 39-year-old married mother of two boys with roots among the Luri people of Khuzestan. She has been a Christian for six years, along with her husband and sons.

"I have a brother in Scandinavia who's a believer," Farah told me. "When my sister visited him, she too became a Christian. I listened to my sister talk about Jesus. She used to say to me, 'We know 100% that we will go to heaven.' She spoke boldly to me, and I argued with her, but I also started reading the Bible. My sister told me that God is love, and I wondered, *Who is this God?*

"The Bible reading began to influence me. I compared everything I read in it to the Qur'an and saw that the Bible was better. I spent a lot of time thinking about John 14 where it says that Jesus is the only way. During this time, I also watched the *JESUS Film* and the *God is Love* film.

"I was torn, but started to pray in Farsi (Persian) to God, and stopped doing *namaz* (Islamic prayers). I prayed, *If this is of you, God, let me know.* Then as I watched the *JESUS Film*, my heart opened. At the end of the film, I prayed the prayer. Since then, a great change has come into my life."

New Testaments

When Nadia read the New Testament that her cousin had given her, she said, "I felt my heart open like an old door, and I understood every verse with all my being." In today's Iran, the New Testament or any evangelistic material in the Persian (Farsi) language is illegal.

The first Persian-language New Testament was produced in the early 19th century by a young Anglican missionary named Henry Martyn. Martyn had been inspired to missions by the Baptist pioneer William Carey. After leaving England, Martyn went to India where he collaborated with Carey and gave himself to translating the New Testament into Persian.

In 1810, facing exhaustion, Martyn set out from India for a sabbatical in England. On the way home, Martyn stopped in Iran and, through the British ambassador's office, delivered his

Persian New Testament to the Shah. A few months later, in 1812, Martyn died in eastern Turkey trying to get back to England. He was 31 years old.[29]

Martyn's 1810 translation of the New Testament contributed to the emergence of small numbers of Muslim-background believers reached through the ministries of Anglican, Presbyterian, and other missionaries in the 19th

Henry Martyn   and 20th centuries. After the 1979 Islamic Revolution, Persian-language Bibles were banned. Muslim leaders in Iran allowed the New Testament in their country only in the languages of the indigenous Assyrian or Armenian communities. Authorities believed the archaic Syriac and Armenian languages to be sufficient barriers to prevent witness to the Persian-speaking Muslim majority. With the advent of the Internet and easy reproduction of video, audio, and print media, this Persian-language barrier is breaking down. One church member in Iran admitted to distributing thousands of copies of the *JESUS Film* (which is the Gospel of Luke) in Persian. Revealing the hunger, or at least curiosity, for the gospel, he also reported, "only two persons refused to take a copy."[30]

To expedite the spread of the Bible in the country, Elam Ministries published a modern translation of the New Testament in 2003. Less than a decade later, a million copies were in print and either in the hands of Persian-speaking Muslims or on their way.[31]

Jesus Visitations

After inviting Jesus into her life, Nadia experienced something far different from the rote Islamic prayers and legal prescriptions that had characterized her life as a Muslim. She could sense that, "Jesus's work started inside me." Even more significant than Iranians' yearning for freedom or their disdain for the Islamic state, the single-most powerful factor in the spread of the gospel in Iran has been encounters with the living person of Jesus Christ. Some meet him through dreams or visions, others through healings or answered prayers. Some, like Nadia, experienced a deep inner peace and sense that Jesus was at work within them, transforming their lives from within.

When 23-year-old Reza's Muslim-background Christian friend introduced him to Jesus by telling him that God loved him, it was accompanied by a vision. "Behind my friend," Reza said, "I could see Jesus Christ. It was very beautiful. Jesus didn't talk to me in the vision, but with his eyes he seemed to say, 'Come to me. I have chosen you.'"

Ali Akbar is a 30-year-old Muslim-background believer with large sad eyes who found sanctuary as a refugee in the home of an Assyrian Pentecostal. "As a follower of Jesus," he said, "the security police were very angry with me. They took over our phones, homes, bank accounts, everything.

"Because I was a leader in our house church, I was arrested. They interrogated me so severely that my stomach began to bleed and my blood pressure dropped. I was rushed to the hospital where the doctor said I would die. They couldn't give me a blood transfusion because my blood pressure was so low they couldn't get the needle into a vein.

"Then suddenly I felt very warm like a fire was in my body. My blood pressure became normal again. The Muslims all thought that, since it was the time of Ashura (the Shi'ite holy day in the month of Muharram), that Hussein had healed me. They were shocked, and then sent me home.

"In the elevator as I was leaving the hospital. I saw a vision of a man in a long white gown. I thought I was delirious. Later, though, my mother saw Jesus too, and he said to her, 'I saved your son.' She repented of her disbelief, and all of our family came to faith."

House Churches

House churches have become the primary venue for Muslim-background believers worshiping in Iran today. When Nadia and her family became followers of Christ in 2006, there were few options available for Muslim converts to participate in Christian worship. The Assyrian and Armenian churches in her city were forbidden from admitting Muslim-background members, and besides, they used ancient-language liturgies that were unintelligible to her. Nadia's migration to house church worship has been a path taken by a growing number of Muslim-background believers.

Given the ease with which the government can identify and persecute open churches in Iran, it is not surprising that many Iranian churches, particularly those with Muslim-background believers, have gone underground. Though it is impossible to tell how widespread the house church movement has become, even conservative estimates place the number at more than 100,000 Iranian Muslim-background followers of Christ in the country. Data from interviews with Iranian Christian refugees, and the number of correspondents to satellite Christian television programs give reason to believe the figure could be as high as a few million.[32]

Sad-eyed Ali Akbar, whose family came to faith after a vision of Jesus in the hospital elevator, helped to start many house churches before multiple arrests finally drove him from the country. At the time of his flight from Iran, Ali was working with 35 house churches in a dozen different locations in the country. As we prayed together, Ali began to weep. "I am here," he said, "but I do not want to be. My heart is in Iran."

How I See Him

After Nadia and her family fled from Iran, joining thousands of other Muslim-background refugees who had lost everything for the sake of Christ, they were warmly welcomed by the Christian community in the country to which they had escaped. Muslim-background believers and international Christian ministries quickly embraced her family and helped them find their way.

One of the Christian ministries in their new home city offered a Christian marriage weekend for Iranian-background immigrants. The weekend was led by an American named Don who saw it as a way of helping Muslim-background couples re-establish their marriages on Christian principles.

"We called it a Song of Solomon Workshop," Don said. "It was designed to help these Muslim-background couples move their relationships from a Muslim worldview to a Christian understanding of love between a husband and wife."

Don recalled, "One of the exercises was for a husband to express his love to his wife. I remember Nadia's husband, Sasan, volunteered. Sasan took Nadia by the hand and pulled her to the front of the whole group. He smiled and told her loudly, 'Nadia, I love you,' and then kissed her publicly in front of everyone. The group laughed and cheered for them."

I asked Nadia about the event. She blushed, "That was the first time in our marriage that Sasan told me that he loved me."

Then Nadia lowered her eyes and spoke softly. "It was shortly after that marriage retreat," she said, "that there was an accident in our apartment. I suppose the wiring was not good. When I found my husband's body, he had been electrocuted. His arms and face were terribly burned."

I looked at this woman who had experienced so much death, so much tragedy, so much loss in her life, and wondered how she could bear it. Nadia seemed to sense my question before I could ask it. "It was Jesus's promise," she said.

"'Come to me, all you who are weary and burdened, and I will give you rest' (Matthew 11:28). Jesus has carried me.

"Jesus has given me an unnatural peace," Nadia said. "Though my husband's face was terribly burned, still today, when I close my eyes, I see him handsome and tall and dressed in the best clothes that I always laid out for him."

Nadia closed her eyes and smiled as if hearing Sasan's voice saying once again, "Nadia, I love you."

Small Group Discussion ~ Discover for Yourself

1. What impressions do you take away from this chapter?
2. How is God at work in the Persian Room?
3. Discuss Bishop Haik's story. How does it relate to the bigger picture of what God is doing in this Room?
4. What do you think the future holds for the Persian Room?

the Turkestan room

*This is what the Lord Almighty says:
'Return to me,' declares the Lord Almighty, 'and
I will return to you.'*

Zechariah 1:3

 DURING HIS LIFETIME, Timur Lang's armies were responsible for the death of five percent of the earth's population. Timur Lang (1336-1405), or Tamerlane as he was known to the West, annihilated entire cities of more than a million inhabitants—Delhi, Isfahan, Damascus, Baghdad. After the cities surrendered, he executed their citizens. Historians estimate that, despite the absence of modern-day weapons of mass destruction, Tamerlane's armies of Central Asian Turkic tribesmen killed 17 million men, women and children.[1]

Tamerlane was an equal opportunity killer claiming millions of Muslim and Hindu victims, and had Ming Dynasty China in his sights when he died of the plague in 1405. But the Muslim warlord singled out Christianity in Central Asia for extermination. Christianity in the region had already been weakened by a century of Islamic Mongol oppression when Tamerlane's marauding warriors wiped out most of the remaining Christian communities of Turkestan.[2]

On the steppes of Central Asia, Tamerlane's ancient capital of Samarkand in modern-day Uzbekistan still revels in the magnificent mosques and architectural tributes that rose during his 35-year reign. Tamerlane relocated and repurposed the greatest artisans from each of his conquests to erect and embellish his beloved capital.

One of those monuments was his own mausoleum, the *Gur-e Amir* (Tomb of the King) where Timur was enshrined in 1405. Five centuries later, in 1941, a Soviet anthropologist, Mikhail Gerasimov, exhumed the body of the Turkic conqueror for examination. Upon opening Tamerlane's coffin, Gerasimov discovered on the inside of the tomb a curse inscribed: "Whoever opens my tomb, shall unleash an invader more terrible than I." Two days later, Adolph Hitler's armies invaded Russia in the largest military assault in history. Operation Barbarossa, with a three-million-man invasion force, eventually cost the Soviet Union more than 20 million civilian and military casualties, three million more than Tamerlane had exacted.[3] In November 1942, Timur was reburied with a full Islamic ceremony, and two days later the German army was defeated at the Battle of Stalingrad.

Americans today have little reason to know Tamerlane. However, on April 15, 2013, a troubled pair of brothers brought the 15th-century terrorist's echoes to the Boston marathon.

The brothers, immigrants from Daghestan in the Caucasus region of Turkestan, detonated a pair of bombs near the finish line of the annual Patriots Day Boston Marathon killing three and maiming 264 others. The brothers were from a Muslim Daghestani family named Tsarnaev. Their family and friends knew the older of the two, and architect of the attack, by his first name, Tamerlan.

Tamerlane

Empire of the Steppes

Turkestan is the land of the Turkic peoples. It stretches 4,000 miles across the steppes of Central Asia from its place of ethnic origins in the Altai Mountains on Mongolia's western border to the turbulent communities of the Caucasus Mountains before spilling across modern-day Turkey and into the Balkan states of Europe.

Today, more than 200 million Turkic peoples of Turkestan comprise 227 Turkic people groups residing in 15 nations. The more prominent Turkic groups are the Uighurs of Xinjiang,

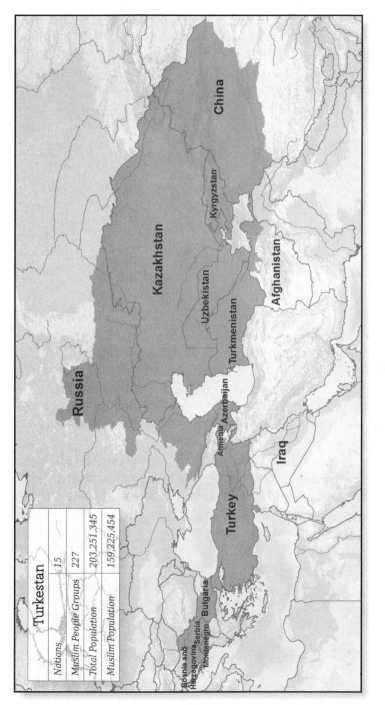

Turkestan

Turkestan	
Nations	15
Muslim People Groups	227
Total Population	203,251,345
Muslim Population	159,225,454

China; the Kazakhs, Kyrgyz, Uzbeks, Turkmen, Azeris and Tatars of the former Soviet Union; and of course, the 75 million Turks of Turkey.

Turkestan is a diverse and conflict-riddled Room. In the far east, Uighurs in China chafe under Communist subjugation. In the west, Turkish Muslims in the Republic of Turkey struggle with Kamal Ataturk's (1881-1938) modernizing reforms. In between, the former Soviet Turkic states have languished and festered, first under Communist control, and today under one-party strongmen.

Since the earliest records of human history, whoever has controlled Turkestan has been enriched by the valuable Silk Road between China and Europe. This lucrative trade route has made this region a battleground between the East and West for more than 3,000 years.

History

The opening act of Turkestan's dramatic history was played out on the steppes of Central Asia and acted out in epic battles with Mongols to the east, Persians to the southwest, Hindus to the southeast, and Russians to the North. Though often the victors, Turkic peoples have lived out their existence on the edge of annihilation. This context of kill or be killed has led them to some of the most extreme acts of aggression and conquest in human history.

Turkic peoples made their first appearance in the West when their raids against settlements in Central Asia pushed Germanic tribes into the crumbling Roman Empire of late antiquity. If the Romans found the Germanic Goths and Vandals to be barbarians, they were even less prepared for the terrifying warriors who had driven them off the steppes of Asia. In the mid-5th century, Europe met those terrors in the person of Attila the Hun, "the scourge of God," who brought the Byzantine Roman Empire to its knees in 434-453.

Islam entered Turkestan following the Arab conquest of the Persian Empire in 651. With the Arab defeat of the Chinese Tang Dynasty armies at Talas (in today's Kyrgyzstan) in 751, Muslims seized control of the Central Asian Silk Road.[4] Five eras mark the subsequent religious history of Turkestan. The first began in 1299 with the founding of what would become the Ottoman Empire. The second unfolded in the reign of Tamerlane in 1360-1405, followed by a century of the Golden Horde rule in Central Asia. The third era was the Golden Age of Ottoman expansion highlighted by the conquest of Constantinople in 1453. The fourth era was one of decline, beginning with the 16th-century halt of Ottoman advance in Europe, and subsequent ascension of Imperial Russia over Central Asian Turkestan. The final period is still unfolding as Turkestan has entered a post-Communist era as part of the Commonwealth of Independent States.

When Sultan Mehmed II raised the Ottoman flag over Constantinople in 1453, it was the fulfillment of a 700-year-old Islamic dream. The Ottomans did not stop with Byzantium, however, but soon set their sights on the remainder of Christian Europe. Ottoman armies rolled through the Balkans, checked only temporarily in 1462 by Wallachia's Vlad III. Vlad, whose paternal surname was Dracul (known to posterity as Dracula), earned the name Vlad the Impaler by defeating and impaling 23,884 Turks on the banks of the Danube River. By 1475, though, Vlad the Impaler was no more, and Ottoman armies continued their advance into Europe.

Suleiman the Magnificent

Mehmed the Conqueror's great grandson, Suleiman the Magnificent, earned the title through his magnificent conquests of Persia and North Africa. Suleiman proved less magnificent when his army of 120-130,000 troops failed to defeat a much smaller force in the Holy Roman Empire city of Vienna. Suleiman's failed 1529 Siege of Vienna marked the end of Turkish Muslim expansion into Europe and the beginning of a long and inexorable Ottoman decline. It also coincided with the rise of Imperial Russia.

Ever since the first Christian Roman emperor in the fourth century transformed the town of Byzantium into his new capital and renamed it Constantinople, it had been regarded as the

"Second Rome." With the fall of Constantinople, Christians in Moscow took up the mantle, declaring their city the "Third Rome." The two cities shared the same Eastern Orthodoxy. The Grand Prinçe of Moscow, Ivan III (1440-1505), sealed the legacy when he married Sophia Paleologue,[5] the niece of the last Byzantine emperor, Constantine XI. Ivan III tripled the size of Russia, and ended the century-long reign of terror by the Turko-Mongolian Golden Horde of Central Asia.

Through the 18th and 19th centuries, Imperial Russia was expanding, largely at the expense of the declining Ottoman Empire. Russia's imperial ambitions also threatened to challenge the British and French control of the Mediterranean. Following a dispute with France over the rights to the Ottoman-held Christian holy sites in Jerusalem, France and Great Britain partnered with Ottoman Turks against Russia in the 1853-1856 Crimean War. The unlikely alliance of majority-Christian nations in Western Europe with Muslim Turkey against Eastern Orthodox Russia foreshadowed the 20th century Cold War of American-led NATO allies (including Turkey) against the Soviet Union.

In 1856, in exchange for British support against Russia in the Crimean War, the Turkish Sultan agreed that Muslims in the Ottoman Empire were free to convert to Christianity and be baptized. In response to this unprecedented opportunity, England's Church Missionary Society started a new outreach

Joseph Stalin

to Muslims in Constantinople (now Istanbul). Mission historian K.S. Latourette reported, "A few conversions were made, but a storm of persecution clouded the initially bright prospects." By the end of the 1870s, "mainly because of shortness of funds" the opportunity was lost and "the Constantinople station discontinued."[6]

Though 20th century Communism initially offered greater autonomy to Turkestani Muslims, the official Communist position that viewed religion as "the opiate of the masses" eventually turned against Islam. Over the next eight decades Communist assaults upon Islamic institutions weakened the educational and societal infrastructures that have always been vital to Islamic civilization.

In the post-Communist era, local presidents-for-life have emerged in each of the former Soviet Central Asian Republics and created varying degrees of totalitarian regimes.[7] Though the formal constitutions in each of the new republics of Uzbekistan, Kazakhstan, Kyrgyzstan, Turkmenistan and Azerbaijan profess freedom of religion, Islam remains the religion of the great majority. In order to curry favor from this majority, these governments have proven more than willing to crack down on Christian minorities.

If local Muslims became too militant, though, they too could feel the sting of the government whip. Islamic radicals are routinely targeted for suppression by these post-Communist dictatorships, because they know how quickly radical Islam can trigger a violent reversal of power.

The Nature of the Movement

As the Soviet Union loosened its grip prior to its final collapse in 1989, thousands of evangelical Christians from the West made their way into the former Communist empire to share their faith. A mere 25 years later, Turkestan, which had known no movements to Christ in its 1300-year-Islamic history, was now home to multiplying new movements of Muslims to Christ.[8]

While Western evangelists in the post-Soviet era played a significant role in the gospel's spread, they were preceded by a half century of vibrant Christian witness from hundreds of thousands of ethnic German Baptists, Mennonites and Pentecostals. Interviews with many of Central Asia's Muslim-background followers of Christ revealed that it was these ethnic German believers who first showed them the love of Christ, decades before Western evangelicals arrived on the scene.

Where did these ethnic German evangelicals come from? How did they land in the heart of Muslim Turkestan? The largest German immigrations into Russia could be traced back to the rule of Catherine the Great (1729-1796), who was an ethnic German from Prussia. Catherine invited open immigration for Germans and exempted them from military service. This made her offer particularly appealing to the pacifist Mennonites and Baptists who poured into Russia over the next century. She also allowed them to evangelize non-Christian minorities so long as they did not proselytize the Orthodox.[9]

By the twentieth century, two million ethnic Germans—many of them Baptists, Mennonites and Pentecostals—were living in Russia. However, most of these German Baptist and Mennonite evangelicals did not enter Turkestan until 1942. That was the year that Adolph Hitler turned his Nazi war machine against the Soviet Union.

Catherine the Great

Suddenly, Joseph Stalin (1878-1953) found the presence of two million ethnic Germans in Russia to be problematic, so he relocated them to Central Asia. He perceived a similar threat in the Far East where hundreds of thousands of ethnic Koreans had emigrated to Siberia during the 19th century to work in the underdeveloped timber and mining industries. Though Koreans were not Japanese—and were in fact bitter enemies of the Japanese who were occupying Korea at the time—they did look like Japanese. So Stalin's solution for them was the same. Half a million were relocated to the Soviet Central Asian states of Kazakhstan, Kyrgyzstan and Uzbekistan.[10]

In the decades following the collapse of the Soviet Union, hundreds of thousands of these indigenous Soviet-Germans relocated to Europe and the Americas, though as recently as 1999, there were still 353,441 ethnic Germans in Kazakhstan and 21,472 in Kyrgyzstan.[11]

Both the ethnic Germans and Koreans would come to play significant roles in the gospel transmission to Muslims in Turkestan. Though the Koreans were not Christians at the time, they would later provide a key cultural bridge to the post-Soviet arrival of hundreds of foreign evangelical Koreans who were able to easily connect with them and lead them to Christ.

As an ethnic Christian community, the Germans had a more immediate gospel impact. Though these evangelistic Germans saw relatively few Muslims actually come to faith, many of today's converts recall these pacifist witnesses as the first Christians whose arrival was not backed by an invading army.

Coming and Going

Today, Turkestan is home to several Muslim movements to Christ. Some are struggling to survive, while others are approaching a critical mass of many thousands. Though their total numbers are minuscule in comparison to Turkestan's 200 million Muslims, their very existence, which would have been inconceivable a century ago, marks a historic change in the 1300-year-old story of Islam in the region. Two decades ago, when the Iron Curtain had just collapsed, one could find only the beginnings of a couple of movements in the Soviet Union's Turkic republics.

As thousands of American, European and Korean evangelicals took advantage of Mikhail Gorbachev's new policies of *glasnost* (openness), they crossed paths with hundreds of thousands of ethnic German Protestants who took advantage of the same policies to evacuate Central Asia and return to either Russia or their native Germany. The tenure of these reluctant witnesses in Central Asia had lasted only about five decades, but while they were there, these German Protestants faithfully presented Christ to the Muslims around them. For this reason, history may yet identify the atheist Joseph Stalin as the greatest gospel deployment agent in the history of Turkestani evangelization.

Western missionaries who arrived after the collapse of the Soviet Union in 1989 had only a brief window before new regimes in Turkestan began clamping down on their witness. Through their witness, though, these Western evangelicals showed Muslims a Christian faith that was not part of a colonization effort. Many Muslims saw, for the first time, a faith that was neither an extension of the Orthodox Christianity of the Russian Empire nor the British imperialism of the 19th century's "Great Game".[12]

Because they were interested in reaching people rather than conquering territory, these Western evangelicals gave attention to specific languages and cultures of the Turkestani peoples. So, instead of arriving in the region with a Russian or German-language witness, they learned Uighur, Kazakh, Kirghiz, Uzbek and other Turkestani languages. More importantly, they saw to it that the gospel was translated into contemporary contextualized versions of each of these languages. This meant, among other things, that rather than use the Russian word for God, *Bog*, or the German *Gott*, they translated God's name as *Khoda*, the Turko-Persian term used for God by Muslims across Central Asia.

They also made sure the gospel was available in non-literary forms through such media as the *JESUS Film* translated into local Turkic languages. As the window began closing on Western missionary presence in the region, these local-language gospel resources remained behind to fuel a new stage in Turkestani church history.

From Yours to Mine

Eighty years of Marxist education conveyed a consistent message to the youth of Central Asia: Islam came to you at the point of a sword, and religion is nothing more than a tool for manipulating the masses. Though the former point could not be debated, it also reminded Turkic dissidents that Islam could once again be used to challenge the repressive nationalist dictators who ruled over Turkestan.

By the start of the 21st century, beachhead communities of new believers from several Turkic people groups were established across much of Central Asia. In the more open republics, new associations of Baptists, Presbyterians, Lutherans, Pentecostals and others registered their presence with the government. In the more restricted countries, new believers met secretly in homes and apartments. Most of the early converts were young adults. Doubtless some of them were attracted to the development programs that the Western Christians offered. Some saw these foreign relationships as avenues to a better life in the West. When Western (and Korean) organizations offered church buildings and pastoral subsidies to local leaders, the motivations for conversion became even more clouded.

In the early years of the 21st century Turkestani regimes used the threat of Islamic extremism to justify ever-tightening government control. At the same time, to pacify Muslim majorities, these nationalistic governments periodically expelled foreign Christians as well. Christian witness and church development were suppressed in many countries and outright banned in others. Christian advance, which had initially been vibrant, slowed, then plateaued and declined. Many wondered if the Turkestani spring was already slipping into winter.

In some republics churches were shuttered and disbanded; in others, the foreign leaders were expelled, leaving the communities to make their way under fledgling local leadership. However, rather than cause the communities to shrivel and die, the new crisis brought about changes in the way the gospel spread in Turkestan. No longer possible to rely on Western leadership and institutions, indigenous Turkic leaders began to emerge. These new leaders, though less formally trained than their Western predecessors, had the advantages of being native: their language was flawless, their residence irrevocable, their worldview identical, and their skills for living under persecution well honed.

Many of the open churches in Turkestan went underground where they thrived. Smaller house churches began multiplying. Unable to receive foreign donations and funding for projects, Turkestani believers are discovering new ways to be and do church. The results are promising.

I spent an afternoon with a group of underground Christians in a Central Asian city. I asked them, "How can Western Christians help?" A middle-aged man spoke up, "I think Western Christians could help us set up our own businesses, not financially support us directly, just help local believers to get started in their own businesses. We know that many Westerners just want to do the easy thing. They want to give money, because that is their business. They receive donations and must give it away. But if we have our own business, then we can help others. We know better whom to help and how to help."

Another added, "I think sometimes support can make people become lazy. People don't have the motivation to do the ministry. They just stay at home and say, 'I will get the support this month.'"

He continued, "Like drug addicts, local Christians can get support addicted. When American agencies start providing humanitarian aid, this is also very bad. It makes sense to help, but...."

A woman said, "When there is a crisis, medical treatment is okay, but just giving food or clothing just corrupts people."

A young leader quickly added, "We don't want to say that they are doing something wrong. They want to help, to do something very good. But there are consequences. For example, the government is saying that every believer just gets $100, and they are lazy. And I think, in some cases, it is true."

New Gospel Pathways

When asked what God had used to bring them to faith in Jesus Christ, Turkestani Muslim-background believers talked about the role of dreams, the importance of having a New Testament in their own language, watching the *JESUS Film*, and other factors. But the most important thread linking each testimony was an encounter with a living Christ who heard and answered their prayers. Unlike the empty offerings of Communism or secular atheism, Christ touched a deep place in their soul that nothing else had ever filled.

The dissolution of Communism removed much of the social safety net for the masses in the Soviet Union. Under Communism, government provisions for education, health-care, food, housing, employment and pension, though mea-ger, were nonetheless provisions on which many relied, and languished. When a market-place economy removed many of these provisions it posed a seismic shift for millions of former dependents on the State.

The result of this shift was a much more vulnerable society. Problems of unemployment, family crises, crime and alcohol abuse peppered the stories of most of those who were interviewed. Many testimonies revealed lives that had bottomed out before finding a Savior and new guidance for daily life in the person of Jesus Christ.

Though all those interviewed were from an Islamic background, most admitted that it was only a nominal, cultural identity. It was the religion of their people, in contrast to the atheism or Orthodoxy of the Russians, but meant little to them personally. Their lives were filled with material concerns, and were often empty. Unlike the Arab and Persian worlds, Turkestani Muslims struggled with alcohol abuse and its corrosive effects on their families and personal lives.

Today, scattered across Turkestan, there are more than a dozen Muslim movements to Christ of at least 1,000 baptized believers or 100 churches among their people. Gone are the days when these churches, Bible schools, and development projects are led by foreign Christians. While each movement is different, there is a pattern of independence and dignity, as the movements are finding their own leadership, their own styles of worship and community, their own flavor.

One of those flavors is a spirit of thankfulness to God, even in the face of extreme persecution. In one of the more embattled movements, believers had to travel hundreds of miles through circuitous routes to a city located in a more open republic in order to be interviewed. Of the dozen who were interviewed, only two had been significantly influenced by foreigners.

A believer named Bek told a story similar to others we heard. It was not one thing, but several touches that steered his journey to faith. As a child Bek had been sick and spent a lot of time in the hospital, leaving him with a fear of death and a hunger to find God. Bek tried to do this through reading the Qur'an, but could not understand Arabic. Through subsequent high school and military service, he drank alcohol and lived a partying lifestyle, but none of this satisfied him.

A local believer from a Muslim background befriended Bek. This believer's life was different: he had a peace within him; he didn't drink alcohol; he often read from a book. When Bek asked him what he was reading, he gave Bek a gospel tract in their own language entitled "Where Does Your Soul Go?" After Bek read it, he wanted to know more. So he went to his friend, who invited him to an ordinary house for a meeting with several other young persons. There they sat on the floor, praising and thanking God. After a while, they asked Bek if he wanted to accept Jesus, and he did.

"When I arrived home," Bek said, "I told my wife all that had happened. She did not understand. 'You are not a Russian,' she said, 'so why do you preach these things?' So I quietly prayed for her.

"Some time later, my mother-in-law became sick, so we went to the village to visit her. She had thyroid cancer and had been unable to eat for nearly six months. She had grown so thin that her husband began preparing for her burial.

"I prayed for her in Jesus' name, and she said, 'I want to repent and accept Jesus.' We wept and prayed with her. Then, God healed her. Everyone was so surprised. It was a great miracle."

Several other believers from one of the movements testified to a background of broken homes, alcohol, drug addiction and crime before coming to faith in Christ. The greatest miracle, though, was the change in their own lives.

Mamduh came to faith after a 20-year addiction to heroin. By the time a fellow Turkic believer shared the gospel with him in 2002, he was ready: "I accepted Jesus into my heart and my life changed. At that time, I stopped all kinds of drugs." When Mamduh's friends heard about his new faith, they avoided him, but soon they could see the positive changes in his life. "You are becoming a different man," they said. And that encouraged Mamduh to continue.

Another Turkestani believer began his interview with an admission: "I was a thief, a hooligan, a fighter. I was one of the worst sinners. I was imprisoned four times for crimes I committed. But God saved me from all those things. I didn't understand it then, but I understand it now."

Most of those interviewed had no contact with Western or foreign Christians. Those who had known some Western and Korean Christians spoke of these relationships in the past tense, and not always in a nostalgic manner. Though times were easier and ostensibly better when their Republic was more open to the West, their faith was also conflicted by mixed motives and peripheral issues.

Those who had intimately related to Western Christians spoke positively of the evangelism, discipleship and theological training they had received in Bible institutes that were now closed. But they no longer received funds and rarely saw Western Christians, and when they did, they kept their distance lest they draw undesired attention from the heavy hand of the security police.

A large Pentecostal church building that had once drawn hundreds of worshipers every night of the week was now closed. Those who had worshiped there now met wherever they could in groups of two and three. Nonetheless, they kept track of the growing numbers of new believers and cell groups. They set prayerful goals for reaching more. "Our networks now number about 3,000," their leader told me, "of whom, about 1,000 have been baptized."

He continued, "These days, we don't dare carry Bibles with us openly. We gather in groups of two and three, and use our smart phones to download Scripture from the Internet. We meet long enough to read a passage, discuss its meaning, then encourage and pray for one another. After that we disband."

One of the Turkestani brothers saw my look of concern and flashed a sympathetic smile. "Don't worry," he said. "We are rejoicing in Christ. We have a saying, 'When you are perse-cuted, thank God that you have not been thrown into prison. If you *have* been thrown into prison, thank God that you have not been beaten. If you *have* been beaten, thank God that you have not been killed.'" He paused, and smiled again, "And if you *have* been killed, thank God that you are with him in heaven."

Return of the King

On a warm spring day in the dusty town of Samarkand, Muslim families with children on their break from school line up outside of the Gur-e Amir (Tomb of the King) to see the sepulcher where Tamerlane has been buried for more than six centuries. As they approach the jade-colored sarcophagus, parents pause to tell their children of their illustrious ancestor who cemented the preeminence of the Muslim faith across Turkestan and crushed all other competing religions.

Gur-e Amir Tomb

A few old men and women stop to lean against the tomb and whisper a prayer or solicit a *baraka*, a blessing, from the famous Turk.

Unnoticed by them is a young Muslim-background follower of Jesus Christ with a cross necklace tucked into his undershirt. He awaits his turn before leaning against the tomb to whisper the words slowly, as if old Tamerlane could hear:

"We're back."

Small Group Discussion ~ Discover for Yourself

1. What impressions do you take away from this chapter?
2. How is God at work in the Turkestan Room?
3. What was the significance of the gospel momentum shifting "From Yours to Mine" in Central Asian Turkestan?
4. What do you think is the future of Muslim movements to Christ in Turkestan?

the
West Africa
room

Blessed are the peacemakers,
for they will be called sons of God.

Matthew 5:9

 IN 1967 WHILE European and American college students were protesting the escalating Vietnam War, five thousand miles away, 23-year-old Faith Slate was changing the world in a different way, serving as a two-year missionary "Journeyman" in West Africa. Forty-five years later, as a retired missionary, she remembered, "a most significant event that had a great impact on the future—that took place in June 1967."

During the school year, Faith taught missionary children, but in the summer vacation months she trekked out to the villages with Maddie Granger, a veteran single missionary who was fun and fearless. The two women spent the night in the villages, preaching the gospel every day, and as many as 12 times on Sundays. Weekday mornings, they held literacy classes and offered a rudimentary clinic where they saw lines of patients.

"Now mind you," Faith explained, "both of us were teachers, not doctors."

"Until today," Faith said, "I can clearly picture in the line a strikingly beautiful woman with a sick baby on her back. She was the first nomadic Muslim from the north that I had ever seen up close." Maddie told Faith that the woman had walked 25 miles for their medical help. Maddie gave the very weak baby something, perhaps some vitamins, and then handed the infant to Faith.

"Here," Maddie said. "He's yours."

"But what do I do?" I protested.

"First," Maddie said, "pray—hard.

"Then," she said as she handed me a tin of Peak milk and a tiny spoon, "try giving him some milk."

Faith did pray, and pray. Then, to her delight, the little boy began accepting spoonfuls of milk.

"After my care," Faith said, "the mother smiled a beautiful smile, wrapped the baby on her back and walked the 25 miles back home to her village."

Faith continued, "I finished the summer with Maddie, resumed my teaching responsibilities, then went back to America where I attended seminary, got married, and later spent years with my husband as missionaries in Zambia. But I often wondered about and prayed for that Muslim woman and her baby."

When Faith arrived, Protestant missionaries had been working in West Africa for more than a century, the Catholics even longer. Both groups had aimed their work at the responsive Animistic peoples along the coast. The Muslims of the north were not so eager to receive a witness from those they deemed to be polytheistic (because they were Trinitarian) Western colonizers.[1] Missionaries had more than enough challenge discipling the Animism out of their converts while bringing to them the more obvious benefits of Western schools and hospitals.

By the late 1950s, though, a curious pattern began to emerge in several of the Protestant missions. In separate, independent initiatives, it was particularly single women missionaries, like Maddie Granger and Faith Slate, who began venturing out beyond the compounds and institutions of the coastal ministries and engaging the Muslim peoples of the North.

Two Oceans

West Africa is a tale of two oceans: the Atlantic to the west and the great Sahara Desert to the north. For thousands of years, these two oceans have insulated the peoples of West Africa from outside civilizations.

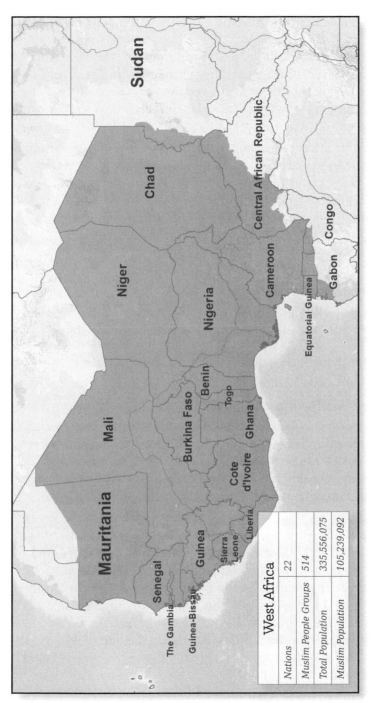

West Africa

West Africa	
Nations	22
Muslim People Groups	514
Total Population	335,556,075
Muslim Population	105,239,092

Long before the Atlantic brought Portuguese explorers to the region on their way to the lucrative East Indies spice trade, Arab camel caravans, "ships of the desert," crossed the Sahara to exploit West Africa's bounty in gold, ivory and human cargo. When the Arabs reached the West African edge of the Sahara, they aptly called it the *Sahel*, the Arabic word for "coast" or "shore."

Just as European colonizers established a string of trading posts along the Atlantic coast in Conakry, Freetown, Abidjan, Accra, Lagos and Monrovia, so too did the Arab and Berber traders establish caravan outposts along the Sahara shoreline in Sahel cities of Timbuktu, Djenne, Gao, Sokoto and Kano.

As West Africa entered the 21st century, the two oceans continued to define a region that is predominantly Christian in the south, along the Atlantic coastal zone, and Muslim in the north, along the savannah lands of the Saharan Sahel. Both Christian and Muslim populations have swollen with the arrival of Western healthcare and education, causing the two cultures to spill their adherents into the battleground zone between north and south. There the spiritual fate of millions of West African Animists has yet to be determined.

Human Trafficking

West Africa's isolation from the outside world has shrouded its early history. By the time of the Muslim advance across North Africa in the 8th century, a trans-Saharan trade was well underway, allowing the exploitation of the valuable gold, ivory, salt, and slave trade.

Arab historians in the 9th century described a powerful Ghana Empire[2] rich in gold, and guarded by a military that "could put 200,000 men into the field, more than 40,000 of them archers," noting their "cavalry forces as well."[3] The Ghana Empire and its successor Soninke and Mali empires positioned themselves on the border of modern-day Mali and Mauritania, between the riches of West Africa and the Mediterranean markets to the north. By the end of the Middle Ages, Mali was the source of almost half the Old World's gold.[4] In exchange for West Africa's riches, Almoravid Berbers of Morocco and Algeria introduced Islam to West Africa.

Faith and fortune have always co-mingled in West Africa. Slavery was the great wound in the region that, in many respects, has never fully healed. The exploitation of the weak by the strong stretches deep into human history, and indeed slavery existed in West Africa long before Arabs and Europeans globalized it.

Human trafficking peaked in the trans-Atlantic slave trade of 1500 to 1866, when Europeans and Americans exported 10 to 12 million mostly West Africans to the New World as slaves. Added to the victim toll were the one to two million Africans who died in transit across the ocean, and a further six million men, women and children killed in the wars and slave raids that acquired the human cargo.[5]

By the end of the 19th century, European, American and Arab participation in the slave trade was effectively over.[6] What remained, however, was residual suspicion and hostility between the descendants of the slave trade's victims and those who prospered as co-conspirators. The same tribal hostilities that prompted Africans to deliver fellow Africans to Arabs, Europeans, and Americans as slaves, persisted long after the slave trade ended. It is this legacy of internal ethnic conflict that refuses to heal and continues to plague the region to this day.

Human Trafficking

Colonization

West African colonization began in the 19th century, when King Leopold of Belgium set off a European "Scramble for Africa" in his own quest to acquire an African colony. Before the great land grab was over, European powers had carved out colonies from Egypt to Cape Town.[7]

Britain and France (and Germany prior to World War I) divided the peoples of West Africa into Anglo and Franco-African colonies and protectorates. While Europeans focused their interests along coastal trading ports, the arid interior of the region continued to live as it had for centuries. Muslim people groups on the edge of the Sahara retained ancient allegiances to Muslim sheikhs and feudal rulers under varying degrees of Islamic law and social customs.

Global decolonization followed soon after the end of World War II, but did not effectively reach Africa until the end of the 1950s. Ghana gained its independence in 1957, followed by Guinea in 1958. Then in 1960, 17 additional African nations, including 11 in West Africa, gained their independence, followed by Sierra Leone in 1961. In contrast to the West, these are still young nations. By comparison, at this stage in its history, America was still decades away from the outbreak of its own Civil War. All of these challenges still lay ahead for the new nations of West Africa.

The Resource Curse

West Africa's treasures of natural wealth in gold, diamonds, and, more recently, oil, have been both a blessing and a curse. While these raw materials have helped to jump start the new economies, they have also produced what some economists call the "Resource Curse" or the "Paradox of Plenty."[8] Having a valuable, non-renewable source of wealth allows those who control that wealth to ignore a social contract with the people. While those controlling the valued resource may act with little regard for public opinion, they soon find the need to suppress the public in order to maintain their control. The curse of resources has been graphically illustrated over the past three decades in Liberia, Sierra Leone and Nigeria.

In 1980, Master Sergeant Samuel Doe led a rogue band of non-commissioned officers to murder and replace democratically elected President William Tolbert of Liberia. Tolbert had been a Baptist preacher and past president of the Baptist World Alliance. The man who killed him, Samuel Doe, was also a Baptist. Nine years later, Doe was tortured and killed by a rebel leader, Prince Y. Johnson, who purportedly sliced off Doe's ears before murdering him. Johnson subsequently had his own Christian conversion experience, and become pastor of an evangelical church. Today, Johnson holds an elected seat in the Liberian Senate.[9]

The man who succeeded Samuel Doe as president of Liberia in 1990 was Charles Taylor. Taylor was an American-educated Baptist lay-preacher and one of the 20th century's most notorious war criminals. The architect of two civil wars in Liberia and one in Sierra Leone, Taylor was convicted in 2011 at the international criminal court in The Hague for terror, murder, rape, sexual slavery and conscripting thousands of child soldiers.[10]

Samuel Doe

The Christian identity of some of West Africa's most notorious tyrants is a reminder that entanglements between financial, political and religious interests are not limited to Islamic despots, but are common to the human condition regardless of religious affiliation.

Liberia's two civil wars, between 1989 and 2003, claimed 250,000 lives, more than 12 percent of the nation's population, and spilled over to neighboring Sierra Leone and Guinea, where it extracted a further 50,000 lives and created more than a million refugees.[11]

The Liberian civil wars were rivaled in brutality only by the Sierra Leone conflict. In 1996, Sierra Leone's democratically elected Muslim president, Alhaji Ahmad Tejan Kabbah adopted the campaign slogan: "The Future is in Your Hands." The opposition Revolutionary United Front (RUF) responded by chopping off the hands of villagers who supported Kabbah. More precisely, the RUF rebels kidnapped and terrorized thousands of children whom they beat and plied with cocaine to desensitize them before forcing them to kill their own parents and then take a place on the front lines of battle.[12]

Ahmad Tejan Kabbah

At stake were millions of dollars in gold and diamonds.[13] Among the gentle people of Liberia and Sierra Leone today, it is difficult to imagine the brutalities that erupted only a decade ago. Yet there are few persons in either country who were not scarred by or implicated in those years of chaos between 1980 and 2003, leaving one to wonder what will be the next *casus belli* or trigger that will set the peoples of the region against one another.

That trigger may already be revealing itself in neighboring Nigeria, where Christians in the oil-rich south of the country contend with Muslims in the impoverished north.

While Christian schools and hospitals undeniably improved life quality in West Africa, markedly extending life expectancy and reducing infant mortality rates, they also produced a population explosion for both Muslims and Christians. Added to this population boom are ecological disasters brought on by the expanding Sahara and a shrinking water table. Lake Chad, for example, on Nigeria's northern border, declined in size from 9,700 square miles in 1983 to less than 580 square miles in 2001; many predict that the lake will disappear entirely before this century's end.[14] Islamic groups such as *Ansaru, Boko Haram,* and *Movement for Oneness and Jihad in West Africa* are simply the latest militant vehicles addressing the disparities in the country.[15]

Nigeria's *Boko Haram* has gained the most press attention in recent years. *Boko Haram* or "Western Education is Forbidden" is the Hausa shorthand name for the "Congregation and People Committed to the Propagation of the Prophet's Teaching and Jihad." Boko Haram was formed in 2001 by Mohammed Yusuf as a militant movement aimed at implementing *sharia* law and combatting Westernization. Yusuf was arrested and killed by Nigerian police in 2009, but over the next three years Boko Haram militants went on to kill more than 1,600 persons. They targeted Christian churches, school children and moderate Muslims who cooperated with the government.[16]

The Nature of the Movements

The nature of the Muslim movements to Christ in West Africa is different from those in many other Rooms in the House of Islam. Unlike the Arab world with its ancient Christian communities that stood in stubborn contrast to the relentless march of Islam, Christianity in this part of the Muslim world arrived more recently and appears to be the more vital force. Much of Islam, on the other hand, appears spent and desperate. The desperation can be seen in the terrorism of such groups as Boko Haram and Ansaru.

In contrast to many other Rooms in the House of Islam, most of West Africa still has legal systems that espouse separation of religion from state, offering a more level playing field for Muslims to come to Christ and vice versa. As a result, one finds Muslims who have come to Christ scattered throughout churches in West Africa, as well as Christians who have converted to Islam.

Christians have not been shy about sharing their faith with Muslims, except in the fiercely Islamic states in the north that are pressing militantly for the imposition of *sharia*, Islamic law. These Muslims interpret the advance of southern Christian tribes as an act of domestic colonization and an invasion of Western culture into their homeland.

Though there are several Muslim movements to Christ in West Africa, one must be careful not to assume they are all the same. One could view them in three categories: (1) in predominantly Christian areas, (2) among folk Islamists, and (3) in predominantly Muslim areas.

Along the Atlantic coastal zone where Christianity is dominant, churches have little impetus to contextualize or accommodate the gospel message to Muslim sensibilities. These coastal communities are more connected with the Western world with its trade, cultural influences, and popular Pentecostal expressions.

Across this coastal zone, many individual Muslims have come to Christ and been baptized. To do so, though, has meant extracting themselves or being forcibly expelled from their Muslim families and communities. The churches most effective in this kind of winning of Muslims have been those that have taken an all-encompassing approach to their faith. To assimilate a Muslim-background convert the church must replace all that the convert has lost: his family, his job, his wife (or prospects for one), and children. Unless a church is able to accept such a holistic challenge, it has little hope of retaining the Muslim convert.

Muslims who are drawn to these vibrant Christian communities become one of them, typically exchanging their Muslim names for Christian ones, and leaving behind their Islamic traditions. One could only guess as to how many individual Muslims are scattered throughout the tens of thousands of Protestant and Catholic churches of coastal-zone West Africa.

In both the Muslim north and the Christian south, African Tribal Religion still occupies the beating heart of many ostensibly Muslim and Christian adherents. For many West Africans who are neither Muslim nor Christian, daily life is a struggle with witchcraft and sorcery. The practical question they face is, "What religion is powerful enough to protect me from the spiritual forces around me?" Western expressions of Christianity which emphasize rational precepts, doctrines and programs have little currency in such an environment, yet when the gospel boldly offers the power to defeat the challenges of curses, physical illness, mental illness, and demonic possession, it is welcomed. At present, the movements within this Animistic buffer zone still vacillate between superficial Muslim and Christian loyalties and tend toward the faith that helps them overcome the spiritual darkness that surrounds them.

The deeper one goes into the Muslim heartland, the more one finds Muslim movements to Christ that are indigenous and contextualized to the Islamic community. These converts typically do not reject their Muslim culture, for to do so would be to reject their core ethnic identity. To be a Fulani, a Kanuri, a Susu, a Bambara, a White or Black Moor is to be a Muslim. To reject this core identity is tantamount to suicide. Consequently, the Muslim movements to Christ in the north have a much more tenuous identification with the Christian religion and culture, while still exhibiting a deep commitment to the person of Christ and to the authority of the New Testament.

Challenge of Wineskins

Though thousands of Muslim-background converts have been assimilated into Christian churches through marriage, evangelism and attraction to the Christian faith and fellowship, there remain problems. Thousands of other Muslims have embraced Jesus Christ, but have not been willing to leave their Muslim family and tribe to join one of the Christianized tribes.

The challenge for many of these Muslim-background believers stems less from fear than from love. A young Muslim-background follower of Christ from a large and ancient Muslim people group revealed a deep gash in his forehead where his uncle had struck him with a machete. When asked, "Why have you not left?" he replied, "I will not leave until my family has come to faith." That was more than a decade ago. Today, there are more than 5,000 of his Muslim community who have come to faith in *Isa al-Masih*, Jesus Christ.

Other obstacles to these movements come, not from Islamic intolerance, but from traditional churches. These churches often fail to address the lifestyle and culture of Muslims who are coming to faith. In one case, several thousand nomadic Muslims came to faith in Christ and met regularly in discipleship groups for years before they were allowed to be baptized. The problem was not their unwillingness to be baptized, but a church polity that said, "Unless you are baptized into one of our denominationally registered churches, by one of our ordained pastors, you cannot be baptized." For many Muslims who desired Christian baptism, though, joining one of those denominational churches meant abandoning their own people, and being abandoned by them.

These checks and balances were woven into local church polity over 150 years as bulwarks against heresy and immorality, both real and anticipated. Few could have imagined, though, that these checks might also impede thousands of Muslims from being baptized at all.

How God is at Work

Response to Injustice

Often enough, it is injustice within the Muslim community itself that leads Muslims to turn to Christ.

Fatima's father was a *marabout*, a Muslim holy man. Now she is a 32-year-old widow with three children. Her 90-year-old husband died two years earlier. Her oldest child was born when she was only 14. She herself was married at age 12.

Fatima said,

> My mother forced me to marry this elderly man, though she knew I did not want to marry him. My mother used a magic potion on me to force me to marry him. After my mother died, I began to have many conflicts with the stepchildren in our home. Many of these children were older than me—children of other wives.

After experiencing repeated dreams that drew her toward Christ, Fatima determined to seek out Christians to help her understand.

> I went to a woman who was living nearby and told her about my dreams. She said I should go to the pastor and he could explain it to me. The local Baptist pastor encouraged me to give my life to the Lord. He said, I have often called out to Jesus, but I have never seen him like you have.

> After I came here, I had several visions of the Lord and I decided to go to church. Since I started going to church, it has not been easy. My husband went to my aunts and said they should prevent me from going to church.

> I have been experiencing very serious persecution from the stepsons. They have cut off all of my support. They don't even support my own children now. As we speak, they are in the court of law. I am facing very serious persecution. Even when I listen to Christian radio, my stepsons criticize me.

> If not for the Lord, I would be dead right now. . . . God only knows what I am going through.

Fatima wrung her hands and wept.

Another Muslim-background woman confided:

Because of the way the Muslims treated me, it moved me to go to church. After my husband died, the Muslim landlords gave me three days' notice to pay an increased rent before they would kick me out. I found another place to rent.

I started going to church and saw the life in the church, how it was different. My life was changed. I repented of my sins. All of my children are now a part of the church as well. One of my children is a leader in praise and worship.

Marabout Holy Man

In these and similar testimonies, one observes a pattern. When the Muslim community mistreats one of their own, that person is more inclined to find an alternative sanctuary in the person of Christ and the Christian faith.

West Africa's troubled history has shown us that Muslims have no monopoly on injustice and inhumanity, and current actions by Muslim vigilantes reveal that the violence will likely not end any time soon. On May 24, 2013, on a busy London Street, a 20-year-old man of Nigerian descent named Adebolajo nearly beheaded an unarmed 25-year-old off-duty soldier, after ambushing him with a butcher knife.

Camera-phones recorded Adebolajo's ranting rationale and broadcast it for all the world to see on multiple cable news channels: "We swear by almighty Allah we will never stop fighting you. The only reason we have done this is because Muslims are dying every day. . . . This British soldier is an eye for an eye, a tooth for a tooth."

Perhaps as shocking as the grisly murder was the fact that Adebolajo was a convert to Islam from the Nigerian-British Christian community where he had been known as Michael.[17]

The ideological struggle in West Africa is unlikely to end any time soon. Both Christians and Muslims will continue to be challenged to pursue the highest ideals of their own tradition lest those they mistreat convert to the faith of their rival.

Self-Discovery

Another path to faith in Christ for Muslims has been the discovery for themselves that Christ is who he claims to be. Unlike the Qur'an, which can only be truly represented in the Arabic language, the Bible is translated into the local language.[18] More than one Muslim-background believer commented: "I do not understand Arabic or the Qur'an. But I understand the Bible."

When asked, "What do you say about Jesus?" a young man replied, "The Qur'an says, 'If you are in doubt, ask the people who were before you.' So, if Muhammad was told to ask the people who were before him if he was in doubt, I see Jesus as someone who clears my doubt. Jesus is someone who says you cannot come to the Father except through Him. I accept this; He is the truth and the life."

Another Muslim convert offered this insight: "As Muslims, all we did was five memorized prayers. But there was no assurance of heaven. No one could give me a good answer. This is what prompted me to look into who Jesus was."

In response to the question, "Who is Muhammad?" a Muslim-background believer said, "I know that when the Prophet Muhammad died they buried him. But when Jesus died, he rose up and God took him to heaven. Jesus is the Son of God, and Muhammad is the son of the world."

Generally speaking, Muslims reject the Christian message of who Jesus is. They have been taught that these Christian testimonies are ignorant and wrong. When they discover for themselves, though, it is a different matter. Once they encounter Christ, through answered prayers, dreams and their own reading of Scripture, they find a living Lord whom they cannot ignore, and for whom they are willing to die.

Christian Prayer, Love, and Witness

Still others have come to Christ through witness in Christian schools and charitable ministry, prayers and simple friendship with classmates. A Muslim-background man in his 30s reflected on his own pilgrimage: "Two Christian friends helped me to know who Jesus was. We used to play soccer together. I wept at what Jesus had done for me, and at night I dreamed about him. I found the answer of how to go to heaven in Jesus."

A 32-year-old Muslim-background pastor was asked what God is using to draw Muslims to faith in his community today. "Love is the major thing," he said. "Muslims don't really practice love and charity." He continued, "First, you must love them, then you pray for them. When they learn that God answers their prayers, they renounce Islam and follow Christ."

A 22-year-old woman from a strong Muslim background has now been following Jesus for eight months. She said, "Christianity is so sweet. I love the way Christians treat each other. Jesus is now God to me. He answers my prayers."

I asked a young woman from a strong Islamic family, who disowned her when she became a believer, "Following Jesus took a lot from your life, didn't it?" She replied adamantly: "NO. Now I can preach, I can sing, I can talk to people about Jesus. That is exciting to me. I am a changed person now. I am no longer a part of the world."

Inside and Out

The future of Muslim movements to Christ in West Africa is by no means assured. Challenges come from both external and internal factors, and it remains to be seen how and if the emerging movements will effectively overcome these challenges.

Externally, militant Islamic groups such as Boko Haram and Ansaru have determined to eradicate Muslim movements to Christ. To this end, they have destroyed churches and missionary outreach, murdering Muslim-background converts as well as those who seek to bring them to Christ.

On the one hand, their harsh treatment of missionary outreach and conversion has had a chilling effect on Christian witness. The ongoing threat of violence has compelled many Christians to take a wait-and-see approach to the Muslim interior.

On the other hand, as we have seen elsewhere in the House of Islam, Muslim violence can also prompt Muslims to turn away from Islam and seek a more peaceful faith. It is for this reason that the temptation for Christians to adopt a *jihadi* ethic and exchange an eye for an eye poses one of the greatest challenges to Muslim movements to Christ in the region. If Christ is no different than Muhammad, where then is one to turn?

Internal challenges also pose grave threats to these newly emerging movements. Perhaps more than in any other Room in the House of Islam, faith and fortune have been deeply intertwined in West Africa.

Though Muslims pay a great price to leave their communities to follow Christ, the Christ that they follow is sometimes offered to them as a "Bless-me-Jesus." While God has undoubtedly used healings and answered prayers as a means of drawing countless persons to faith in Christ, the allure of health and wealth in *this* life has created what has been called the "Prosperity Gospel" that is sweeping through many churches in West Africa.

Pastors of some of West Africa's so-called "Prosperity Churches" have themselves become multi-millionaire advocates of a gospel that promises health and wealth to faithful followers.[19] On the road ahead, Muslim-background disciples of Christ will be challenged to follow the Christ of Scripture and not get lost in the ephemeral trappings of a prosperity-driven gospel.

Further internal challenges stem from the very freedoms that these new believers find in Christ. Muslim critics of Christianity in West Africa accuse it of being chaotic and lawless. Given West Africans' history and the tragic record of corrupt, yet nominally Christian, regimes in Liberia, Nigeria and Sierra Leone, these charges are difficult to dismiss.

Another internal challenge that both Muslim- and Christian-background believers must address is that of community. Followers of Christ from a Christian background have developed some of the most vibrant churches in all of Christendom, but they remain culturally miles apart from the unreached Muslim people groups they seek to reach. So long as a Muslim man or woman is willing to leave his home, family, community and tribe to become a part of the Christian community, they are welcomed.[20]

But should extraction, expulsion from one's own people, be prerequisites for conversion? In movements to Christ, it is not the individuals, the single converts, who represent the nature of a true movement. It is the communities, beginning with the families that produce the swelling ranks of true *movements* of Muslims to Christ.

In 1969, a Muslim-background believer named Malam Yusufu from a Fulani royal family observed,

> Some of our converts before they receive the gifts of the New Birth fall back, because in the process of the unnecessary sacrifice of their own way of living they have become individualists, emphasizing the individualistic approach, and have lost the care and love of their natural community and the sense of belonging. That is what brings out the remark often heard (from Muslims), 'Look, they are the people who separate men and women from their villages and family.' They do not belong any more.[21]

Faith's Fruit

In 1974, Faith Slate, now Faith Wells, and her husband, Peter, returned to West Africa where Faith had served as a Journeyman. Their assignment was to start a high school for African students. As she had done with Maddie seven years earlier, Faith ventured with her husband into the Muslim villages of their area.

In 1980, after the New Testament was translated into one of the local Muslim-language dialects, Peter and Faith experienced a breakthrough.

"In early 1980," Faith said,

> we were in the village . . . visiting some of the Muslim-background believers when we saw a group of young Muslim teenagers from the nomadic Muslim people in the north. We told these young men about the school we had started. The boys took us to meet their families. Immediately, I recognized the beautiful smile of the woman I had met in the village clinic thirteen years earlier. Her son, that little baby I had held and prayed over, was now standing before me a tall and handsome boy of 13.

Faith continued the story,

Two years later, this teenage boy and his older brother were among the first 17 Muslims from that nomadic people group that my husband baptized in 1982. Eventually his mother, a beautiful woman named Bosha, also became a believer. In fact 80 people from her village accepted Jesus Christ. After his baptism, the young man took as his Christian name the name of our son David. He later went on to Bible school and is now pastor of a Baptist Church near Omore.

Faith and Peter have long since retired to America, but today, among that nomadic Muslim people group that Faith first touched as a young woman, there are more than 10,000 baptized believers.

Small Group Discussion ~ Discover for Yourself

1. What impressions do you take away from this chapter?
2. How is God at work in the West Africa Room?
3. How has the Christian community positively and negatively impacted the spread of Muslim movements in this Room?
4. What do you think is the future of Muslim movements to Christ in West Africa?

the Western South Asia room

The wolf will live with the lamb, the leopard will lie down with the goat, the calf and the lion and the yearling together; and a little child will lead them.

Isaiah 11:6

 AHMED KNEW WHAT he had to do. His teachers at the madrasa had made it clear to him. He had to kill the Jew man.

Weeks earlier Ahmed had been sitting on the floor in his brother Nasir's apartment in Kebirabad, meditating on the familiar verses from the Qur'an that he had long ago committed to memory. Nasir was one of the millions of rural Muslim villagers who had ventured to the South Asian city of Kebirabad in search of work. Along the way, Nasir had made friends with persons from other countries, other cultures, and other faiths. It was this cultural pollution that brought Ahmed to the city to check on his brother.

Before noon, Nasir entered the apartment accompanied by a middle-aged Westerner. "This is my friend Ted Moore," Nasir said. Ted extended his hand and offered his best smile to the expressionless Ahmed.

Without lifting his hand, Ahmed turned to his brother and replied in his tribal language, "He is *kafir* (a pagan)." Nasir was embarrassed by the boldness and venom in his brother's voice.

After Ted left, Ahmed demanded, "Why have you brought this Jew man into your house?"

"He is not a Jew," Nasir began, "He is an *angrezi* (a Westerner)."

In fact, Ted was one of the few Western Christians still living in the country, trying to find ways to communicate the gospel in a land that had grown steadily more and more hostile to the West.

"No!" Ahmed replied sternly, "He is a Jew. He is a *kafir*. If you do not leave this Jew, then you should leave us."

Instead, it was Ahmed who left, returning to the mountain village where he reported to his Islamic teachers about the Jew-Christian-*kafir* who had befriended his brother.

"Your brother is with Islamic enemies," Ahmed's teachers told him. "You should kill him. Do not wait."

Ahmed replied without hesitation, "I will do it."

Islam was Ahmed's life. When he was only four years old, his father had committed him to a madrasa where he learned Arabic before he learned to read his own language. By the time Ahmed was nine, he had become a *hafez*, one who had memorized the Qur'an. What had been difficult for a young child was now easy for the 21-year old young man. "I was happy to go deeper and deeper into Islam," he later reported. "My teachers said, 'Come, we will put you in a class to learn more about Jews, Christians, and *kafirs*.'" When Ahmed agreed, they put him in a class that taught him all kinds of ways to kill people.

It was not long afterward that Nasir arrived at Ahmed's family home in the mountains. This time a different Westerner, a friend of Ted's named Jason Hanson, rode on the back of Nasir's motorcycle.

In Ahmed's report to his leaders, his narrow Islamic education left him with few categories for classifying outsiders who were a threat to the faithful. He described Jason to his madrasa teachers as "a tall Pharaoh who is also a Jew." Ahmed's teachers told him he must kill the man.

Ahmed pulled Nasir aside and said, "If you want to live, take your friend and go."

But Nasir resisted.

So Ahmed told his family not to make any food for them, and Nasir's mother suddenly threw a cup at Nasir, cutting

Western South Asia

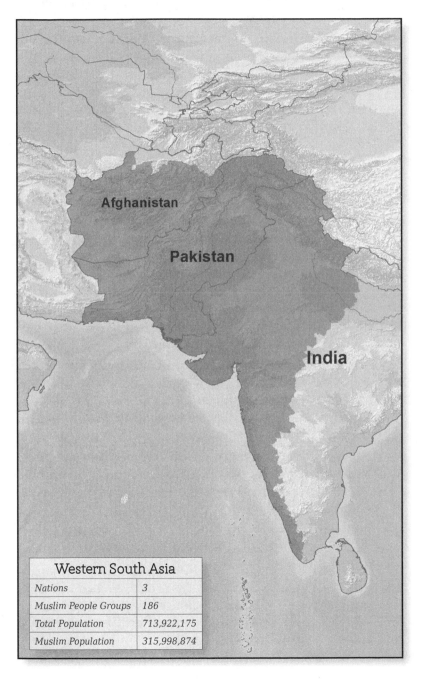

Western South Asia	
Nations	3
Muslim People Groups	186
Total Population	713,922,175
Muslim Population	315,998,874

open his head. Nasir took Jason by the arm and said, "We must go." For a year Nasir did not come to visit, feeling that his family had died to him.

Meanwhile, back in the mountains, Ahmed's teachers informed him, "Now your practical training is completed. You have given your body to Allah without reservation." Ahmed was now a *mujahid* (an Islamic warrior). It was 1996, and Ahmed was preparing to die for Allah on battlefronts such as Afghanistan or Kashmir. But something interrupted his deployment; Nasir and Jason had returned.

Ahmed told his teachers, "My brother had the gall to come again to my home with the *kafir*-Jew Jason." This time, though, Ahmed was happy that his brother was there, because his first assignment as a *mujahid* would be to kill the Jew-man.

With this aim in mind, Ahmed treated Nasir and Jason warmly, shaking their hands, chatting with them, all the while devising a plan to kill them. Ahmed talked with Jason about the Qur'an and Islam, encouraging Jason to convert to Islam. Jason was friendly, but unmovable; he even tried to persuade Ahmed to consider the teachings of Jesus.

That evening, Ahmed told his teachers, "I am ready to kill my brother and his friend." So they gave him two men to assist him. Together they crafted a plan to kill Jason first, and then Nasir. When the sun began to set, Ahmed was to bring Jason to a place of ambush. Ahmed said, "I will bring this Jew-man to you, and together we will kill him."

All day, Ahmed treated Jason with kindness. So, late in the afternoon, Jason was not surprised when Ahmed asked him, "Would you like to go for a ride with me?" Jason was pleased, and accepted the invitation.

But Nasir was worried, "No, Jason, you shouldn't trust him. Don't go." But Jason was looking for ways to befriend Ahmed, so he went along.

To help Jason relax and lower his guard, Ahmed first took Jason around the village to meet some of his relatives. Then he drove the bike out to the rural countryside. There he left the road and drove up a narrow trail into the mountains. After they passed to the other side of the mountain, Ahmed stopped the motorbike and parked it near where he knew that his friends were waiting in ambush.

Ahmed told Jason to walk down the hill with him. The plan was for Ahmed to keep talking with Jason, while his friends came up behind Jason and cut off his head. Jason later admitted that he had no clue that something was about to happen. He was puzzled, though, "Why are we here?" he asked Ahmed. At that moment, Ahmed and Jason looked into one another's eyes, and Ahmed saw something that stopped him. He didn't know what it was, but something in Jason's eyes made Ahmed abandon his plan.

Over Jason's shoulder, Ahmed could see his friends emerging from the bushes, awaiting his signal. Instead, Ahmed grabbed Jason's arm and said, "Let's go. Now!" The two quickly mounted the bike and sped off, leaving Ahmed's friends chasing after them.

They reached Ahmed's home without a word. Ahmed went straight to his brother and demanded, "Take your friend and go, or tomorrow you will take his head. And I will kill you as well."

Fault Lines

Nearly one out of every five Muslims on earth lives in Western South Asia. Comprising the nations of Afghanistan, Pakistan, and the western states of India, Western South Asia's total population of 714 million makes it the second most populous Room in the House of Islam.

Bordered by the Iranian plateau on the west, the region's northern boundary is framed by some of earth's highest summits in a fist of peaks appropriately called the Pamir Knot. These snow-capped giants form an impregnable wall stretching eastward from the Karakorum Mountains through the Hindu Kush and Tien Shan ranges before anchoring themselves in the Great Himalayas. From their snowy summits flow the five great rivers of the Punjab, which have given life to some of earth's most ancient civilizations.

Home to more than 300 distinct ethno-linguistic people groups and languages, Western South Asia features some of earth's most fractious cultural fault lines. Dravidian, Indo-European and Turkic peoples press against one another generating domestic heat and friction that only seems to dissipate when a foreign invader threatens their homeland.

In the 19th century, Afghanistan was a battleground between ambitious Russian and British Empires. In the 20th century, America and the Soviet Union reprised these roles in Cold War contests that led to back-to-back proxy wars. Generations of war hardened the Afghan people and left them with few certainties apart from Islam and their local tribe.

Mortimer Durand, 1903

Many of these tribes were divided along Afghanistan's 1600-mile porous border with neighboring Pakistan, which guaranteed that any conflict in one country would never remain isolated from the other. The border was based on the 1893 Durand Line, named for the British foreign secretary who negotiated it on behalf of British colonial India with an Afghan official who claimed to speak for scores of competing Afghan tribes. In fact, most of those tribes never knew the line existed, and would never have agreed to an invisible barrier that separated them from their kindred tribesmen.[1]

Pakistan, which literally means "Land of the Pure," was named by Choudary Ali, an independence activist, in 1933, out of an acronym representing the five major ethnic groups of the country: **P** for Punjabi, **A** for Afghani (Pushtun), **K** for Kashmiri, **S** for Sindhi, and the final -**stan** for Baluchistani. Curiously missing from Choudary Ali's acronym was the East Pakistan Bengali peoples, whose ethnic omission eventually contributed to the Bangladesh War of Independence in 1971. East and West Pakistan were wrenched out of British India at midnight on August 15, 1947, as havens for Muslims from India's Hindu majorities.[2]

Within days, half a million unfortunate Muslims, Hindus, and
Sikhs lost their lives simply for
being on the wrong side of the
British line of demarcation. The
great fertile plain of the Punjab
was particularly hard hit with as
many as seven million Hindus and
Sikhs fleeing to safety in the East,
and a similar number of Muslims
scrambling to the West.[3] The Punjab remains divided, with lingering
memories of hurt and hate. Since

Choudary Ali (1895-1951)

partition, more than 60 years ago, Pakistan has maintained
a continual state of readiness for war with its massive Indian
neighbor to the east.

Today, Indian Muslims, particularly those along the western
border states facing Pakistan, live under a shadow, viewed as
latent enemies within their own country. The resulting distrust
makes them easy targets of discrimination from their more
populous Hindu neighbors. More often than the outside world
knows, this discrimination boils over into violence.

Such was the case in 2002 in the west-Indian state of
Gujarat where 60 Hindu pilgrims were burned to death in a
train fire that Hindu nationalists
blamed on Muslim militants. Hindus responded with a rampage
through Muslim neighborhoods
that left 2,000 Muslims dead. Gujarat's chief minister at the time,
Narendra Modi, did little to stem
the violence, and so was hailed by
Hindu extremists as a hero. Today,
in 2013, Modi is a leading conser-
vative-party candidate to be the
next prime minister of India.[4]

Narendra Modi

More recently, militants who
were recruited from Pakistani slums and trained in radical
madrasas, like the one that trained Ahmed, extracted their

revenge on India. In November 2008, 11 terrorists associated with Pakistan's *Lashkar e-Taiba* (Army of the Righteous) unleashed a three-day jihad in Mumbai, India's most populous city, killing or injuring nearly 500 Indian citizens and police.

Since the birth of the two South Asian states in 1947, India and Pakistan have fought openly for the northern border state of Kashmir. With wars in 1947, 1965 and 1999, this region remains the subcontinent's most volatile flashpoint for what many fear may be the first nuclear war of the 21st century. Today, generations of ordinary citizens in Western South Asia continue to be plagued by violence that undermine efforts for peace and stability in the region. Yet it is in this cauldron of conflict that God's Spirit is breaking into the lives of men and women and offering a different path forward.

Turning Points

Soon after Indian and Pakistani independence in 1947, both countries began expelling Western missionaries. Those who remained were often saddled with tight restrictions forcing them to limit their attention to local Christian minorities or institutions such as hospitals and schools that consumed their every waking hour. Little time was left to address the lost masses of Muslims that continued to grow at one of the fastest rates in the world.

Despite these challenges, 150 years of Christian missions made important strides toward sowing the gospel within Western South Asia. Like the leaven in the lump, the gospel's influence expanded, almost invisibly, but pervasively.[5]

When Western colonizers withdrew from the region, gospel witness was free to be accepted or rejected on its own merits rather than for any perceived advantage that might be accrued by association with a foreign occupier.

Though twenty-first-century Western South Asia now has its own indigenous Christian population, most of these Christians come from Hindu backgrounds, and have little in common with the Muslim majorities around them. It remains to be seen whether or not they will carry forward the mandate of the Great Commission to the masses of Muslims who dominate this region.

Foreign Christians who remained in the region mostly did so without an overt missionary identity. They now collaborated with local partners and with a swelling number of Korean and even Chinese Christians to once again engage one of the greatest concentrations of non-Christians on earth. This time, rather than approaching the region politically, they reframed Western South Asia in terms of their distinct language and ethnic communities. The aim of these post-missionary missioners was to ensure that each people group, and each language community, had some opportunity to hear and respond to the gospel.

To this end, they launched multiple Scripture translation projects, including oral Bibles for non-literates, radio broadcasts in many of the region's larger trade languages, gospel recordings on cassette, and the widely viewed *JESUS Film*.

Beginning in the late 1990s, with people like Ahmed, the gospel contagion spread beyond foreign missionaries to local Muslim individuals who had grown weary of war, killing, retaliation and hatred. Desperately searching for a different *sharia* (way of life) from the one that had produced the hellish existence in which he found himself, Ahmed's heart, followed by many, many others, opened to a different way.

Today, less than two decades since that turning point began, the number of Muslim-background-faith communities in Western South Asia may number in the tens of thousands. An unpublished indigenous survey, highly disputed by many, was conducted in 2010, revealing tens of thousands of baptisms over the past decade and a half.[6] This branch of the Muslim-background movement to Christ claims to have spread across 20 language and ethnic groups and spilled over into eight countries.

Ahmed's story is significant, not only because it is one of the first, but because it is typical of the transformation of a life from a sharia that sanctioned killing and terror to a sharia whose guiding principle is love.

The stories that emerged from the Western South Asia Room in the House of Islam were among the most brutal and violent thus far collected. For this reason, we checked repeatedly to see if these stories were, in fact, exceptional or simply representative of what is actually happening in the region. Though there are certainly corners of the region where violence has not brutalized and radicalized the population as much as it has in these stories, these stories are not extraordinary, but rather all too typical, for the Western South Asia Room.

Ahmed's Turning

The same Ahmed who had vowed to kill his brother Nasir and "the Jew-man," Jason, was now seated beside me, helping me understand what God was doing among his people.

"When I was only four or five," Ahmed said, "my father threw me into the madrasa to get a proper Muslim education."

"Why do you say he 'threw' you?" I asked.

"Because I was forced. Each of my brothers before me had been sent to the madrasa, but they escaped. So when my father took me, he left early in the morning, while it was still dark, so that I would not be able to find my way home."

The madrasa was a boarding school located some distance from Ahmed's village. His entry began a process of Islamic education that would continue until Ahmed was 18 years old. During the first six years of his education, he was allowed to visit his family only three times.

"My brothers could not memorize well, but I had a good memory. So, at age six, I was assigned to memorize the Qur'an, in Arabic, a language I did not understand."

Class began at four in the morning and Ahmed would often study until midnight. "If I ever tried to escape from my classes, I was beaten. It took me three years to memorize the Qur'an, but I succeeded.

"When I turned 12, after my *qaeda* (base) of Islamic study was behind me, my father let me come home to visit once a week." Two years later, at the age of 14, Ahmed enrolled in a secondary madrasa in the massive city of Kebirabad. It was after completing his secondary studies in Kebirabad that Ahmed would meet his brother Nasir's Western friends (the *Jew men*) Ted Moore and Jason Hanson.

It was important to Ahmed's family that he completed his preparation to be an imam for good reason. They believed an imam could bring seven persons with him into heaven. "Our family was large," Ahmed explained. "Counting me, there were eight of us. If I did not complete my studies, who would bring my family into paradise?"

Back in the village, Ahmed's friends were angry with him for failing to carry out their plan to murder Jason. Ahmed's Islamic teachers railed against him, "How can you protect Islam if you cannot kill one man?" "I'm sorry," Ahmed said. Next time I will do better." "It's okay," they said, "let us make a new plan."

Ahmed continued, "'This time let's do more. Let's find all of the Jews who are behind what is happening, and kill them all.' They said, 'First let us train you some more and then we will send you back to Kebirabad to kill your brother and the others.'

"When I returned to Kebirabad I stayed in the home of Ted Moore. During the day, I would leave Ted's house, to try and find out how many connections there were to my brother in Kebirabad. My brother took me to another Western Christian's apartment and then another and another. Then I saw their church building where they met. I wrote to my teacher and said, 'In Kebirabad there are many Jews and they have many connections.'

"During this time, Ted Moore tried hard to get through to me. He invited me to lunch to talk about Islam. For a year we talked about many things. He was trying to share with me, and I was trying to convert him to Islam. Over time, I came to understand that Ted and Jason were not Jews; they were Christians.

"When I returned to my village, my teachers said, 'You need more practical mujahedeen training, and then you can choose whether to go to Afghanistan or Kashmir.' I chose Afghanistan. It was near the end of 1997. The training was for one and a half months, and then I went into Afghanistan. In those days the Taliban were everywhere. In those days, everyone loved the Taliban. I was a Taliban.

"We were sent to the cities to impose *sharia* (Islamic law). If we found women out in public, we were to smack them on the bum with sticks six times, and to strike eight times anyone that we found not observing the *azan* (the call to prayer).

"Once we caught a fellow and beat him three different times (eight blows each time) because he was walking during *namaz* (prayer time). He was crying out, 'My wife is dying, I must go to get a midwife for her. I did the *namaz* in my home already.'

"In the evening only a few of our mujahedeen would return. So many were being killed. We were fighting Shi'as, whom we suspected of being supported by the Russians.

"Our teachers had told us that we were protecting Islam from kafirs, but I could see that we were killing other Muslims.

"Two things affected my heart. The first was killing a baby girl. We had been sent to kill the Shi'a in a village, and we ended up killing the entire village. I picked up a little baby girl, maybe one or one and a-half-years old. She held my finger, before I killed her with a poisoned knife."

Ahmed saw my stunned reaction.

"We believed," he said, "that killing the enemy was like killing a snake. To kill a snake was to grow Islam.

"Another killing that deeply affected me was when they taught me how to cut off a person's head. They brought out a man with a bag over his head. They poured sand all around him. Then they pushed him to his knees, and pressed a knee into his back, forcing his head back and exposing his throat. I put the knife on his throat, and heard him panting in terror. I put the blade on his throat, as the others around me were shouting, '*Allahu Akbar,*' '*Allahu Akbar,*' again and again.

"I dropped the knife. I could not do it. They said, 'You must do this, or we will kill you.'

"I said, 'I will not,' and ran away.

"My friend came after me and said, 'Just hold him, and we will kill him.' So I held that man as they cut his throat. This affected me deeply. I walked away alone, and when my friends could no longer see me, I cried.

"That night they put me on watch duty. All through the night the image of that man haunted me, and the baby girl haunted me.

"So that night I ran away. I said to myself, 'Ahmed, this is not your life.' I walked and ran all night and all day and another night. When I came close to a village, they saw that I was wearing Taliban clothes. They kissed my hand and brought me milk and gave me a place to sleep. They said, 'We love the Taliban. Stay here with us.'

"I told them, 'I am looking for a way to get back to my home.' After another seven hours of walking I came to a train station. The people on the train loved me because I was Taliban. They said, 'Sit wherever you want, because you are Taliban.' They brought me food and I fell asleep. I was so tired that I slept past the stop at my village, and did not awake until I had reached Kebirabad.

"The people on the train said, 'We did not want to disturb you. You are serving Allah, so we are serving you.' I stopped at a police station and gave them my gun. They said, "We will keep it for you. You will need it again." I told them, 'No. No. I don't want it.'

"Then I made my way to the home of Ted Moore. I did not know that Ted and Nasir had been praying and fasting for me for three days. Ted and Nasir took care of me, and I slept for two days.

"When I woke up, I told Ted that my heart was changing. I said, 'Ted, let's swap. I'll give you my Qur'an, and you give me your Bible. Then I'll see for myself, and we can talk.'

"I returned to my village, and for a year I studied the Bible, while Ted studied the Qur'an. In between, we would write to each other. One day during Ramadan, I had been studying the Bible very earnestly when my mother called me to break fast for the evening.

"That night I had a dream. Through the little window in my room, I saw a big light come through, and it had a face. The light spoke to me and said, 'I am sending my three people to you. Listen to them, and whatever they say, do it.' Three times I had this dream.

"The next morning I saw Ted Moore, Jason Hanson and my brother. In those days we had no phones to connect quickly. They had no way to know about my dreams.

"Unlike Jason's first visit, this time I was serving and loving them. I was beginning to change. I told Ted and Jason about my dream.

"I said, 'Please brothers help me. Satan has put me in a very dark place. How can I find the truth?' So they shared openly with me that Jesus was God. They urged me to come out of the darkness and into the light and love of Jesus. I told them I would first go and talk with my family.

"It was during the *eid* (Islamic festival) that I went to talk with my family. I told them, 'When I was four years old you threw me into the madrasa and said I would be responsible for the family. If this is true, will you accept any decision that I will make?' They all said, 'Yes, because on the Judgment Day, you will be the responsible person.' So I said, 'Here is my decision. I am changing. I'm taking all of you out of this dark life. I am giving you the *sahih* (true) Islam.'"

Ahmed later said that he saw himself as a Muslim, but one who was following Jesus outside of Islam. In Ahmed's mind, a real Muslim was one who was truly submitted to the will of God, and this was how he saw followers of Jesus. It was they who were truly submitted to the will of God; all other Muslims were following a false path.

"Ahmed's family replied, 'Whatever you decide we will accept it.' I said, 'We will follow Jesus.' They said, 'Then we will.'

"It was 1998, when Jason, Nasir and Ted baptized me in the name of the Lord Jesus."

The following year, in 1999, a devastating flood washed through the mountains not far from Ahmed's village. Ted Moore was one of the first responders. While there he contracted Japanese encephalitis and died a few days later.

God's Tribe

Jalal was a 43-year old man from a small town in the mountains of Western South Asia. Asked if he has a family, Jalal was guarded, "Yes, I have family." The people from Jalal's background don't like to reveal information about their family. There is a continual fear that government or vigilantes will discover their precious secret and wreak havoc on them.

Jalal explained that he came to faith in 2007 and has been a follower of Isa for six years.

Here is his story.

"In my childhood I did no studies," he said. "My father was a fighter for our tribe. From my childhood I traveled with him from place to place, because my father had many enemies. My father taught me how to read the *Qur'an Sharif* (the Noble Qur'an). Many people who cannot read," he explained, "learn to read the Qur'an.

"As I traveled with my father, we were sometimes moving guns and sometimes food from mountain to mountain, I was helping him and growing up in the mountains. My father was very proud of me. He put his gun in my hand and said, 'After me, you will own this gun.' After my father died, I became the elder of the gang.

"The people in our villages honored me for protecting them from government capture. One day, though, a great flood swept through our villages. The flood washed away animals, homes, and families. I could do nothing to protect my people.

"After the flood, outsiders — not foreigners, but countrymen from another tribe — came to our area to try to help. When this happened, I told my gang, 'We must go and protect our people. We don't know these outsiders, and perhaps they will take away our women and our possessions. We must protect them.'

"We watched over the relief effort through binoculars. We saw some of these outsiders touching our women in inappropriate ways. So we came down to the village and attacked them and said, 'No one from the outside can come here to help. We will help our own people.'

"The third day of the flood, another group of outsiders came, but they were all wearing *shalwar kameezes* (local attire). One of our gang members asked them, 'Who are you?' They said, 'We have come to help.' So we said to them, 'No one from the city can come and help.' They replied, 'We are not from the city, we are tribal people like you.'

"Because they were tribal people, like us, we allowed them to help. We knew that they would respect our women and our possessions. They started moving our people and animals to higher ground and a safer location.

"I watched through the binoculars, until I saw that they had finished moving everyone, but these tribal outsiders were not leaving. So I came down from the mountain and said to them, 'Now you must go.' But my own villagers came to me and said, 'No, we do not want these people to go. They are good people.'

"I said, 'If they do not leave the village in two weeks, I will kill them all.'

"My villagers were caught in between. They liked the outsiders, but they also respected me. As I warned them, I said, 'You know that if our tribes begin fighting, we will not stop.' I again demanded, 'We do not need any more help.'

"Because I was a wanted man, I returned to the mountains, but I kept my eyes on the village. Over the next few days, groups of five to eight people started coming into the village. At night, I learned that they were sharing ancient stories about the prophets of old. My people reported these things to me.

"The more I heard, the more angry I became. So one night, I went down to the village and burned the tents of the outsider tribals. When they ran from their tents, I beat them, shouting at them, 'Go!' Then I returned to the mountains and waited for them to retaliate.

"After they put out the fire, these tribals sat down with some of the villagers. They opened their book, read it and began praying together. I was watching closely, expecting this action to be followed with a call to battle, but they did nothing more than read and pray.

"For the first time in my life I was actually worried that a tribe would attack me. I was afraid that they must be a powerful tribe, and that they would come and smash me like an elephant crushing a crop. For a week my gang and I hid in the mountains. Then one day, I decided to send one of my men to them as an emissary.

"He found the outsider tribe ministering to the people as they had done before. My man said, 'We told you to leave. We beat you. Why have you not left, and why are you not seeking revenge?' They said, 'We are only helping. We are not interested in revenge. If you kill us, that is up to you. We are not going to fight back.'

"When my messenger reported this to me, I became very angry. I made plans with my group to go down and kill them all. So we launched another attack. We shot at them, but instead of killing them, the bullets fell short, but still managed to injure their feet. We had decided that if we killed one or two of them, the others would leave, but this didn't happen. Those who were injured they took to the hospital. And we retreated again to the mountains.

"Now I was certain that their tribe would come and attack us. It was not normal for a tribe not to attack. I said to my group, 'We must run away now,' and we retreated deeper into the mountains.

"The next day, our own village members were very angry with us. They took up guns and came into the mountains looking for us. They entered my camp with some of their young children with them, and cried to us saying, 'Why are you trying to kill those people? They are good people.'

"I warned them, 'I will never allow those outsiders to stay. They are planning to take over our village.'

"Then my villagers returned with guns, and I thought they were going to kill me. But they were just talking to me and warning me. But my heart was like a rock. They said to me, 'If you do not stop this attack, we will kill you, or we will tell the authorities where your camp is, and they will kill you.'

"So for a year I stayed away, but continued watching the village. In my heart, though, something was happening. Finally, one night I came down to the village and sat down with these tribal outsiders and listened to them.

"I saw in my village that there were some mosques. I knew that the flood had washed away all of the mosques, but these outsiders had rebuilt mosques out of brush. We sat in one of these mosques and I asked them, 'Why are your people not afraid? Why do you not fight for your tribe?' They said, 'No. We do not fight against you. We are God's tribe.' I had never heard this before. I said, 'No. God does not have a tribe.' But I thought about these things.

"They were changing many things in my tribe, teaching them how they could help each other. They were looking for empty lands to which they could relocate the flood-affected families. They were building schools.

"One day I asked them, 'What is this new tribe that you are calling God's tribe? I expected your tribe to come and kill me, but it has not. Tell me, what is this new tribe?'

"They told me many stories about prophets and then about Jesus. I learned many things from them.

"One evening as they were sharing with me about their tribe, something happened to me in my heart. I thought about my many sins, my many killings and beatings of people.

"Then I began thinking about Muhammad's life. I wondered if this was Muhammad's tribe, the killing and beating of people? The tribe they described, God's tribe, was a very good tribe.

"I realized I had nothing. I had been living in the mountains all my life with nothing.

"I listened for another eight months before I led my gang down out of the mountains. We watched a movie that night with them. It was in my own tribal language, the first movie in my language I had ever seen.

"I watched as many strong tribal fighters watching the movie were moved to tears. It was clear to me that this was a holy movie. I instructed my gang to put our guns in the corner, out of respect for the movie. We watched the whole movie. For the first time, I was seeing the life of *Hazrat* Isa al-Masih.[7] After the movie, my hands were trembling as I took my gun and led my gang back into the mountains.

"We camped in one place in the mountains for the next three months. One of my gang said, 'Why are we not moving?' I said to him, 'I do not want this life any more.' And with that,

I went down to the village. It was on a Friday. The group was praying and reading the *Kalam* (the Bible) together. I joined them.

"After four hours, as they finished their gathering, I asked them, 'What is the punishment for me, that I can receive the punishment from this group for my sins against you? I beat and shot you. What is the punishment that your faith says I must pay for the big sins I have done?'

"They said to me, 'No. There is no punishment for you. We love you.'

"One of them, who was about my age, came to me and hugged me and kissed me on the cheeks. He said, 'God forgave you.' I said, 'But how?' He said, 'If I tell you, will you accept it?' I said, 'Yes! For many months I have not been sleeping.' He said to me, 'Walk the true life.' I said, 'How can I do this?' He replied, 'Take baptism and walk with us.'

"I turned to my gang and said, 'If I accept this new way, will you follow me?' And they all said, 'Yes, master.'

"My villagers became very happy and gathered all around me. I threw down my gun. I asked my gang, 'Can you throw down your guns?' They did, and we all received baptism that day.'

I probed further, "Jalal, who is Jesus to you?"

"Jesus is in my life. He is a shadow. I'm living under his shadow and I feel peace. He is God. My body is given to him. I believe that he came for our sins because I was a big sinner."

"And who is Muhammad to you?" I asked. "What does the Qur'an mean to you?"

"People are saying that Muhammad is a prophet, but he's not a prophet in my life. *Saidna* al-Masih (*Saidna* means "our Lord") is God and his life is a model for me. Muhammad is just a man. The true Qur'an is the Bible."

I asked Jalal, "Tell me about your jamaat. When do you meet and what do you do there?"

"We meet every Friday. Our jamaat is focusing on those things that are coming from Islam into the believers' lives. We are saying, 'Take out all of those things that are from Islam and take on Saidna Isa's sharia.' We read the Bible and take it into our life."

A Second Awakening

So far, all of my interviews had come from men. Women in this corner of Western South Asia are rarely seen by outsiders. There is a saying in these mountains: "You must not eat another meal if there is a 16-year-old daughter in your home who is not yet married."

Unlike some parts of the Muslim world, where sequestering wives and daughters is explained as a testament to their great value, these men harbored no such illusions. Women were only treasures in the sense that they were property. Yet their value was rarely higher than that of a horse or prized goat.

An American Christian who spent many years among these people explained that the gap between men and women is even greater than any ethnic divide or tribal separation. Up to this point, he said, this Muslim movement had been almost entirely a men's movement. So even after these men come to faith in Christ and are born again, they still have little to say to their wives. All of his married life a man may have never had a meaningful conversation with his wife. Now suddenly he has had this tremendous spiritual change, he's been born again, but if he goes home and tries to speak to his wife about it, she will think him crazy. He has no meaningful relationship with her. If she discovers his faith in Isa, she would likely leave him, or report him to the imam.

Ahmed explained, "In our culture, women are like shoes. We just wear them, and then when they are old we throw them out."

"Among our people," he said, "when a boy turns 18 years old, his father is thinking, *My son is grown now, I must find a wife for him.* So he goes out and finds a wife for his son. When he brings the girl for the marriage, the boy is thinking, *She is not mine, because my father and mother chose her for me.*

"And many times, the mother will say to her son, 'I bought this girl for you and she is mine. Don't listen to her. Just come and sleep with her and then go.' The mother and father teach the son not to trust or confide in his new wife. They tell him, 'She is your first enemy. If you give her lots of information, she will use it to kill you.' So we do not tell our wives what we are doing, where we are going, or what we are thinking."

Ahmed continued, "If a woman does something that does not please her husband—perhaps the food is late, or the animals are not properly cared for—the husband and his brothers will grab her by the hair and drag her through the streets to the cemetery, and we would bury her alive." Ahmed said, "This is not a story from long ago. This happens now. For any number of reasons, we men would do this."

For the believers in this movement, this is changing, though it still has a long way to go. The turning point was all too recent; it happened in June 2008. Western missionaries, Joe and Donna had arranged for an education consultant, a young teacher from the West named Rachel, to lead a workshop for a dozen women from tribal Muslim villages. They hoped to train the women to become teachers in places where there are no schools.

Donna recalls, "The weather was very hot, but we wanted to be culturally sensitive, so Rachel and I wore clothes that covered us from head to toe. Then we traveled the hour across town from where we were staying to a Catholic retreat center where the teaching conference was to be held. The retreat center was quite affordable because of the lepers who frequented its fresh springs; this also ensured its privacy from curious outsiders.

"On the first day, to our surprise, instead of twelve women, we were met by twelve men!

"The men, husbands of the twelve women who were expected to come, had grown uneasy at the thought of their wives journeying to the city without their protection. So, at the last minute, they vetoed their wives' participation and, not wanting to disappoint the foreigners, went in their stead."

The first day was a bit of a fiasco. The tribal men were aghast at the thought of two women, even Western women, teaching them anything. To their translator, Ahmed (the same Ahmed whose story is related above), they muttered, 'Can women really teach us?' As was their custom, the men averted their eyes, never looking directly at the two fully cloaked instructors who stood perspiring in front of them.

It was during lunch that an unexpected change trigger was tripped. The twelve men, like everyone in their culture, do not talk over meals. So while they sat at one end of the dining table, silently devouring their rice and dhal (lentils), Ahmed tried to carry on a polite, though awkward, conversation at the other end of the table with Donna and Rachel.

The conversation stumbled along until Ahmed casually asked the two women, "Should we not be beating our wives?"

The two women stopped eating. Donna said, "I thought he must be joking, and I looked up to see if he was smiling. But he was quite earnest. So I said, 'No, of course you should not be beating your wife!'

Ahmed replied innocently, "Well, what does the Bible say about this?"

Donna was speechless. She had never been asked this question. Rachel returned to her food. Donna drank some water, before saying, "Let me look into this and I'll let you know what I find."

The afternoon sessions passed with the same dubious effect as the morning session. As Donna and Rachel returned to their hotel, Donna's mind was already absorbed with searching the Scriptures to answer Ahmed's question, *What does the Bible say about this?*

That evening, rather than escape their cramped quarters for fast food and air-conditioning, Donna insisted on pouring over the Bible. As God directed her to relevant Bible passages, she sent them by text message to Ahmed's phone at the conference center.

Her first text:

Genesis 2:18-24   "For this reason a man will leave his father and mother and be united to his wife, and they will become one flesh."

Donna filled the hours that followed with what the Bible had to say about God's love for women and his desire for his people to love them too.

Ephesians 4:17-32 "You were taught, with regard to your former way of life, to put off your old self. Be kind and compassionate to one another."

Ephesians 5:25-33 "Husbands, love your wives, just as Christ loved the church and gave himself up for her."

1 Corinthians 13 "Love is patient, love is kind. It always protects, always trusts, always hopes, always perseveres."

Genesis 29:31-35 "Surely my husband will love me now."

1 Timothy 3:2 "Now the overseer must be above reproach, the husband of but one wife, temperate, self controlled."

Scriptures and provocative questions continued to fly from Donna's cell phone to Ahmed's across town, an hour and nearly 2,000 years away. She worked feverishly knowing that the country's power grid was scheduled for an outage at any time.

When the electricity finally failed, and she could no longer see her Bible, Donna laid back on her cot in the darkness, and wept.

The next morning the two women arrived at the retreat center shortly after breakfast. Before they proceeded with their program, Ahmed explained to them that no one had slept that night. "All night," he said, "we were talking about these things that you sent to us. We talked about what Jesus was saying about women, and how we should change, and how we should treat our wives."

After the men gathered in the training room, one of them stood up. He turned his head to one side, because it was against his culture for others to see the tears glistening in his eyes. He said, "I have made many, many wrong things with my wife, and I have been participating in the killing of women."

When the other men heard what he said, they began to speak. One after another, they stood and said, "I will not beat my wife." "I will not beat my wife. "I will not beat my wife, and

I will stop others from beating their wives." They added, "And we will tell our wives where we are going each day." They said, "After today, we will treat our wives with respect."

Could it be as simple as that? "It has not been easy," Ahmed admitted. "It has not been easy for me. That was a big change for us. Since we had begun studying the word of God, we didn't think about what it meant to the women. We were reading it, but focusing on what was happening in our culture as men, how could we change it? We knew it would be very difficult for us to change it. But we were not thinking that God might also be calling women. We were just happy in *our* life. Men, men, men, men's jamaat; men's training; men's ministry."

With the close of the teacher conference, a women's movement was launched. The male leaders of the movement started requesting more training that would encourage reaching the women. They didn't have to look far.

Joe shared with Ahmed insights he had learned from Nik Ripken, whose book *The Insanity of God*, explored the effects of persecution in the Muslim world.[8] Examining case studies from around the world, Nik learned that failing to disciple the women in a movement had dire consequences in times of persecution.

Ahmed said, "We learned that when the persecution becomes severe, and the men are killed or put in prison, our wives would be given over to the mosque or to the tribal leaders. Our children would have no one to teach them the way of Jesus. Within a short time, our movement would cease to exist."

Joe added, "Ripken taught us that women are the key to the movement's future."

This made sense, even to the most hardened men. "Things are changing," Ahmed said. "Last year, more than 100 jamaat leaders said to me, 'I no longer beat my wife.'" Today, though it remains smaller than the men's movement, the women's movement has started hundreds of women's jamaats, and is growing at the same pace as the men's movement.

"In the history of any movement," Donna's husband, Joe, said, "there are big turning points. This teacher training was a big, big turning point." It had nothing to do with training teachers. It began with a question from a local follower of Christ to a Western Christian woman, "Should we not be beating our wives?" But the turning point came with the response, "We will do whatever God says."

Small Group Discussion ~ Discover for Yourself

1. What impressions do you take away from this chapter?
2. How is God at work in the Western South Asia Room?
3. Discuss Ahmed's story. What did God use to bring him to faith?
4. What was the turning point for the movements in this Room?

the Arab room

...the whole creation has been groaning as in the pains of childbirth right up to the present time.

Romans 8:22

 ON A HOT Ramadan night in August 2011, rising above the ancient mosque and university that serve as the theological heart of the Arab Muslim world of old Cairo's al-Azhar district, one could hear the Voices of Inspiration from Brooklyn, New York, singing: *Amazing grace how sweet the sound, that saved a wretch like me. I once was lost but now am found, was blind but now I see.*[1]

The event showed what could have been in the Arab world, a peaceful interchange of faith and respect between two ancient peoples. Just six months earlier, hundreds of thousands of Muslims and Christians joined forces in the streets of Cairo demanding the ouster of 30-year dictator Hosni Mubarak. But when Egypt's Muslim majority elected the Muslim Brotherhood's candidate, Mohamed Morsi, to the presidency, the collaboration began to unravel. Eighteen months later,

Al Azhar Mosque

protesters again took to the streets, this time calling for Morsi to step down.

In both instances, activists used social media—Facebook and Twitter—to mobilize and organize the demonstrations, then used camera phones to video military atrocities, uploading the images to the Internet through which they spread them to the world.

For good and bad, hostilities that had remained bottled up inside the Arab world for generations were now vented, connected, and channeled to bring about change in the Arab world.

al-Watan al-Arabi (The Arab Nation)

There are many ways to classify Arabs. In ancient Semitic languages predating current historical nationalities, the word *Arab* (Hebrew *'ereb*) was used to connote the desert and the people who lived there.[2]

In its broader sense, *Arab* has come to mean any person or persons who speak a version of the Arabic language. This constituency is now vast. In the century following the death of Muhammad, Arab armies extended an empire greater than Rome at its peak, assimilating into their culture and language more alien peoples than any other culture in history.[3]

Hagar and Ishmael

Arabs today are an amalgam of races and nationalities that each bear testament to this conquering legacy. Coffee-colored Moors in Mauritania call themselves Arabs and speak a Yemeni dialect brought to them by Bedouin warriors a millennium ago. Aboriginal Berbers in Libya's *Jebel Nefus* (Mountain of Souls) now claim only Arabic as their native tongue. Pharaonic Egyptians, Nubian Nilotics, Syro-Phoenician Lebanese and Balkans of Mameluke descent have all been assimilated into the orb of the great *al-Watan al-Arabi*, the Arab Nation.

From their roots, Arabs are a Semitic people, elder brothers to the Jews, tracing back to a common father, Abraham. Throughout their history they weave in and out of the

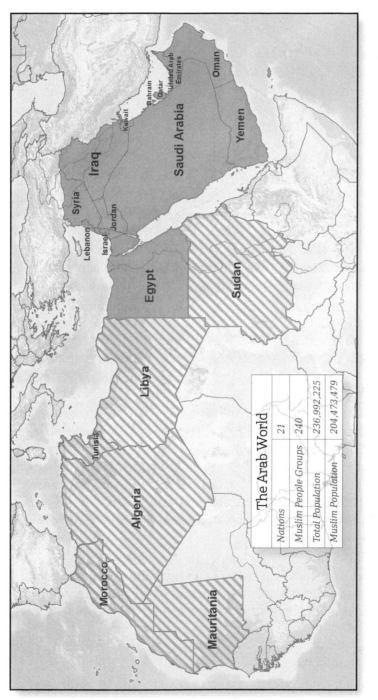

The Arab World

The Arab World	
Nations	21
Muslim People Groups	240
Total Population	236,992,225
Muslim Population	204,473,479

biblical record, from the story of Abraham's son Ishmael (Genesis 16:11ff), to the Midianite wife of Moses, Zipporah, daughter of Jethro, an Arab Midianite priest who gave refuge to the fugitive Moses (Exodus 2:18-22).

Today, spanning many nations and ethnic peoples, Arabic speakers comprise the fourth or fifth largest language group in the world.[4] In reality, the Arabic language is a family of languages. Though Modern Standard Arabic is the written and official language used throughout the Arab world, its colloquial versions vary widely from Morocco to Iraq, and many Arabic-speaking inhabitants of the Arab world find the 7th-century vocabulary of the Qur'an to be almost unintelligible. Illiteracy remains the bane of the Arabic-speaking world. More than half of all Iraqi, Mauritanian and Yemeni citizens are illiterate, with illiteracy among women in those countries as high as 76 percent.[5]

The Arab League counts 22 member nations stretched over five million square miles with a population of more than 400 million citizens. Some 237 million of these citizens speak a dialect of Arabic as a first language. When adding all those who rely upon Arabic as the untranslatable language of the Qur'an, the number swells to 1.6 billion.[6]

Though many Westerners still view "Arab" as synonymous with "Muslim," more than five percent of the population of the Middle East are Christians, and the majority of the Arab population in North and South America are Arab Christians, not Muslims. Much like the English-language pilgrims who arrived before them, these Arab Christians in the Americas came to the new world either fleeing persecution or seeking greater economic and social freedoms.[7]

Arab Muslims view their history as evidence of God's miraculous hand. A band of semi-nomadic religious warriors emerging from the scorching sands of the Arabian Peninsula to defeat and conquer the greatest military powers in history lend weight to such a lofty interpretation.

Within two decades of Muhammad's death, Arab cavalry had overwhelmed frontier-hardened Byzantine armies in the ancient cities of Damascus, Jerusalem, and Alexandria.

Undaunted by a Persian Empire that had stifled Roman advance for eight hundred years, the vastly inferior Arab militia swept across the Persian Empire with one decisive victory after another.

Arabs today are acutely aware of their proud history, which has made their current state of affairs all the more painful to accept. Over the centuries, the great Arab empire has been conquered and subjugated by Persians, Mongols, and Ottoman Turks, but in each case it was the Islamic faith that ended up conquering its conquerors.

All of this changed with the encroachment of Europeans, who were neither Muslim nor inclined to embrace Islam. The first European forays into the Arab world were 11th and 12th century Crusaders whose victories proved to be ephemeral. Rather than convert the Arabs to their Catholic faith, Crusader atrocities actually provoked many indigenous Arab Christians to switch allegiances and join the Muslims to defend their homeland.

Vasco da Gama's circumnavigation of the African continent in the 15th century opened a new chapter in the Arab world. By the 19th century, non-Muslim European powers had colonized virtually every corner of the Watan al-Arab, unleashing a wave of Westernization from which the region has yet to fully recover.

Consternation over centuries of Arab world decline led to an internal call for a return to pure Islamic ideals. Islamic fundamentalisms surfaced across the Arab world. Salafism, from the Arabic *salafi*, literally 'ancestors,' urged a return to pristine Islam. Wahhabism had its roots in a similar impulse the 18th century Arabian Peninsula. In the twentieth century, Egypt's Muslim Brotherhood took shape, later giving birth to al-Qaeda.

Vasco da Gama

Other Arabs sought a renaissance through pan-Arabism. Michael Aflaq (1910-1989), a secular Christian Arab from Syria, helped to form the *Baathist* (Resurrection or Renaissance) Party in 1947 with the aim of uniting all Arabs in a common cause of development and emergence from centuries of colonial malaise.

Contemporary Arab nationalist leaders, such as the Assads of Syria, Mubarak of Egypt, Kaddafi of Libya, and Ben Ali of Tunisia, are all seeing or have seen the end of this experiment in Arab nationalism. Likewise, Arab monarchies in the Arabian Peninsula, Jordan, and Morocco are under pressures to change. Islamic fundamentalism, on the other hand, despite the global war on terror, remains vibrant. The fate of the Arab world is clearly yet to be written.

The final two pieces in the Arab contemporary drama are oil and Israel. At the dawn of the 20th century, no one would have imagined that these two factors, the exploitation of oil and the establishment of a Jewish state in Palestine, would be the most significant forces shaping the Arab world well into the 21st century.

Prior to the 1938 discovery of oil in Dhahran, Saudi Arabia, the primary source of income in the Arabian Peninsula was the Hajj tax collected from pilgrims visiting Mecca and Medina. Today, Saudi Arabia controls 20 percent of the world's known oil reserves,[8] and with it an enormous amount of wealth and influence. Oil wealth in neighboring Arab emirates has constructed fabulous city states out of the desert that would make Aladdin's genie envious.

Arab petrodollars have also poured into the advance of global Islam. Beginning in the 1980s, King Fahd funded translations of the Qur'an into all the world's languages and offered money for the construction of mosques and Islamic centers in cities and villages on Muslim frontiers around the world. Arab billionaires have not been reluctant to fuel the Muslim *dawa* (mission enterprise) with their newly acquired wealth.

Hundreds of millions of petrodollars have also gone to political concerns: Palestinian causes, the Taliban in Pakistan, and Sunni insurgents battling the regime of Alawite president

Bashar al-Assad in Syria. As the dominant Islamic ideology of Saudi Arabia, fundamentalist Wahhabism has perhaps been the chief beneficiary of Arab oil wealth.

Oil wealth has also fueled economic disparities within the Arab world, prompting oil-rich monarchies to impose ever-tightening controls on the subjects within their domains.[9] Everyone living and working in the oil-rich Arabian Peninsula does so with the knowledge that they are living in a police state that has grown paranoid to the threat of social and political unrest.

Since 1948, Arabs have viewed and used the establishment of the state of Israel as a rallying cry for Arab unity and jihad. Though uneasy peace treaties have been forged with Israel's neighbors, Jordan and Egypt, popular opinion in the Arab world continues to view the Zionist state as an injustice to Palestinian Arabs and simply the latest Crusade by the West into the Holy Land.

Arab Spring?

On a Friday morning, December 27, 2010, in the central Tunisian town of Sidi Bouzid, a 26-year-old-street vendor named Mohamad Bouazizi stepped into the middle of noonday traffic, doused himself in gasoline, and set himself ablaze. Angry and hopeless after repeated harassment for selling vegetables on the street without a permit, Bouazizi's act of desperation set off a wave of protests that eventually swept through the Arab world. Riots broke out in 19 of the 22 Arab nations, toppling heads of state in Tunisia, Egypt, Libya and Yemen. Before it was over, anti-government protests spread to Algeria, Morocco, Mauritania, Mali, Sudan, Syria, Jordan, Iraq and Turkey.[10] In the six months following Bouazizi's death, at least 107 other Tunisians attempted to kill themselves in protest by self-immolation.[11] The Arab world today is seething. Population stresses, economic disparities and political oppression have churned the region to a boiling point with no end in sight.

Mohamed Bouazizi

The Arab world today has a poor record of human rights and democratic freedoms. According to the Pew Forum, even before the so-called Arab Spring, the Middle East and North Africa region was the most politically and socially oppressive region on earth. Since the outbreak of the Arab Spring, conditions have worsened considerably.[12]

How God Is Bringing Them

Abouna Zakaria Botros (Father Zechariah Peter) is a 79-year-old, exiled Egyptian Coptic priest who infuriates Muslim fundamentalists. His satellite broadcast television programs and daily Internet chat rooms have led thousands of Arab Muslims to turn away from Islam and place their faith in Jesus Christ.

Father Zakaria

Raised in Alexandria, Egypt, Zakaria was imprisoned twice in the 1980s for preaching the gospel to Muslims. In 1989, Egyptian courts gave Zakaria a life sentence, which was rescinded under the condition that he leave Egypt never to return. After a series of wanderings that took him to Australia, England and then America, he began hosting a television talk show called *Truth Talk* in 2003. By 2008, his live 90-minute program was reaching 60 million Arabs a day on the *al-Hayat* ("The Life") satellite television station.

Not content to merely preach the gospel, Zakaria increasingly took on the challenge of exposing "the ugly side of Islam." Zakaria was determined to reveal the lies and contradictions within Islam, something that would have been inconceivable in the pre-Internet, pre-satellite television era. "My program is to attack Islam," he says, "not to attack Muslims, but to save them because they are deceived. I love Muslims, I hate Islam."[13]

Zakaria's attacks have earned him the title "Islamic Public Enemy No. 1," and a purported bounty of $60 million on his head.[14] A Christian in Egypt smirked that Muammar Kaddafi had offered to pay $60 million to anyone who could just answer Zakaria.[15]

How many Muslims have actually come to faith via Zakaria's ministry is disputed. What is evident, though, is that Zakaria's ministry coincides with a great awakening of questions within the Arab Muslim world. Two decades ago, a cleric or teacher in the Arab world could dismiss student questions with a curt, *"Mafish liih!"* ("There *is* no why!") or *"Isaal Allah!"* ("Ask Allah!").

Today, Arab Muslims *are* asking Allah. Satellite television channels such as Al-Hayat, Alfadry, Sat-7, and the Miracle Channel report thousands of letters, emails and tweets from inquiring Muslims. On his website chat room at www.islam-christianity.net, thousands of Arabs routinely ply Zakaria with questions about Islam and Christianity. When he doesn't have an immediate answer for them, Zakaria encourages his chatroom correspondents to, "Look it up for yourself on St. Google." For many Arab Muslims, it is the first time a man of the cloth has ever given them permission to find the answers for themselves.[16]

Nasr

One of the skeptics influenced by Abouna Zakaria was the 64-year-old chain-smoking grandfather who sat across from me. His road to faith was a winding one.

"I had a little print shop in my house where I had printed 2,000 books over the years on sharia law. When I began to hear Abouna Zakaria talk about the problems with the Qur'an, I went and got one of my books and started studying it to see if what he was saying was right. I found that, not only was it true, but that the Qur'an and sharia were filled with these kinds of problems."

Nasr's relationship to Christ actually began seventy years earlier in a strange way. Before Nasr was born, two of his siblings died shortly after childbirth. For some reason Nasr's parents determined that, if they had another child, they would baptize it. A baby girl, Nasr's sister, was born healthy and they secretly had her baptized in an Orthodox church.

A few years later, Nasr was born, but he was sickly. It was around those days that Nasr's sister had a dream that she and her mother would go to a certain mountain and sacrifice a goat, and this would somehow save the infant Nasr from death. Not long after this, the little girl showed her mother the mountain she had seen in her dream. Together they set out for the mountain where they sacrificed a goat. When they returned home, they quietly took Nasr to the church and had him baptized. "And here I am," Nasr smiled.

"I grew up as a Muslim," Nasr said. "I even became a *hafez* (one who has memorized the Qur'an) and was well respected in the Muslim community. In the course of my lifetime I was politically active, and a leader among my people."

Then one day, after hearing the attacks on Islam by Father Zakaria, Nasr realized that Islam was not the way, that it was a lie. "Most of my life was behind me now, so I asked myself, *Why are you waiting? What do you have to lose?* I began talking to my relatives and friends, urging them to question what they had always been taught. Within a few years, I had led 21 of them to faith in Jesus."

It was around that time that Nasr contacted the television station that had broadcast Father Zakaria's message, asking for someone to come and teach him more.

On the other side of town, an American missionary named Tim had been praying for God to direct his next steps in ministry. By his own admission, he had tried everything to reach Muslims, but with little success. He had used a polemical approach, a friendship evangelism strategy, even a highly contextualized Insider approach for reaching Muslims. Though the latter had gained him many Muslim friends, it had failed to see any Muslims come to faith in Christ. Then God led him to Nasr.

"I was given two choices to follow up on by the television broadcaster," Tim said. "One was a college-educated young professional, the other a 62-year-old retiree. My head said, *Go with the young man,* but my prayers led me to Nasr."

Tim committed himself to the service and spiritual development of Nasr, teaching the elder brother how to listen to God, interpret his word, and walk obediently in the Spirit. Tim's role was that of "shadow pastor," a vision caster, sounding board and encourager, never the high profile leader. Nasr proved to be a visionary leader. Within a year, the old man had organized hundreds of groups of Muslims who, like himself, were questioning Islam and open to discovering Jesus.

Nabila

Nabila is a petite woman who entered the room cloaked in an *abaya* (full covering) that obscured her form. Shedding her burqa and her grey silk *hijab* (head covering), her face looks much younger than the 43 years and seven children she has borne. Now wearing blue jeans and a sweater, she could be a suburban housewife from any city in Europe or America.

Nabila was frank. "I was married at the age of 15. My husband is an Islamic judge," she said, "a terrorist." Nabila's husband had no knowledge of her faith in Jesus. Though her Salafi father curtailed her education at grade six, she has a passion for learning. "Life is a school," she said.

"I've always loved to hear about Jesus, even from a young age. My father would gather us and we loved to pray and fast together. I had a lot of sisters. We would often talk about Jesus. My father taught us that Jesus was going to come back and judge the world and bring everyone together under Islamic law."

Like many Arab Muslims, Nabila's father was not the rock of Islam that he appeared to be in his youth. "Over time, he migrated," Nabila said, "from Salafi to *Ahl Al-Bayt* (Shi'ite) to Baha'i." Her voice softened, "Now, he has Alzheimer's."

What Nabila described was often whispered: Many who are counted as Sunni Muslims are not. They are Shi'ites or Druze, even Communists and atheists, or they are Muslim converts to other faiths such as Christianity or Baha'i. These things they keep hidden.

Nabila continued, "I became a follower of Jesus about two years ago. I wanted to reach the truth, and felt very pressured. For me as a wife, everything was forbidden. My daughters were the same, living under the pressures of Islam. You can't wear perfume or change your clothes. You can't even raise your voice to talk to your husband. Everything my husband says, I must do.

"All of the teachings of Muhammad were against women. I didn't really think about these thoughts when I was young. But Nasr opened my mind; I started questioning these things. I was also getting information from Father Zakaria about the difference between men and women. So women took the first bite of the fruit, but c'mon. Everything is forbidden for a women, but allowed for a man."

She continued, "I want peace and love, this is all I want. I began to ask, *Why is it this way? I am a woman; I think with my mind. My father thought, and he changed his mind. I can think, why shouldn't I change my mind?*

"So my prayer was, *Allah, please fix me in the truth.* After I was baptized, I became peaceful and relaxed. Even my body experienced complete peace and relaxation. Now I can give this truth about Jesus to others."

I asked Nasr what he did to open Muslims' minds to the truth.

Nasr said, "If I am sitting with a Muslim, I might ask, 'What kind of prophet, when he's 53 years old, takes a six-year-old girl as his wife? And he began to have intercourse with her when she was nine. It's disgusting—a little girl.'

I probed, "And you actually ask a Muslim these questions?"

"Of course. Why not? It's written right there. There's no argument."

I continued, "Do you think this is something that you can do, but I, as a Westerner, should not do?"

Nasr laughed, "No, no, no, no, no. I can do this, because I am a Muslim."

I was struck by this casual admission, 'I am a Muslim,' by a man who had now given his life to dismantling Islam. "So you can do this because you are in the community, but for me to do it. . . ."

"Listen, all these are, is questions. I'm not offering them answers. I'm not trying to hang them up. I'm just asking questions that are very clear."

I continued, "But there again, you can do this because you are in the culture?"

"Yes," Nasr said. "There's a barrier against you. The first thought that comes to their mind when you question the Qur'an, is that you are against them, because you are an American."

Nasr went on to explain that he used these questions, questions that are provided by the Qur'an and the Hadith itself, to determine who is open to the truth and who is not.

I asked Nasr how many Muslims had now been baptized through his ministry. Without hesitation he replied, "There are 2,845 that were baptized this past year. All of these baptisms occurred in 11 months. In 11 months we have gone from 21 to 2,845."

Sabri

Sabri is a 50-year-old deputy leader in the movement; he is married with five children. Like Nasr, Sabri is a heavy smoker, and blends easily into the millions of Arab Muslims living around him. He was raised in a strong Islamic environment but was not a very religious person. He only followed what he thought was right and wrong. He has been a follower of Christ for a year and eight months.

Sabri said, "I was just a normal guy when I received the message from Nasr. I began to see the truth from a lie, and I wanted to follow the truth. I could see that our religion wasn't right, and now all of my children and my wife are believers. I was the judge in my home, the referee in matters of religion, but not in the way of the sword, but with love."

I asked, "How did you lead your family to faith?"

He said, "I just sat with them and compared the Bible and Qur'an with love, and eventually they understood and I baptized them. They were able to see step by step; you bring them in slowly and let them have that time to think about it."

"How has your life changed?" I asked.

"Now I am very peaceful inside. I have love for others and they love me."

"Tell me about the movement," I said.

"There are just under 400 persons in my town that I am responsible for. I've also got two families here in this area. I have 24 persons responsible underneath me; I'm about to add my 25th. We keep the groups really small because it causes problems when the groups get large."

I asked Nasr why he thought so many Muslims were turning to Christ today.

"In the past even if you said 'hello' to a Christian, it was a shameful and forbidden thing. Neither could you share in their holidays. Today, the situation is changing. People are opening the Internet and asking questions. They are beginning to think.

"A larger number of people are understanding the truth, but they are afraid to say publicly because they may lose their heads. There are a large number of secret believers. When the parties of terrorists and the Islamic Brotherhood surfaced with the Arab Spring, people could see how violent Islam is. The world is seeing this. We need people to say to the masses, 'Come.'"

Amal

Amal is a 21-year-old college graduate who has been a follower of Christ for nearly two years. She is single, but anticipates marriage soon.

Amal spoke with a clarity and confidence that belied her youth, "When I was young, I would always have this pressure on me and I'd think, *There's something wrong with this.* I'd try to escape the pressure. But when I would try to do something, I'd be told, 'Don't do that. It's shameful or forbidden.' Even to give my opinion was not allowed.

"As I got older, I wasn't convinced that Islam was right. It was just formalities, rituals and words. I read the Qur'an, but I couldn't really understand it. I thought, *There's so much terrorism and killing of innocents.*

"In the Christian faith, I saw that there was love and peace, but in Islam there was just fear of doing the wrong thing. It was an unhealthy fear of God, fear that God was going to get me for the things I did. I compared how we lived under Islam and how Christianity treated people. I could see that there was truth in Christianity."

"What happened next?" I asked.

"I was able to see the difference between the truth and a lie. I began to open the Internet and search. I looked at Rachid and Abouna Zakaria's teachings.[17] Brother Nasr also had a big place in my life. I wanted to know how people could come into the way of Isa. Nasr gave me an *Injil* (New Testament), and I began to read it. Things I didn't understand I would take back to him and he'd explain. That was the beginning.

"Then I started having visions of Light. I would always see Light. I would sit by myself and pray, *God I want to know the Truth. Please give me the truth to come to you.* Then God opened up to me and showed me the way of Jesus, the way of peace and truth and love."

She continued, "Today I have seven groups that I lead. There are about 35 total in these groups."

I asked Amal, "Who is Jesus to you?"

She replied, "He is the Father to us. He is my friend. My love. He is my Lord God."

"And who is Muhammad?" I asked.

Without hesitation she replied, "I don't see him as a prophet. He didn't come to give us a message from God. He gave us thoughts out of his own mind, dependent on his own ideas. He gave people something that he wanted, not something that they wanted or that God wanted."

I asked Amal and Nabila if they had experienced persecution. Amal replied, "If they had any idea of even the oxygen that we are breathing right now it would be a big problem for us. I am not going to marry anyone other than a believer. No one will tell me what I must think. This will be difficult, because my father is a strong, strong Muslim and will want to know that my husband is a devout Muslim."

Less than a year later, Amal's father gave her as a wife to a man from a strong Muslim family. Before her first year of marriage was over, Amal's new family discovered her faith in Christ. They responded by beating her to learn the names of those through whom she had come to faith in Christ. Then they sequestered her from leaving the house. She has not been seen since.

How They Live Their Faith

The question, *How are they living out their faith?* can be answered in a single word: discreetly. Despite Nasr's bold probing questions that he uses to awaken Muslims to the deceptions in their own religion, he takes seriously Jesus' admonition to be "as wise as serpents."

Muslim movements to Christ in many Arab countries have an ambivalent relationship to the evangelical and ancient churches around them. Several of the testimonies shared by these Muslim-background converts attest to the different quality of life they witnessed in the lives of Christians. "They love one another. They have peace in their lives," were common observations. At the same time, these traditional churches were under constant pressure from Muslim-dominated governments to avoid outreach to Muslims.

"They are afraid," Nasr said. "When someone from a Muslim background comes to them and says, 'I want to become a Christian,' they say 'No.' They are afraid of the secret police. At times the church will even turn people in to the government when they say they want to be a Christian."

Nasr went on to explain that when he became a follower of Christ, "I tried to go to the churches and they told me, 'No, you can't join our church.' They gave me the name of someone involved in Human Rights, and said maybe they can help you. But with the churches it was a dead end." So Nasr turned back to satellite television and to the Internet.

After partnering with Tim, and seeing the movement grow, Nasr used his skills as a political activist to multiply the movement. "We always meet in small groups," he said. "There are five persons in each group. Some of the people know each other and some do not. We do this because we don't want people coming just because their friends are a part of it. We want to know that everyone is committed to what we are doing.

"So if someone falls into the hands of the Secret Police, he falls by himself, we don't want him to bring others down with him. If someone is caught by the secret police they won't be guilty of any crime, but they will be able to respond with love and peace to their captors. If peace is a crime, we all are criminals."

"And what do you do in your groups?" I asked.

"At the beginning of the meeting we pray. We have accountability next; we ask, 'What did everyone do this week in terms of sharing with people?'

"New believers go through the process of learning how to share their faith. We teach them the five prophet stories from the Bible that lead to a gospel presentation. Then they study together from Luke and Isaiah.

"We also ask them, 'What were the sins that you committed, or what were the sins that you walked away from this week?' For the sins that they confess, we say, 'Okay, we're going to ask for forgiveness for the sins committed this week.' After we do prayer and accountability, we do our lesson. In their lesson, they study the Bible. After reading the passage in the Bible, everyone goes around the room and has an opportunity to say what he believes or understands from the passage of Scripture.

"After they study it together, and everyone starts to get a clear picture of what it means, everyone in that group then takes it to the groups they are leading. We're working under the assumption that everyone in the group has another group that they're meeting with. So you have a group that you are served in and a group that you serve.

"After we finish the lesson, we talk about what everyone is going to be doing this next week that you should be doing. We really focus on teaching and training people how to do their Christian service: we're watching their behavior, how they move and how they talk, so that we can begin to identify the potential leaders for the future. In order to encourage everyone in prayer, at the end we take prayer requests, and then every week or in every meeting, each person has a turn in leading out in the final prayer so that everyone is learning how to pray. So they pray for all of the prayer requests of the group, but each time it's a different person doing the praying."

The *Mukhabarat* (secret police) is everywhere in the Arab world, and they are just as quick to infiltrate and arrest a docile network of Muslim-background-Christ followers as they are to corral a cell of al-Qaeda terrorists. For this reason, the Muslim-background believers are leery of foreigners with questions and outsiders whom they do not know.

One of the women I interviewed proved later to be just such an infiltrator. Unlike Nabila and Amal, this woman's responses to my questions were strained, incomplete, evasive. At the time, I attributed her nervousness to my being a foreigner asking intimate spiritual questions.

A wave of persecution broke out eight months later that movement leaders were able to trace back to the informant. But Nasr's organizational plan proved to be effective as the informant's small group was quickly identified and isolated from the larger movement.

Further persecution followed, though, that eventually pushed Nasr out of the country under threat of imprisonment or death. Nabila was soon forced out as well, leaving behind her husband and seven children.

I Know Where I'm Going

"Four years ago I thought Jesus was only a man, but after what happened to me, I now know that he is my God. When you have heard my story, if you were not already a Christian, you too would have faith in Jesus."

So began Mahad, a 58-year-old retired Arab businessman who has been a follower of Jesus for three years. So compelling was Mahad's story that he had led members of 70 households to Christ. Many of these new believers have now led their entire families to faith as well. Mahad leads this network of believers in Bible study and worship as they grow in their understanding of Christ.

"As a university student," Mahad said, "I studied business management, but I also studied Islamic apologetics. Though I was a hafez, and had memorized the Qur'an, I still had questions. So I studied other religions. I concluded that all religious books were manmade, except for the *Injil* (the New Testament).

When I read it, I felt that it was not manmade. Though I did not have a strong faith, I did believe that it was true. I suppose you could say I believed, but did not follow."

Returning from university to his village, Mahad became a successful businessman and local politician. "Eventually, I grew one of the largest businesses in this country," he said, "but then something happened that changed everything for me. My wife, whom I loved with all my heart, died. When she died, a part of me died as well. I became very depressed. I sold my business. I no longer had a reason to live."

Mahad's depression eventually took a toll on his physical health. "About four years ago," he said, "I went to see a doctor who referred me to a heart specialist. 'You should have come sooner,' the cardiologist said. 'One of your arteries is closed.'

"As the doctors prepared for open-heart surgery, they told me my chances of survival were no better than five percent.

"As I went under the anesthesia, I was afraid. The heavens seemed to open up before me and I started praying, but I didn't feel any peace. Just as I was losing consciousness, I called out, 'Jesus,' three times.

"Immediately, I felt a peace that I was going to go into surgery and come out.

"While I was under the anesthetic, I had a vision. I saw the most beautiful green meadow I had ever seen. Standing in the meadow, I saw Jesus beside my wife holding her hand. They both looked so happy. She smiled when she saw me and motioned for me to come to them.

"It was like I was walking above the ground toward the meadow. I felt such joy. I knew that this was my wife and that she was with Jesus. My wife was always very beautiful, but I've never seen her more beautiful than she was in this vision. I also knew that in the real world I must have died, but that was all right; I was going to be with them.

"When we were just a few meters apart, my progress toward them stopped; I started falling away, and they started receding from me. I didn't want to go back. I knew it meant that the surgery was a success, but I didn't want it to succeed.

"I will never forget that vision. When I woke up, my children were all around my hospital bed. I couldn't speak, so I asked my daughter for a pen so I could write down what had happened. I closed my eyes and prayed that I could go back. But later I woke up again in my hospital bed.

"The surgery was successful, but since that day, my heart has been tied to Jesus. Before the surgery, I was afraid of dying. But now I know that I will go to be with my wife and with Jesus."

Mahad's story raised another question. Mahad's family had been known in their village as Muslims.

"Your wife," I asked delicately, "was she a follower of Jesus too?"

"Yes!" Mahad exclaimed with great excitement. "She loved Jesus." Mahad sent his son away to bring something from the back room. "My wife always loved Jesus and she loved Mary too. She never talked to me about it, but she always wanted them close."

Mahad's son returned with a plaster figurine of Da Vinci's Last Supper, the kind sold to tourists in the market.

"She bought this many years ago," Mahad smiled. "When we get to heaven, we will ask her about it."

Small Group Discussion ~ Discover for Yourself

1. What impressions do you take away from this chapter?
2. How is God at work in the Arab Room?
3. What are some of the biggest barriers and bridges to faith in this Room?
4. What are some of the unexpected ways that God is at work in this Room?

PART 3:
in the house of war

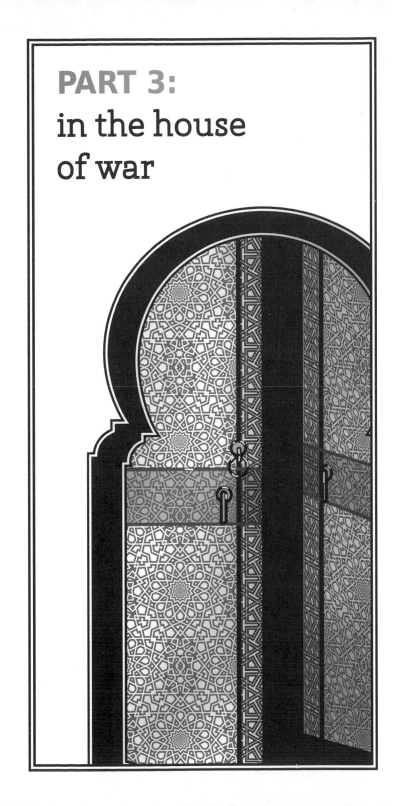

looking back

 WHAT HAS OUR journey through the nine Rooms in the House of Islam revealed? We have much to learn from the ways God is at work. Before we do, though, let's revisit the ten critical issues introduced in chapter three to see how our study has fared.

Security Concerns

Our concern for security has proven to be well founded. In addition to the martyrdoms, wars, persecutions, and brutalities that occurred as a daily fact of life for so many in the House of Islam, there have also been incidents that were directly related to those who contributed to this book.

Among those we interviewed, several individuals were abused during the course of this book's production simply for being followers of Christ in the House of Islam. In two instances, the nation's *Mukhabarat* (secret police) drove two network leaders of Muslim-background-Christ followers from their homes and countries under threat of a prison sentence or death.

Two Christian missionaries who assisted my interviews were arrested and imprisoned before eventually being expelled from the country. Their arrest was for allegedly inciting civil unrest—by encouraging Muslim movements to Christ.

One Muslim convert in East Africa, a dynamic evangelist, shared dinner with me on Christmas night 2011. Three months later, a neighbor to whom he had been witnessing poisoned him. By God's grace and the quick response of a Christian doctor, this brother was brought back from the brink of death.

In a South Asian country, someone abducted the brother of a movement leader whom I befriended and interviewed. Whether the abduction was a kidnapping by jihadis or an arrest by government agents is difficult to say. "In this country," I was told, "arrest and kidnapping are the same." What we do know is that those who took him tortured him for five months in ways that cannot be recounted in this book. He was released, but as a fraction of the person he had been.

Finally, there was the young Arab woman, 21-years old, who boldly told us she would not marry a non-believer. A few months later, her devout Muslim father forced her to do just that. Less than a year later, her new family uncovered her faith in Christ and beat her into silent submission.

These are the threats facing every Muslim who turns to Christ. This reality of persecution remains the great crucible that is both proving and purifying their faith. As we look back through these nine Rooms, I urge the reader to join me in praying for those who have cast their destiny with Christ at the risk of everything.

Scope of the Project

What began with a vague sense of 25 or so potential Muslim movements to Christ expanded until we had identified 82 movements across the scope of Islam's shared history with Christianity. The first of these did not occur until 13 centuries into the Muslim-Christian encounter.

Centuries	Number of Movements	Percentage of the Total
7th - 18th	0	0
19th	2	2
20th	11	13
21st (1st 12 years)	69	84

A skeptical eye might guess that there are more Muslim movements to Christ today because we keep better records now or we are looking carefully for the first time. The facts, as we know them, do not bear this out. Previous generations took mission record keeping even more seriously than we do today. Missionaries during the great age of Western colonial expansion often kept daily journals of their work. Church baptismal and burial records were more carefully maintained prior to the modern era than are government census records today. Reports of a Mohammad or Abdullah changing his name to Peter or George would have been a cause for celebration, and could hardly escape notice.

Even a couple of generations ago, when students and faculty of the West's most prestigious universities, Harvard, Yale, Princeton, Oxford, and Cambridge, were occupied with the great global mission enterprise, they could point to no Muslim movements to Christ prior to Sadrach Surapranata's 19th-century breakthrough. A careful reading of Joseph Schmidlin's *Catholic Mission History*, the multi-volume *New Catholic Encyclopedia*, or K.S. Latourette's monumental seven-volume *A History of the Expansion of Christianity* revealed no additional movements to our record.

Our study, on the other hand, was able to confirm 82 Muslim movements to Christ through the course of history, of which, at least 69 appear to be current. Historically, we know that at least three of these past movements—the 19th century Sadrach and Shaikh Zakaryas movements and the post-1965 Indonesian movements—have been assimilated into other Christian work. Of the 69 contemporary movements, my collaborators and I were able to draw interviews from 45 of them, 65 percent of all the contemporary Muslim movements to Christ. Prior to this study, I interviewed Muslim-background-Christ followers from four other Muslim movements to Christ.

In the end, the scope of the project proved to be manageable, but just. Collecting these interviews required a quarter million miles of travel by the author, plus countless additional miles by collaborating partners around the world. The scope included more than 1,000 interviews drawn from 33 ethnolinguistic people groups in 14 nations.

Phenomenological Approach

At the outset of this book, we determined to take a phenomenological approach to the subject, which we defined as a descriptive method that suspends judgments until the phenomenon
of Muslim movements to Christ has been carefully described.
The reader will have to judge for him or herself whether or not
we accomplished this purpose. By couching each of the movements, and the interviews drawn from them, in descriptions of
their respective Rooms in the House of Islam, we aimed to show
how the unique context of each Room contributed to the movements that arose within them.

To ensure accuracy of understanding, multiple experts
from within each region reviewed the author's descriptions of
each of the Rooms in Part Two of the book. These experts have
spent years, and in some cases a lifetime, within the Rooms
described in this book. The contributions of these experts were
invaluable aids to correcting and clarifying the complexities of
each Room and the histories that have shaped them.

As one might expect, the experts did not always agree with
the author or with one another. This is the nature of exploring
regions of the world that are controversial and nuanced, and
remain largely veiled to full understanding or analysis. To
quote the Apostle Paul, "For now we see as through a glass,
darkly; . . . now I know in part" (1 Corinthians 13:12, KJV).
Hopefully, this current description will give rise to deeper and
better understanding in future studies.

View of Islam

The study revealed that, while Muslims share a common
Qur'an and Hadith, the Muslim world is complicated. General-
izations about Islam are better suited to the critique of Islamic texts than to the understanding of individual Muslims and
their communities. Realities range from secular and apathetic
cultural Muslims in many countries to the devout Qur'anic
Muslims who are also coming to Christ in significant numbers.

We also discovered the inadequacy and inappropriateness
of trying to fit all Muslim-background followers into a stati-

cally captured C1 to C5 scale of conformity to a preconceived scheme of understanding. An Insider in Saudi Arabia, if transported to Dallas, Texas, may very well transform into a church deacon. People are messy creatures.

There is an evil in Islam, as with all religions, when it is used to control and manipulate its followers or incite them to violence against those who would exercise their freedom of conscience to embrace a different way. Islam today is perhaps the most intrusive and egregious world religion at squelching nonconformity of belief. We must remember, though, that Islam is probably no more controlling than was Roman Catholicism in the Middle Ages or, closer to home, Puritanism in the early years of Anglo-American history.[1] One can only hope that Islam, too, will experience a reformation in its relationship to its adherents, allowing them the freedom to think, believe, and choose for themselves.

Definition of Conversion

One of the first questions that Christians ask when hearing about these movements is *Are they real? Are Muslims really turning to faith in Jesus Christ, the same Jesus Christ that we Christians know and love?*

In light of the biblical definitions we established in the "Critical Issues" chapter of this book, the most meaningful answers to this question are found in the lives and testimonies of the Muslim-background believers themselves. These testimonies reveal that the same Jesus, the one experienced and worshiped by Christians around the world, is the same Jesus whom these Muslims are discovering, the same Jesus of the New Testament to whom they have given their lives.

At the same time, some of these Muslim-background followers of Christ are less enamored with the labels of "Christian" and what they perceive to be "the religion of Christianity." While many Muslim-background followers of Christ are being assimilated into churches that do associate with the Christian religion, others are not. Others still are on a journey, one that began before their faith in Christ, when Christians and Christianity were regarded as enemies. Perhaps someday these same enemies will be regarded as family and friends. This is the reality of Christ followers within the House of Islam. Knowing and understanding that reality will help us better engage it.

For many Muslim-background believers who live in hostile, anti-Christian societies, identifying with the Christian religion would quickly accomplish two things: (1) their removal from those family members and friends they long to bring to faith in Christ, and (2) their immediate execution. Many have chosen not to identify themselves as Christians in order to expand their witness to their Muslim friends and family. Others have seen in Christianity a cultural or political association they choose not to embrace. Nonetheless, each of those surveyed and presented in this book profess to have been captured by the person of Jesus Christ, have followed him in baptism, and are seeking to live out their lives in a new way because of their relationship to him as their Savior and Lord.

The question of true conversion is a question of life transformation. For most of those interviewed, the transformation began immediately. Prayers were answered, lives were changed, and the implications of that change have challenged and shaped their lives and relationships in ways that continue to unfold.

Definition of a Movement

This study has strictly confined itself to movements of Muslim communities to faith in Christ of at least 1,000 baptisms over the past one to two decades or at least 100 new church starts in the same period. For that reason, Muslim-background believers have not been assessed in those parts of the world where they have been assimilated as individuals into existing open Christian communities or, on the other end of the spectrum, where persecution has been so severe as to provoke an anonymous response to Christ.

What does this have to say about those converts who fall outside the scope of this study? What does it say, for example, about the thousands of anonymous Muslim-background believers who have met Jesus in a dream or listened to a radio or television broadcast and privately given their lives to

Christ? Or, on the other hand, what does it say about those Muslim converts who have taken on a new identity as ethnic Christians worshiping with other Christians in more traditional churches? It says very little, as both of these polarities are beyond the scope of this study. They remain fodder for another study, an important, but very different study. Perhaps someone reading this book will be inspired to explore such a topic.

Motivations for Conversion

This critical issue contains both positive and negative dimensions. The positive aspect seeks to understand the many factors God is using to draw Muslims to himself. We will explore that question in the next chapter.

The other side of this question, the negative side, would seek to uncover ulterior motives that might have prompted these movements. The question, frankly stated, is *What role did money have in these movements?* After hearing the stories of sacrifice and martyrdom, the question may sound vulgar, but the question of money and its role is a legitimate one. If these movements are the result of financial enticements or rewards, what hope is there for their continuation, much less for their growth?

The first response to the question is to return to the threat of capital punishment that awaits any Muslim who converts to faith in Christ. Are there sufficient financial incentives that could overcome such an existential threat?

There is no doubt that many individuals, both from Muslim and Western backgrounds, come to faith without a full understanding of the gospel and its implications. Many of these, like the young Muslim-background college student we interviewed in South Asia, testified, "I prayed to Jesus to make better grades, and he answered my prayers." People sought Jesus for healing, blessing, salvation, truth, peace, forgiveness, and other reasons. But what about for financial gain?

We did interview some widows in West Africa who were victimized by their Muslim communities after their husbands died, and then found justice and a new family of faith in the Christian world. One might see this as financially motivated. Many of the Iranian refugees fleeing their country's economic collapse are seeking better economic opportunities somewhere else. That many of those same economic refugees are also either followers of Christ or came to faith in Christ after they left Iran appears to be more coincidental than cause-and-effect.

Much more common, though, were the stories of converts who lost everything for the sake of following Christ. This is the normal way that the Muslim community treats apostates: they take away everything. We interviewed persons whose communities had beaten them, arrested them, tortured, shunned, poisoned them, and stripped them of their jobs, possessions, and families. These were far more normal outcomes than gaining financial rewards for their decision to follow Christ.

Limitations of This Study

It remains tempting to emphasize the significance of how God is at work in the House of Islam. We are witnessing an historic, unprecedented moment in salvation history. Even from a secular vantage point, we have never seen so many Muslim individuals or communities in so many different places move toward faith in Jesus Christ. These facts cannot be denied.

But let me here anticipate and acknowledge valid critiques that will rightly come. As we stated in Part One, the total number of Muslims who have come to faith in Christ is statistically almost insignificant. Only a tiny portion of the Muslim world, less than one-half of one percent of Islam's 1.6 billion adherents, has turned to follow Christ. *A Wind in the House of Islam* will truly be significant only if it is reporting a hinge moment in history, the beginning of a breakthrough to a growing number of Muslims turning to faith in Christ.

Furthermore, despite efforts to gain a balanced demographic range of interviews (young/old; educated/uneducated; urban/rural; male/female; leader/layperson), this goal was only partially achieved. Nonetheless, I have tried to present in this book those interviews that do reflect the diversity within the movements themselves. Consequently, you have heard stories from these nine Rooms from men and women, young and old, highly educated and illiterate, urban and rural, leaders and laity.

The Author's Bias

Before entering this study, I shared my personal biases as an evangelical Christian who submits my own faith and practice to the biblical authority and the uniquely exclusive salvation claims of Jesus Christ as revealed in the Bible. On the one hand, holding this faith position compels me to filter every testimony and event through my own faith presuppositions. Hopefully, though, my personal faith position has not clouded the presentation of what is happening in these Rooms nor impeded readers from making their own assessments of where and how God is at work.

In the chapters that remain, I will re-engage this faith position as we explore together the spiritual lessons, implications, and applications of the ways God is at work in the Muslim world.

Desired Outcomes

Before beginning this journey, we set forth four goals or desired outcomes for this study.

1. To accurately describe these movements.
2. To learn the ways God is at work across the Muslim world so that we can better participate in these movements.
3. To encourage those Muslims who are coming to faith in Christ by helping them to see how God is drawing Muslims to Christ across the Muslim world.
4. To challenge Christians everywhere not to fear and hate Muslims, but to engage them with the gospel of Jesus Christ.

Our pursuit of the first goal took us through each of the nine Rooms in the House of Islam, filtering them through the ten critical elements we've reviewed above. We took the time to examine the complex environment of each Room, its history, ethnography, religious and political dynamics. After framing the context for each Room, we listened attentively to the testimonies that arose from the movements contained within them.

In the next chapter we will tackle the second goal, identifying the hows and whys of these movements. As we do, we will also be exploring the most common questions that arise from our study: *Why are these movements occurring today? What is God using today to draw Muslims to faith in Jesus Christ?*

Small Group Discussion ~ Discover for Yourself

1. In light of the "Ten Critical Issues," what surprised you most about how God is at work in the House of Islam?

2. What are the implications of these surprises for how we can participate in God's work in the Muslim world?

how & why

 SO HOW AND why are these Muslim movements taking place today? What is God using to bring hundreds of thousands of Muslims to Christ? Why is it happening now, and why not for the past 13 centuries? And finally, how can we be a part of it?

Volumes could, and probably should, be written to examine this moment in salvation history. We have never seen a time like this before, and we have much to learn. While I do have insights and lessons I have gained from these surveys and interviews, I am confident that I have gleaned only a fraction of what God would have us learn.

Rather than pretend to exhaust this subject here, I want to invite you to participate in a Wiki-analysis. A Wiki-analysis, like the online *Wikipedia,* invites contributions from far and wide. I believe all of us have something to contribute, and together we can all know more.

Consider this your invitation to log into the book's website: www.WindintheHouse.org and offer your insights: *How is God at work in the House of Islam? Why is it happening the way it is today? Why did it take 1300 years for this turning to begin? How can, could, and should, we be a part of these movements?*

Let me offer some immediate observations to start the conversation.

Ten Bridges of God

(1) Faith - "Now faith is being sure of what we hope for and certain of what we do not see. This is what the ancients were commended for" (Hebrews 11:1-2). It all begins with faith. We can believe, even when we do not see, even when the evidence is absent. It is this kind of faith that has motivated missionaries through the ages as well as today to enter the House of Islam and share the gospel. Earlier generations of missionaries remained faithful in their witness, even though the great majority of them "did not receive the things promised; they only saw them and welcomed them from a distance" (Hebrews 11:13).

How much faith was needed for them to leave their homes and cultures to raise their children in the House of Islam, whose legacy has been to assimilate millions of Christians into their communities? Countless faithful witnesses in ages past did not see the movements we are seeing today, yet their exemplary pursuit of a harvest that they "welcomed . . . from a distance" laid a foundation for the great movements that are occurring in our day, and to them we owe a debt of gratitude and belated celebration.

Exemplary faith is also being demonstrated by those Muslim-background brothers and sisters who daily walk in the way of Christ while the path of countless others around them is dictated by Islamic sharia. These movements are built upon the pure faith of those who have "not loved their lives so much as to shrink from death" (Revelation 12:11).

What about us? This is the remaining question to be answered. Too often, we have diluted the meaning of faith to mere mental ascent, agreement with a particular point of view or doctrinal formula. This is quite different from the faith described in the book of Hebrews or lived out today in the House of Islam. Faith in those depictions is nothing short of bold obedience, even when that obedience may result in death. It is that higher call of faith, that biblical call, that leads the faithful to discipleship and service in the House of Islam today.

(2) Prayer - "The prayer of a righteous man is powerful and effective" (James 5:16), and "The weapons we fight with are not the weapons of the world. On the contrary, they have divine power to demolish strongholds" (2 Corinthians 10:4). Aisha, a Muslim-background follower of Christ from the desert sands of North Africa, was once asked to account for the reason so many Muslims in her land are now coming to Christ. "I believe," she said, "that the prayers of people all over the world have been rising up to heaven for many years. In the heavens, these prayers have accumulated like the great clouds during the monsoon season. And now they are raining down upon my people the miracles and blessings of salvation that God has stored up for them."

Prayer has been the first and primary strategy for virtually every new initiative into the Muslim world. It is the great unseen force that has both stimulated Christians to venture into the House of Islam and pierced the hearts of Muslims whom they encounter there.

Prayer changes us as well as those for whom we pray. Prayer draws us near to the heart of God, and near to the heart of God are countless Muslims in need of a Savior. If the Holy Spirit is the wind that is blowing through the House of Islam, then prayer is one of the ways we spread our sails and catch that wind.[1]

Praying missionaries have infused prayer into the DNA of the movements they help to launch. Countless Muslims who have prayed for Allah to reveal to them the truth are finding that truth in Jesus Christ. In Christ, they are discovering the One who loves them and answers their prayers in personal ways they had never experienced in the rote prayers of Islam.

(3) Scripture - "For the word of God is living and active. Sharper than any double-edged sword, it penetrates even to dividing soul and spirit, joints and marrow; it judges the thoughts and attitudes of the heart" (Hebrews 4:12). Though Christians have possessed the Bible for two thousand years, it is only now reaching the inhabitants of many Rooms in the House of Islam, and it still remains unavailable in the heart languages of many Muslim people.

Scripture in the local language has been instrumental to every movement we have examined. If he has not already read it, the first thing a new Muslim-background believer wants to do is read the Bible for himself, or if he cannot read, he often learns to read for this purpose. We are only beginning to see the effect of the broad dissemination of Bibles, New Testaments, and Scripture portions into the languages of Muslims around the world. As this effort continues, the response is likely to follow.

Sadrach's pioneering movement in Indonesia came on the heels of a new Indonesian Bible translation. Shaikh Zakaryas's visions of Christ in Ethiopia drove him to a Swedish Mission bookstore from which he obtained a New Testament in his own language. It is no coincidence that the earliest Kabyle-language Bible translations and the *JESUS Film* (which is the Gospel of Luke in video format) quickly fueled an indigenous movement to Christ in Algeria, or that the distribution of a million Farsi-language New Testaments in Iran or the appearance of a Musulmani Bible translation in Bangladesh resulted in movements among each of their respective peoples.

Much of the Muslim world remains illiterate, but new initiatives to provide the Bible through storying, the *JESUS Film*, and radio and television broadcasts hold forth the promise that Holy Scripture will continue to ignite and fuel movements across the Muslim world.[2]

(4) Holy Spirit activity - "Unless I go away (Jesus said), the Counselor will not come to you; but if I go, I will send him to you. When he comes, he will convict the world of guilt in regard to sin and righteousness and judgment" (John 16:7-8).

Jesus assured his followers that it would be good for them that he would leave them, because he would send the Counselor, the Holy Spirit, whose presence would not be limited to a single human body. The Holy Spirit, Jesus promised, would be like the wind, able to go wherever it pleases (John 3:8).

Myriad Christians serving among Muslims have found that it pleases the Holy Spirit to blow through the House of Islam. God is visiting these Muslims through dreams, visions, and answered prayers in the name of Jesus. Virtually everyone who has worked in ministry to Muslims can attest to the pervasive presence and work of the Holy Spirit.

Perhaps Christians should also be thankful that Muhammad endorsed the value of dreams in his own life, prompting Muslims worldwide to give a credence to dreams that is no longer current in the more secularized Western world. Whatever the reason for their listening to dreams, what is clear is that God is using this avenue to stir the souls of countless Muslims to look beyond their faith to the One who offers them salvation and new life.

A colleague has been serving God among Muslims long enough to have heard countless testimonies of dreams in which a "being who shone bright as light" appeared to them, beckoning them to come to him. In a recent encounter with a Muslim man who had experienced such a dream, my colleague simply opened his Bible to the story of Christ's transfiguration in Matthew 17 and invited his Muslim friend to read the first two verses: "After six days Jesus took with him Peter, James and John the brother of James, and led them up a high mountain by themselves. There he was transfigured before them. *His face shone like the sun, and his clothes became as white as the light*" (Matthew 17:1-2, emphasis added). Startled by the discovery, the Muslim responded, "That's the guy, the guy in my dreams! Who is this?"

(5) Faithful Christian witnesses - "Therefore, since we are surrounded by such a great cloud of witnesses, let us throw off everything that hinders and the sin that so easily entangles, and let us run with perseverance the race marked out for us" (Hebrews 12:1). Though we have said it before, it bears repeating here that faithful Christians—not only in the recent past, but also through the ages—laid the foundation for much of what is now happening. In terms of devotion to prayer, evangelism, ministry, faithfulness to the word of God, and personal sacrifice, these pioneers stand as giants.

Too often, Evangelicals in the West have failed to recognize the impact of those from other traditions who have come before us. Many faithful followers of Christ in Roman Catholic, Assyrian Orthodox, Nestorian, Armenian, Ethiopian, Coptic, and Mennonite traditions have appeared in the testimonies of today's Muslim-background movements to Christ. Whatever flaws we find with these traditions are overshadowed by the continued existence of Christ and the Holy Scriptures, which they have retained faithfully through the years and passed on to Muslim seekers around them.

(6) Learning from the Body of Christ - "Come follow me," Jesus said, "and I will make you fishers of men" (Matthew 4:19). A good fisherman, upon approaching an unfamiliar fishing hole, will ask those who have successfully fished there, "What are they biting? How deep did you set your lure? What time of day did you catch them? Was it near to the shore or in the deep water?"

One reason we are seeing movements to Christ today that we were not seeing in centuries past is we are conducting outreach to Muslims in ways that differ from ages past. Gone are the crusades, inquisitions, and colonial conquests that sought to expand the kingdom of God by expanding the kingdoms of men. With the separation of church and state in many countries today, the gospel is free to be accepted or rejected on its own merit, rather than as a referendum on the governing political power that is pushing it. Into this new environment, gospel "fishermen" are introducing colloquial Muslim idiom translations of the Scripture, Muslim-focused outreach and ministry, contextualized witness, satellite television and radio broadcasts, prayer walking, Qur'anic bridging, and other innovative approaches.[3] In the movements we have examined, there is clear evidence of lessons learned, shared, and implemented by Muslim outreach advocates from one Room in the House of Islam to another.

Even now, breakthroughs are taking place in some remote corner of the House of Islam that are resulting in many Muslims hearing and understanding the gospel for the first time or prompting them to take that initial step of faith and repentance that leads to salvation. What we often fail to see is that it is the body of Christ that is accomplishing those breakthroughs in the divinely ordained art of fishing for the souls of men and women. When we go to the trouble to learn how the body of Christ is at work in one corner of the world so we can better apply those lessons in another corner of the world, we are not simply being pragmatists; we are being students of the ways God is at work in our world. Only as avid students of God's ways can we truly become the fishers of men he desires and calls us to be.

To become a student is to become like those little children Jesus exalted as examples for his followers.[4] This lesson in humble learning is particularly necessary for those of us from the West who have historically filled the role of knowers and teachers, rather than learners and students. We have much to learn.

(7) Communication - "'Come now, let us reason together,' says the Lord" (Isaiah 1:18). Communication is more than proclamation. Effective communication always has a "together" component. It requires understanding on the part of the hearer as well as the communicator. No breakthrough in this area has been more dramatic than in the field of contextualization. Contextualization means communicating in a manner that is clearly understood in the culture and worldview of those who are intended to hear it.

Christ said, "when I am lifted up from the earth, I will draw all men unto me" (John 12:32). These words were a prophecy of his imminent death on the cross, but also a promise that his gift of atoning salvation would be for all peoples. Too often, those we are seeking to reach fail to hear our message or see the saving work of Jesus Christ because they are distracted by us or our culture.

In the testimonies we hear from today's Muslim movements to Christ, there is a familiarity to their stories, a resonance in the faith we see exhibited in their lives. But there are also significant differences from what we see in our own lives. Many of the cultural expressions of our own faith that have become so familiar to us as to seem inseparable from the gospel itself are strangely absent from these movements. It is these cultural expressions (not the theological or spiritual) that we mistakenly associate with the Christian religion that many of these Muslim-background-Christ followers have balked at accepting.

Neither we nor these newly emerging Muslim-background disciples of Christ have a license to pick and choose elements of the gospel that we will accept or reject. But we and our new Muslim-background brothers and sisters both have biblical precedence for determining that "it is through the grace of our Lord Jesus that we are saved" (Acts 15:11) and not through cultural or even culturally religious behavior.[5] It was the challenge of distinguishing culture from gospel that provoked the first council of the church in Jerusalem (Acts 15:1-21), and this challenge has continued through the centuries.

Effective communicators of the gospel to Muslims have come to understand and appropriate Paul's challenging example to, "become all things to all men, so that by all possible means, I might save some" (1 Corinthians 9:22). And they have used this understanding to effectively communicate the gospel to Muslims in ways that previous generations never received.

At the same time, though, the medium is not the message. The power of the gospel is in the gospel itself, not in the way it is packaged. The same good news "that was once for all entrusted to the saints" (Jude 3) is transforming lives and ushering in movements throughout the House of Islam today. While the gospel has not changed through the ages, what has changed is the way it is being transmitted. Technological breakthroughs in communication are playing an enormous role in the spread of this ancient life-giving message, enabling it to penetrate into societies that are effectively closed to outsiders. The *JESUS Film* and other gospel-centered videos have had an immeasurable impact on the Muslim world. Broadcasts of the gospel message, first through radio and now through satellite television and the Internet, have exponentially increased our ability to offer the gospel of salvation to persons all over the world, many of whom may never meet a Christian face to face.

(8) Discovery - "Taste and see that the Lord is good" (Psalm 34:8). A remarkable and, for many of us, an unexpected way Muslims are coming to faith today is through personal discovery.

Growing up a Baptist, I understood the comment, "You can always tell a Baptist, but you can't tell him much." Though it may not have been intended as a compliment, for me it aptly described a passion for, and commitment to, truths that were not easily shaken.

Muslims are like that as well. Their cultural and religious commitments run deep. They abhor being told they are wrong or that truth is something other than what they have always believed. However, when they discover the truth for themselves, it becomes a part of them, something for which they will lay down their lives.

Muslim movements to Christ are filled with stories of individuals who rejected the truth when someone tried to foist it upon them, but passionately accepted it when they discovered it for themselves. Sometimes it began with a dream. At other times it started with a realization that Muhammad lacked the character and conduct of a godly man, or that the Qur'an, in fact, offered no assurance of salvation.

A number of Muslim movements to Christ were birthed through some form of a Discovery Bible Study, a growing familiarity with the biblical salvation narrative. Through the Bible they discovered for themselves God's plan that began in Creation and continued through the prophets—prophets they recognized—before culminating in the life, teachings, and work of Jesus Christ. By the time these "discoverers" encountered Christ in the New Testament, they were convinced of his authenticity and had given their lives to him in humble submission.

(9) Islam itself - One of the great surprises in the Muslim movements to Christ we examined was that Islam is often its own worst enemy, containing within itself the seeds of its own destruction.

Colloquial Qur'ans - For many Muslims whose testimonies we gathered, their pilgrimage to Christ began with a clear reading, for the first time, of the Qur'an in their own language. For centuries, Muslims have had to accept, and often memorize, the Qur'an in Arabic—the language of Allah. The fact that they did not understand it only enhanced its mystique and the hold it held over them. Now that many of them are able to read it in their own languages, the illusion has been shattered.

Christians who have feared the Qur'an as a rival to the Bible fail to grasp this simple truth: the Qur'an offers no assurance of salvation. For assurance of salvation, one must turn to the person and work of Christ Jesus. So potent is this discovery of the Qur'an's limitations that many Muslim-background-Christ followers have urged the spread of colloquial Qur'an translations as a prelude to gospel witness. As one Muslim-background evangelist put it, "Only after I read the Qur'an in my own language, did I realize how lost I was."

Life of Muhammad - The questionable morality of Muham-mad is a well-known topic among Christians, but remains one of those unspoken secrets in the House of Islam. While there is certainly a place for Christian apologists who boldly point out the amorous appetites and frequent acts of violence by the Prophet of Islam, these revelations are rarely well received by Muslims. When members of their own community present discovery-based questions to Muslims, however, the results have been quite different. In the movements we examined, the best course of action has been for Muslim-background believ-ers themselves to raise these matters. There is ample evidence in their own sacred texts for them to come to the conclusion reached by a group of 20 Muslim leaders in East Africa: "We concluded that Muhammad was not qualified to be a prophet of God."

Islamic Oppression - While the tools of jihad and sharia law have certainly been used to advance Muslim territory, today's Muslims are increasingly repulsed by a religion that imposes its will with force. Muslim brutalities against Muslims in North Africa, the Arab world, South Asia, and Indo-Malaysia have been key stimulants to millions of Muslims questioning the di-vine origins of Islam and turning to Jesus Christ.

(10) Indigenization - "Therefore, go and make disciples of all nations. . . teaching them to obey everything I have commanded you" (Matthew 28:19-20). Jesus did not commission us to teach the nations everything he commanded us; he commissioned us to teach them to *obey* everything he commanded us. The distinction is significant.

Indigenization literally means "generated from within." Muslim movements to Christ may begin with outside stimula-tion, but they become movements only when the new believers own and advance the lordship of Christ themselves.

While contextualization may allow outsiders to communicate effectively with Muslims, indigenization takes over where contextualization leaves off: when those we seek to reach are obeying Christ of their own accord. When this occurs, these new believers take discipleship to deeper levels than outsiders can ever anticipate as they "look to Jesus the author and perfecter of our faith" (Hebrews 12:2).

For those who seek to stimulate and encourage movements, indigenization may mean that Christian outsiders will take a different role than they may have previously envisioned. While Christian outsiders, such as missionaries, must take the initiative for introducing the gospel, their role will evolve as the movement takes root. Rather than remaining the up-front leader, indigenization may require them to be the encourager, vision caster, shadow pastor, servant leader, and trainer of local leaders who will indigenize the movement so that it can engage all of the hidden issues of Muslims that outsiders can scarcely imagine.

Christians who are reluctant to encourage indigenization often do so by appealing to the need for discipleship. There is a role for outsiders in the discipleship process, but it is more about teaching them the importance of obediently submitting to God's word and modeling for them the lordship of Christ in every area of our own lives than about inculcating into them all of the doctrines and practices we hold dear.

True discipleship, discipleship that goes to the deepest core of cultural sins, requires indigenization for its accomplishment. Nowhere was this more graphically depicted than in the Western South Asia Room when the question of whether a man should beat his wife was raised not by knowledgeable outsiders, but by the new believers themselves. When the missionary modeled submission to God's word rather than offering her own advice, the new believers found a path forward.

Indigenization requires us to believe Christ's promise that the power of the Holy Spirit will "lead them into all truth" (John 16:13) and the word of God will render them "fully equipped for every good work" (2 Timothy 3:16-17).

Five Barriers to Movements

A wise missionary once said, "It is often not what you do, but what you stop doing that leads to kingdom breakthroughs." Great barriers to Muslims coming to faith still exist within the Muslim world today. Challenges of sharia, jihad, terrorism, ignorance, and injustice within the Muslim world continue to restrict hundreds of millions of Muslims from the knowledge and saving power of the gospel. However, the greatest barriers to Muslim movements to Christ may be found not in the Muslim world, but within our own ranks.

(1) Contentious Christians - With thousands of denominations today, Christianity is irreparably fragmented, but that doesn't mean it has to be contentious. As an irenic Christian once said, "We don't have to see eye-to-eye to walk side-by-side."

Our human nature has a need to be right, but that needn't imply that all others are wrong. The same Jesus who said, "He who is not with me is against me," (Matthew 12:30) also said, "whoever is not against us is for us" (Mark 9:40). The distinction in Jesus's statements should not be missed. Being against Jesus (the "me" in Matthew 12:30) is never acceptable. But in dealing with the "us" (the community of Christ), we should be more charitable, as was our Lord. Christ's paradox of inclusion and exclusion should, at the very least, leave us with a healthy mixture of humility and grace before we seek to attack others in the body of Christ.

From the earliest years of Islam in the 7th century, Muslim armies took advantage of internal divisions within Christianity to advance the cause of Islam. When the Arab General Amr ibn al-'As led a band of 4,000 warriors into Egypt in 640, he faced overwhelming armies and massive fortresses that should have been more than adequate to defeat his desert fighters. Instead, he discovered a Christian nation that was hopelessly divided over matters of doctrine that had been elevated to irresolvable levels. Catholic Byzantine rulers had used the Chalcedonian dogma as a weapon to imprison Egyptian Christians who refused to submit to their official orthodoxy. Long oppressed by their

Byzantine co-religionists, many non-Chalcedonian Coptic Christians of Egypt preferred the promise of benevolent Muslim rule to the reality of Byzantine discrimination.

Similar divisiveness aided the eventual Ottoman conquest of Constantinople, the capital of Christendom, in 1453. Muslim armies had tried intermittently for eight hundred years to breach the walls of Christendom's greatest city. Yet in the year 1204, European Christians did what no Muslim army had accomplished, when they rerouted the Fourth Crusade to sack Constantinople instead of the Muslim-controlled Holy Land. In a self-destructive act that pitted Western Christian against Eastern Christian, the way was paved for Islam to eventually swallow what was left of the Byzantine Empire, as Christians, not Muslims, first looted the city, destroyed its libraries, stole its monuments, and violated its churches.

If we are wise, these lessons of history will serve as cautionary tales, lest our divisions today distract us from the high calling that is before us.

(2) Fear and Hatred - A missionary couple who served for many years in the Muslim world were on home assignment in the U.S. for a few months and used the opportunity to speak to churches about God's love for Muslims. After speaking in a local church, the couple accepted an invitation to lunch from one of the church deacons. On the way to the restaurant, the deacon spoke candidly, "I hear what you're saying," he said, "about how God loves the Muslims and all, but let me be honest: I think we should just bomb them all."

The deacon's response was not an isolated one. Many Americans, and many Christians in America, are angry and afraid. The still-raw wounds of 9/11, coupled with terrorist bombings in Boston, London, Spain, and elsewhere, seem to demand a response in kind.

From a rational standpoint, how could one not fear the advance of Islam? Look what "they" have done. Wherever Islam has triumphed, dissent has been silenced, and conversion to the Christian faith, or any other faith for that matter, has been punished by death. Islam, as both a religion and an ideology, is a legitimate threat. But Muslims are neither a religion nor an ideology; they are individuals in need of a Savior, individuals for whom Christ died.

The great example that instructs and challenges us comes from Jesus himself. Jesus's instructions to turn the other cheek, go the extra mile, pray for those who despise you, and forgive those who have offended you remain non-negotiables for Christ's faithful disciples today.[6] Following Christ is never easy, and may land one on the cross for the sake of his enemies, but there is an assured triumph and resurrection that follows.

(3) Imitating Islam - Islam was born in a hostile environment, surrounded by enemies who threatened its very existence. Islam canonized 7th-century Arab culture and used military might to advance it as God's ideal for the world. Islam's founders eliminated uncertainties by crafting a religion that legalistically prescribed every aspect of life and conduct, and then launched their followers on a military jihad that continues to the present day.

Christianity began with a different impulse. Called to follow a living Savior and Lord, who declared himself to be "the way and the truth and the life" (John 14:6), Christians set out on an adventure of obedience to a living Christ who promised to be with them always, even to the ends of the age. When we find ourselves threatened, though, we are tempted to follow the path that Muhammad charted: legalistic answers for every aspect of life and violent reactions to those we perceive to be our enemies. When we succumb to those tendencies, we may become more like the Muslims we fear than like the Christ who promised us his power and presence.

Through the centuries, and through countless societies around the world, Christians have embraced cultural patterns of their day that they associated with normative expressions of Christianity itself. Whether it is 10th century Coptic liturgy, 16th-century Mennonite dress, or 19th century American revivalism, each of these cultural adaptations was important for the contextualization of the gospel in its day and time. But when these adaptations become normative and synonymous with the gospel, we have a problem. When we fail to see that our culture, even our Christian expression of our culture, is not the same thing as the gospel, we may identify those who practice their Christian faith differently than we do as aliens and enemies.

The gospel transcends each of the world's societies and invites believers to repent of their own path to salvation and participate in the salvation and way of life God has made for us in Christ Jesus. However, when we regard our particular expression of Christian culture as the norm for all Christ followers, and adopt oppressive or even violent means to impose those cultural patterns—as we did during the Crusades, the Inquisition, and the more recent Colonial Era—we are mimicking the path of Islam rather than that of Christ. In doing so, we run the risk of forfeiting the power, blessing, and promise extended to those who go out in Christ's name and in Christ's way.

From its 7th century inception, Islam has spoiled for a fight, and invited Christians to do the same. Given our great might, wealth, and military advantage, many Westerners, even Western Christians, are ready to gamble the future on a head-to-head battle with Islam.

It is a fool's wager, and one that Christians should seek to prevent. It is no coincidence that the history of Christian relations with Islam is saturated with war. Whether it was the initial Christian armies from Byzantium fighting against the 7th century Muslim warriors who streamed out of the Arabian Desert, the Crusaders bent on recapturing the Holy Land, the medieval knights who contested Ottoman advance, or the more recent Western colonizers of the 19th century, our history of failure in reaching Muslims for Christ has coincided with our failures to be like Christ to Muslims.

It is also no coincidence that the growing tide of Muslim movements to Christ has come, not at a time of Western hegemony in the Muslim world, but at a time of retreat from colonial and military dominance in that world. The Colonial Era has been followed by an era of trade, commerce, and interdependence. In a time when we have little in the way of incentives to offer Muslims, apart from the eternal blessing of salvation in Christ, Muslims are choosing to come—not to us or "our side"—but to our Lord.

(4) Ignored Injustice - When Christians disregard injustice and dismiss those who are the victims of injustice, we open the door to Islam. This should be for us one of the greatest lessons taken from the history of Muslim-Christian interaction.

When the first Arab Muslim armies rolled across the Middle East and North Africa, they found a region replete with injustices that Christians had long ignored. Jews in Palestine, who had been banished from Jerusalem for centuries by anti-Semitic Christians, were more than willing to reveal to Muslim armies all the secret pathways into the Holy Land, the pathways that led to its conquest.[7] When the Muslim Sultan Umar arrived in Jerusalem, he requested a tour of the Temple Mount from the city's Christian patriarch Sophronius. Expecting to find a holy site, Umar was appalled to discover that Christians had turned the once sacred site into the city's garbage dump, an action aimed at demonstrating to the Jews that their religion was of no consequence. Umar ordered the garbage removed and constructed what would later become the historic Dome of the Rock and al-Aqsa mosques.[8]

Likewise, seventh-century Coptic Christians in Egypt, whose patriarch had been imprisoned for opposing the doctrinal authority of the Catholic Church, swung open the gates of Alexandria to Arab invaders under the promise that Muslims would allow them to worship freely.[9]

As Muslim armies marched across North Africa, they found thousands of slaves whose families had been owned for centuries by generations of Christian patricians. Though Muslims did not reject the institution of slavery, and would later become some of the world's last champions of the slave trade, they immediately saw in the unjust conditions an opportunity they could exploit. The Islamic conquerors informed these slaves that no Christian was allowed to own a Muslim slave, prompting thousands of Christian slaves to win their freedom simply by converting to Islam.[10]

Injustices perpetrated or simply tolerated by Christians persist today, and Muslims are not slow to identify these inroads, while offering Islam as the solution. On the contrary, when Christians are proactive and move to combat social injustice, both at home and abroad, we inoculate our communities against Islamic incursions. And more importantly, we honor the cause of Christ. In the same way, many of the Muslim movements to Christ we are witnessing today have occurred because of unaddressed injustices that have been ignored within the House of Islam, prompting Muslims to find refuge and justice in the person of Christ.

(5) **Ignorance and Apathy** - Most Christians admit to knowing little about Islam or the ways God is at work in their world to reach Muslims. Too many others simply don't care. For centuries, Americans have had the luxury of living in a hemisphere far removed from the old war with Muslims that beleaguered Christians in Europe for more than a thousand years. All of that ended on September 11, 2001.

Since that time, Americans have found themselves engaged in two wars with predominantly Muslim countries while fighting a seemingly interminable Global War on Terror with Muslim militants both at home and around the world. We can no longer indulge the luxury of ignorance and apathy.

The Fullness of Time

These five barriers will continue to challenge Muslim movements to Christ in the days ahead. It remains to be seen whether or not Christians will be able to overcome these barriers to bring the good news of Jesus Christ to the Muslim world. At the same time, the 10 bridges we've identified represent a convergence taking place today in ways that may be unique in history.

Not all of the bridges are new. Movement catalysts such as faith, the prayers of God's people, the Holy Spirit's work, heroic Christian witness, and internal fractures within Islam itself have likely not changed since Islam first appeared on the scene nearly 14 centuries ago. Even the prevalence of Jesus dreams may not be new. It is possible that Muslims have had dreams of a "Being as bright as the sun" for centuries. What was different in the past is that these Muslims were left with no solution to the enigma of the dreams that haunted them.

Today these Muslims with restless hearts face a different prospect. Internet access, satellite television, globally dispersed Muslim migrations, local-language Bible translations, oral, video, and culturally indigenous witnesses to the power of the gospel have changed the equation. There may be no *single* answer to the question of why Muslim movements to Christ are occurring in the House of Islam today. Instead, it may be that the Holy Spirit is orchestrating all of these elements into a fullness of time that is ushering in an unprecedented *Day of Salvation* for Muslims.

There is so much to learn from the ways God is at work in the Muslim world; so much, in fact, that we have only begun to introduce the subject in this single volume. The reader is encouraged to listen again to the stories that have emerged from these Rooms. Discover for yourself what God is doing and how he is doing it. Then ask yourself, *How can I be a part of what God is doing? What is my role? How can I contribute?*

The good news is that God has not ignored nor ever ceased to care about Muslims. His Spirit has been blowing steadily through the House of Islam, and the wind is building. It is time for us to shake off our slumber, our ignorance and apathy, and catch up.

Small Group Discussion ~ Discover for Yourself

1. Do you agree with the author's *Ten Bridges*? Why or why not?
2. What other bridges would you add to this list?
3. Do you agree with the author's *Five Barriers*? Why or why not?
4. What other barriers would you add to this list?

our response

 THE ISLAMIC JURIST Abu Hanifa (699-767) first coined the term House of War (*Dar al-Harb* in Arabic) to describe the non-Muslim world in contrast to the House of Islam. He intended the distinction to give Muslims the mindset they should possess as they engaged those nations that had not yet submitted to Islam.

It is in this House of War that Christians find themselves today seeking a response to the immigration of thousands of Muslims into Europe, Asia, Africa, and the Americas. They are our neighbors, our classmates, our colleagues at work, and our friends. Christians who never envisioned going to the Muslim world are finding that the Muslim world has come to them.

Like Islam, Christianity was also born in a context of war. From its inception, hostile opponents sought to crush the movement that the Galilean carpenter had launched. Unlike Muhammad, though, Jesus rejected the temptation to take up arms, and chose a different path.[1] He did call his followers to battle, but it was a battle of the kingdom of God against the kingdoms of this world, a spiritual battle.

Today, some Christians want to match Muslims in a blow-for-blow contest, argument for argument, an eye for an eye, and a tooth for a tooth. Unlike the embattled flock of the first century, our twenty-first century church is powerful. Christians today follow the world's largest religion, possess its greatest wealth, and lead its mightiest armies. Indeed, we are

no longer "the refuse of the world" (1 Corinthians 4:13) that
we were when we began. And so we are tempted to engage
the challenge of Islam in our own strength. But to do so is to
forfeit the insuperable power that has been willed to us by the
one who took on himself "the very nature of a servant" and
"humbled himself and became obedient to death—even death
on a cross" (Philippians 2:8). For Christ's followers, the way
forward is unavoidable: "Your attitude should be the same as
that of Christ Jesus" (Philippians 2:5).

Taking on the attitude of Christ does not mean we shrink
from the battle at hand. Instead, we must "be strong in the
Lord, and in his mighty power (and) put on the full armor of
God"(Ephesians 6:10-11). God's full armor enabled the perse-
cuted church of the first century to surmount overwhelming
opposition, and it holds forth the same promise for us today.
But we must never forget that our struggle is "not against flesh
and blood," in other words, not against Muslim men, women,
and children, but "against the spiritual forces of evil" that continue to challenge Christ's kingdom.

In the course of this book we have learned a lot about
Muslims and about how God is at work in the House of Islam.
This has been an insightful journey, but if we finish this
journey with nothing more than education and observations,
we have fallen short of the discipleship implications of this
information. Christ's invitation, indeed Christ's mandate,
is for us to be a part of his great work. Christ calls us to
raise our spiritual sails and ride the wind of his Spirit that is
blowing throughout the world.

How do we do this? Here are five practical steps we can
take right now that will align us with God's redemptive activity
among Muslims.

(1) Pray for Muslims.

Prayer changes things, and every Christian can pray for
Muslims. Prayer originates with God and returns to God
on behalf of those who do not know God. When we pray for
Muslims, we begin to see them as God sees them. If you
lack a love for Muslims, pray for them and see how your
heart changes.

If you don't know how to pray for Muslims, begin with what you read or hear in the daily news. Hardly a day goes by that some Muslim tragedy, war, or atrocity doesn't appear in the news. Pray for God to work through these tribulations to bring Muslims to a knowledge of Christ and his salvation. As we have seen in our walk through the House of Islam, God is able to take the violence and injustice that plagues the Muslim world and turn it to good, just as he took the evil and injustice of the cross and turned it into the redemption of mankind.

(2) Support outreach and ministries to Muslims.

Now that you have seen how God is at work in the House of Islam, you have discovered for yourself what God is using. You've seen the importance of missionary and local Christian witness, Bible translation efforts, gospel videos, satellite television, radio broadcasts, compassion ministries, religious freedom advocacy, ministry to refugees, and other efforts.

These ministries are costly. Muslims will not and should not be expected to pay for their own evangelization. That job is up to Christians, Christians from both a Muslim background and from a Christian background. God has placed more wealth into the hands of Christians today than at any time in history. Investing in the fulfillment of the Great Commission is sure to pay eternal dividends. The 21st century movements of Muslims to Christ presented in this book are ample evidence that when we do invest in kingdom outreach among Muslims, God multiplies those investments many times over.

(3) Go to Muslims.

The Bible makes it clear, "How, then, can they call on the one they have not believed in? And how can they believe in the one of whom they have not heard? And how can they hear without someone preaching to them? And how can they preach unless they are sent? As it is written, 'How beautiful are the feet of those who bring good news!'" (Romans 10:14-15).

Movements to Christ do not take place spontaneously. They occur when someone sacrificially responds to God's call and brings to them the good news. Through this book you've learned of 82 Muslim movements to Christ in history and heard testimonies from 45 of those movements drawn from 33 Muslim people groups. You've also learned, though, that there are 2,157 Muslim people groups around the world. This means movements have occurred among only 1.5% of the world's Muslim people groups. There is so much work yet to be done.

(4) Minister to Muslims in your own community.

Jesus said the greatest commandment is to love God with all our hearts, and the second is to love our neighbors as ourselves (Matthew 22:36-40). Today, our neighbors include Muslims. A rich definition of ministry has grown out of the many Muslim movements to Christ around the world; Christians participating in these movements define ministry as "answering the prayers of lost people." This concept of ministry requires us to get to know Muslims, to listen to them, to become their friends.

Thousands of Muslims have left their homelands and arrived as immigrants and refugees in countries with substantial Christian populations. Many of these Muslim men, women, and children are fleeing violence themselves and have lost everything in their war-torn countries. Christians who take this opportunity to befriend and minister to Muslims in these situations are revealing to them a Christ they have never known, and making great strides toward Muslim movements to Christ.

(5) Share the gospel with Muslims.

Prayer and ministry are the perfect preludes to gospel witness. When you've spent time praying for someone and then demonstrated Christ's love to them through ministry, it is natural to "give the reason for the hope that you have." "But" as the Apostle Peter continues, we must always "do this with gentleness and respect" (1 Peter 3:15).

Thanks to the pioneers whose ministries have contributed to the movements explored in this book, we now have many options for effectively sharing the gospel with Muslims: distributing the Bible in their own language, sharing the *JESUS Film*, starting Discovery Bible Studies, practicing Any-3, using Qur'anic bridging, and simply discussing with Muslims their dreams and prayer requests.[2] The single most significant thing Christians have done to stimulate the current wave of Muslim movements to Christ is to prayerfully and obediently engage them with the love and gospel of Christ. This remains the most significant step each of us can take today.

In the years to come, the testimonies in this book will circulate throughout the House of Islam. Already, Muslim-background believers are sensing that the wind of God's Spirit is blowing through their communities. They are discovering that God is doing something extraordinary among their people. The simple knowledge that God has Muslims on his heart has emboldened these new believers to share their faith with their family members, friends, and neighbors.

When we reject fear, anger, and hatred, we cast off the ballast that anchors us to the ground, and we prepare ourselves for the spiritual adventure God has set before us. In the words of the New Testament, "let us throw off everything that hinders us and the sin that so easily entangles, and let us run with perseverance the race marked out for us. Let us fix our eyes on Jesus, the author and perfecter of our faith" (Hebrews 12:1-2).

Then, as we pray for Muslims, support outreach to them, minister to them, love them as neighbors, and share our faith and lives with them, we rise above the spiraling conflict and violence that occupies those bound to an earthly perspective. Soon, we find we have been lifted to a different plane of ministry. Our meager talents and abilities no longer limit us; we have taken flight. We have been caught up by the wind of the Spirit that blows wherever it pleases, and carries us along with it.

Small Group Discussion ~ Discover for Yourself

1. What does it mean to be living in the House of War?
2. How is our style of warfare different from that of Muslims'?
3. What steps would God have you take to advance the gospel among Muslims?

notes

Chapter 1: Something is Happening

1. "Muslim-Majority Countries," in *The Future of the Global Muslim Population*. Pew Research Center, January 27, 2011. Cited 8 August 2013 on the Internet at: http://www.pewforum.org/2011/01/27future-of-the-global-muslim-population-muslim-majority/.

2. K.S. Latourette, *History of the Expansion of Christianity*, Vol. 2, (London: Eyre & Spottiswoode, 1947), pp. 310-311, citing the earlier work of Alfred Von Kremer, *Culturgeschichte des Orients, Vol. II*, pp. 495-6.

3. For a good introduction to motives for conversion to Islam see R. Stephen Humphreys, "The Problem of Conversion," in *Islamic History: A Framework for Inquiry* (London: Princeton University Press, 1991), pp. 273-283. Also, Philip Jenkins, *The Lost History of Christianity, The Thousand-Year Golden Age of the Church in the Middle East, Africa and Asia—and How It Died* (New York: Harper One, 2008).

4. K.S. Latourette, *Expansion*, Vol. 2, pp. 319-320.

5. Andrew Alphonsus MacErlean, "Conrad of Ascoli," in *The Catholic Encyclopedia: An International Work of Reference*, Vol. 4 (Ann Arbor, MI: University of Michigan Library, 1907), p. 258.

6. Latourette, *Expansion*, Vol. 2, p. 365. Conrad of Ascoli's life and ministry is little known. He receives only one sentence in Latourette's expansive seven-volume history. The Catholic saint is said to have desired to preach the gospel to Negroes in Africa. How many of his Libyan converts were Negro slaves and how many of them were Muslims is unknown.

7. "St. Raymond of Peñafort," in *Catholic Encyclopedia*. Cited 28 November 2012. Available online at: http://www.newadvent.org/cathen/12671c.htm.

8. "Raymond of Peñafort," in *New Catholic Encyclopedia*, 2nd ed., Vol. 11, (Detroit: Gale, 2003), pp. 936-937.

9. Latourette, *Expansion*, Vol. 2, p. 326.

10. J.F. Hinnebesch, "William of Tripoli," in *New Catholic Encyclopedia*, 2nd edition, Vol. 14 (Detroit: Gale, 2003), p. 754.

11. Thomas F. O'Meara, "The Theology and Times of William of Tripoli, O.P.: A Different View of Islam," in *Theological Studies*, Vol. 69, No. 1.

12. Latourette, *Expansion*, Vol. 2, pp. 321-323.

13. Latourette, *Expansion*, Vol. 2, pp. 314-315, citing Lea's *The Moriscos in Spain*, pp. 12-31.

14. *Moriscos* was the term for those Muslims who agreed to convert to Catholicism rather than being expelled from the country. The term later became pejorative as these *Moriscos* were suspected of secretly continuing to practice Islam.

15. Joseph Schmidlin, *Catholic Mission History* (Techny, IL: Mission Press, SVD, 1933, p. 584.

16. Ibid.

17. Don Dent, "Sadrach: The Apostle of Java," pp. 2-3. Unpublished paper cited 28 November 2012.

18. Dent, "Sadrach," p. 27, citing Sumartana, Th., *Missions at the Crossroads: Indigenous Churches, European Missionaries, Islamic Associations and the Socio-Religious Change in Java 1812-1936* (Jakarta: Gunung Mulia, 1993), pp. 89-92.

19. Dent, "Sadrach," p. 26, citing Sutarman S. Partonadi, *Sadrach's Community and Its Contextual Roots: A Nineteenth Century Javanese Expression of Christianity* (Amsterdam: University of Amsterdam, 1988), p. 129.

20. Schmidlin, *Catholic Mission History*, p. 591.

21. K.S. Latourette, *Expansion*, Vol. VI (London: Eyre & Spottiswoode, 1947), p. 17, citing Antony Philippe, *Missions des Peres Blancs en Tunisie, Algerie, Kabylie, Sahara* (Paris: Dillen & Cie, 1931), pp. 143, 145, 146.

22. Latourette, *Expansion*, Vol. VI, p. 19.

23. Paul Balisky, "Dictionary of African Christian Biography, Shaikh Zakaryas 1845 to 1920 Independent Prophet Ethiopia," cited on the Internet 8 August 2013 at: www.dacb.org/stories/ethiopia/zakaryas2.html.

24. The term "The Great Century" was coined by Yale missions historian, Kenneth Scott Latourette, in his seven-volume *History of the Expansion of Christianity, op. cit.*

25. The Indonesian killings of 1965-1966 are well documented. For a listing of 15 additional sources on this topic, see "Indonesian Killings of 1965-1966." Cited 28 November 2012. Available on the Internet at: http://en.wikipedia.org/wiki/Indonesian_killings_of_1965–1966.

26. Avery T. Willis, *Indonesian Revival: Why Two Million Came to Christ* (Pasadena: William Carey Library, 1977).

27. The Iran movements will be discussed in much greater detail in chapter eight of this book. See also Mark Bradley's, *Iran: Open Hearts in a Closed Land* (Colorado Springs: Authentic, 2007) and *Iran and Christianity, Historical Identity and Present Relevance* (London: Continuum Religious Studies, 2008).

28. Ahmed Bouzid, "Algerian Crisis, No End in Sight." Cited 2 Dec. 2012. Online at: http://www.library.cornell.edu/colldev/mideast/algbouz.htm.

29. These will be discussed in greater detail in chapter nine. Sources include the Annual Statistical Report of the Southern Baptist International Mission Board.

30. Bangladesh's intellectual legacy took a severe blow when the invading Pakistani military summarily executed thousands of academics, social and political leaders at the end of the war. Nonetheless, Bengalis proudly count three Nobel laureates from among their ranks: Rabindranath Tagore (1913), Amartya Sen (1998) and Muhammad Younis (2006).

Chapter 2: Hinges of History

1. Many advisors influenced the selection of these core questions. Some of those who helped shape the questionnaire included professional researchers who requested that their names be withheld from the published findings. Others, including seminarians, field-based missionaries, global demographers and trusted colleagues helped the author to hone and clarify the questions that follow.

2. To read more about the "Guidelines and Methodology" we developed along the way, visit the website: http://www.WindInTheHouse.org.

Chapter 3: Ten Critical Issues

1. See, for example, Dudley Woodberry's 2007 article, "Why Muslims Follow Jesus," in *Christianity Today*, 10/24/2007, cited on the Internet 26 July 2013 at: http://www.christianitytoday.com/ct/2007/october/42.80.html which surveys 750 Muslim converts to Christianity irrespective of their relationship to movements, and Ant Greenham's 2004 dissertation, "Muslim Conversions to Christ," Greenham, Ant. *Muslim Conversions to Christ, An Investigation of Palestinian Converts Living in the Holy Land.* Pasadena, CA: WCIU Press, 2004, which examines Palestinian Muslim conversions in Palestine.

2. A. Scott Moreau, *Contextualization in World Missions: Mapping and Assessing Evangelical Models* (Grand Rapids: Kregel Publications, 2012), p. 17.

3. Two books that span the range of perspectives for those who wish to explore the topic more thoroughly are Timothy George's *Is the Father of Jesus the God of Muhammad?* (Grand Rapids: Zondervan, 2002) and Miroslav Volf's *Allah, A Christian Response* (New York: HarperCollins, 2011).

4. These, too, are not monolithic, but range from Communists to practical atheists to secular nationalists.

5. These spiritual yet doctrine-averse Muslims bear some phenomenological resemblance to New Age practitioners in the West.

6. Travis's C-Scale was first published in a 1998 *Evangelical Missions Quarterly*, October 1998 article by Phil Parshall under the title "Danger! New Directions in Contextualization." Cited on the Internet July 1, 2013 at: http://www.emisdirect.com/emq/issue-230/1243.

7. David Greenlee, ed., *Longing for Community: Church, Ummah, or Somewhere in Between* (Pasadena: William Carey Library, 2013), pp. 1-66.

8. Though any child raised in a foreign culture is a "third-culture kid," the term applies directly to missionary kids, children who grow up in a foreign culture and so never fully fit into any single cultural worldview.

9. Greenlee, p. 22.

10. Ant Greenham, *Muslim Conversions to Christ* (Pasadena: WCIU Press, 2004), p. 27.

11. This study is not able to fully evaluate the ecclesiology, or doctrine of church, in each of these "worshiping communities," nor does it attempt to do so. That may well be the subject of a subsequent investigation. The primary point to make here is that these are not simply in-

dividual converts, but rather communities of believers whose practices vary widely, but generally seek to adhere to corporate New Testament prescriptions for disciples of Christ. As disciples of Christ, these worshiping communities are, or are becoming, churches.

Chapter 4: The Indo-Malaysia Room

1. Sutarman Partonadi, *Sadrach's Community and Its Contextual Roots, A Nineteenth Century Javanese Expression of Christianity* (Amsterdam: Rodopi, 1990), p. 70. The *Indische Kerk* was the name of the national Indonesian Church established by Dutch Calvinist mission efforts in Indonesia.

2. Partonadi, *Sadrach's Community*, p. 58

3. Ibid., p. 60-62.

4. Ibid., p. 210.

5. The fully adapted *shahada* is: "I believe that God is One. There is no God but God, and Jesus Christ is the Spirit of God, Whose power is over everything." Partonadi, p. 135.

6. Ibid., pp. 134-136.

7. Ibid., pp. 174-175.

8. David Barrett, *World Christian Encyclopedia Second Edition Volume 1* (New York: Oxford Press, 2002), p. 374.

9. Partonadi, *Sadrach's Community*, pp. 25-26.

10. Ibid., p. 28.

11. "Indonesian killings of 1965-1966," cited in *Wikipedia* July 26, 2013 at: www.en.wikipedia.org/wiki/Indonesian_killings _of_1965-66.

12. Avery Willis, *Indonesian Revival, Why Two Million Came to Christ* (Pasadena: William Carey Library, 1977), footnote 5, pp. 9-10. In his correspondence with Willis, Cooley offers numbers back to 1964, predating the coup attempt by a year, leaving us with a conservative estimate of two million conversions following the coup in September 1965.

13. Braithwaite (2010). *Anomie and violence: non-truth and reconciliation in Indonesian peacebuilding*, p. 294. Cited in "Indonesian killings of 1965-66" in *Wikipedia* July 21, 2013 at: en.wikipedia.org/wiki/Indonesian_killings_of_1965-66.

14. Clifford Geertz, *The Religion of Java* (Chicago: University of Chicago Press, 1976).

15.   Barrett, *World Christian Encyclopedia*, refers to these as "statistical Muslims," p. 373.

16.   Willis, *Indonesian Revival*, pp. 8 and 13.

17.   See "How the Churches Grew," in Willis, *Indonesian Revival*, pp. 191ff.

18.   Roger L. Dixon, "The Major Model of Muslim Ministry," in *Missiology: An International Review*, Vol. XXX, No. 4, October 2002.

19.   Both Avery Willis in *Indonesian Revival*, p. 17, and Roger Dixon in "The Major Model" attest to the existence and effect of this "unintentional" evangelism.

20.   Dixon, *Major Model*, p. 8 of 14.

21.   Barrett, *World Christian Encyclopedia*, pp. 374-375.

22.   In November 2011, the church's website and the above quote were found at: http://www.jkiinjilkerajaan.org/lama/index.php. This site as since been removed.

23.   In the interest of transparency: This approach was identified by the author, David Garrison, as a Muslim movements to Christ 'best practice' in 2010, prompting the author to encourage and edit the book by Mike Shipman, *Any-3: Anyone, Anywhere, Anytime* (Richmond, VA: WIGTake Resources, 2012). The book is available from www.ChurchPlantingMovements.com/bookstore.

24.   Jacqueline C. Rutgers, *Islam en Christendom* (The Hague, 1912), p. 239 cited in Partonadi's *Sadrach's Community*, p. 129.

25.   Partonadi, *Sadrach's Community*, pp. 96ff.

Chapter 5: The East Africa Room

1.   Thomas Pakenham, *The Scramble for Africa* (New York: Avon Books), pp. 470-486.

2.   Country-by-country comparisons from David B. Barrett, ed. *World Christian Encyclopedia*, Second Edition, Vol. 1, (New York: Oxford University Press, 2001.

3.   Ibid.

4.   The author has visited the town with the Muslim dawa and al-Qaeda training camps. Its identity is intentionally undisclosed.

5.   These Qur'anic passages are found in the Qur'an, as cited, but it should be noted that the evangelist shared with me only those portions the sheikhs themselves highlighted as relevant to underscore their point that Muhammad was not qualified to be a prophet of God.

6. At the time of this book's writing, the dissertation was in process through Fuller Theological Seminary. For security purposes, I will not name the author here, as he may choose a pseudonym for publication.

Chapter 6: The North Africa Room

1. The company, headquartered in the U.S., is well known, and for that reason will remain unnamed.

2. By 2004, France was home to six million North Africans. See Yazid Sabeg et Laurence Méhaignerie, "Les oubliés de l'égalité des chances," *Institut Montaigne*, January 2004. Cited on the Internet 15 July 2013 at: http://www.institutmontaigne.org/fr/publications/les-oublies-de-legalite-des-chances.

3. Original study conducted by the U.S. National Library of Medicine, National Institutes of Health by Robino C., Crobu F., et al. Cited on the Internet 15 July 2013 at: http://www.ncbi.nlm.nih.gov/pubmed?uid=17909833&cmd=showdetailview&indexed=google. For an overview of the subject, see: "Algerian Demography" in *Wikipedia*, cited 30 January 2013 on the Internet at: http://en.wikipedia.org/wiki/Demographics_of_Algeria#Y-DNA_Haplogroup_frequencies_in_coastal_Algeria.

4. "Historian Robert C. Davis estimated that between 1530 and 1780, 1-1.25 million Europeans were captured and taken as slaves to North Africa. . . ." See Robert C. Davis, *Christian Slaves, Muslim Masters: White Slavery in the Mediterranean* (Houndmills, Basingstoke, U.K: Palgrave MacMillan, 2004). For an overview article, see "Barbary Pirates," in *Wikipedia*. Cited 30 January 2013. Available on the Internet at: http://en.wikipedia.org/wiki/Barbary_pirates.

5. Vestigial memories of these wars persist in the Marine's Hymn: "From the halls of Montezuma, to the shores of Tripoli."

6. Adel Gastel, "France remembers the Algerian War, 50 years on," in France 24, *International News* 24/7. Cited on the Internet 15 January 2013 at: http://www.france24.com/en/20120316-commemorations-mark-end-algerian-war-independence-france-evian-accords. The actual death toll is impossible to calculate with estimates as high as 1.25 million. See an overview under "Death Toll" in the article "Algerian Revolution" in *Wikipedia*. Cited 30 January 2013. On the Internet at: http://en.wikipedia.org/wiki/Algerian_War#Death_toll.

7. The number of deaths remains a matter of dispute with figures ranging from 44,000 to 250,000. See a variety of sources compared and collated in "Algerian Civil War" in *Wikipedia*, cited 30 January 2013. On the Internet at: http://en.wikipedia.org/wiki/Algerian_Civil_War#Death_toll.

8. See their website at: http://www.aceb.net. Cited 29 January 2013.

9. Unpublished report. James Slack and Robert Shehane, eds. "Public Edition of the Church Planting Movement Assessment of an Indigenous People Group on the Mediterranean Rim," (Richmond, VA: Global Research Department of the International Mission Board, SBC, 2003), p. 7.

10. Ibid.

11. Ibid.

Chapter 7: The Eastern South Asia Room

1. See the discussion of the C-Scale and Insider Movements in "Critical Issue No. 4" in chapter 3 above.

2. Some of these OMers (Operation Mobilization missionaries) were Muslim-background believers who went straight to work after coming to faith. Among the literature being distributed was the *Musulmani* (contextualized for Muslims) New Testament whose publication had been promoted by ABWE (Association of Baptists for World Evangelization).

3. To understand this, one must see it through Thomas's eyes. Joining the Christian religion meant immediate expulsion from one's family. Choosing instead to follow Jesus, without changing one's cultural-religious affiliation allowed one to remain with his family and influence them to follow Christ as well.

4. At 10,000 sq. km., The Sundarbans are the largest mangrove forest in the world. By contrast, the Florida Everglades are 1,900 sq. km.

5. Kolkata supplanted the Anglicized name, Calcutta, in 2001.

6. The most commonly circulated number of fatalities in the war is three million civilians with 200,000 Bangladeshi women raped. Only recently has this figure been challenged. It is almost certainly an exaggeration, but the emotional scars of Muslim-on-Muslim violence remain real and a part of the Bangladeshi corporate consciousness. See Sarmila Bose, *Dead Reckoning, Memories of the 1971 Bangladesh War* (New York: Columbia University Press, 2011).

7. The Soviet Navy dispatched two nuclear-armed groups of ships to the Bay of Bengal in early December 1971. The Nixon administration responded by deploying the aircraft carrier USS Enterprise in support of West Pakistan the following week.

8. See David B. Barrett, ed., *World Christian Encyclopedia*, 2ⁿᵈ *Edition, Vol. 1*, p. 98. Barrett estimates the Muslim population to be considerably lower, only 85 percent.

9. In 2012, the Mecca Hajj counted 3,166,573 pilgrims. Though likely not as large, the *Tablighi Jamaat's* masses is still quite impressive. See the Hajj Information Center, cited on the Internet 12 July 2013 at: http://www.islamicity.com/mosque/hajj/?AspxAutoDetect CookieSupport=1. See also "Hajj," on *Wikipedia*. Cited 2 July 2013 at: https://en.wikipedia.org/wiki/Hajj#Transportation.

10. This survey was conducted by one of my collaborating partners.

11. This Qur'anic bridging to the gospel has been captured in Kevin Greeson's *The Camel, How Muslims Are Coming to Faith in Christ!* (Richmond: WIGTake Resources, 2007).

12. For example, many tribal-background Christians dine on pork and dog, foods abhorrent to both Muslims and Muslim-background believers. On the other hand, many Hindu-background Christians would not eat meat of any kind, while Muslims and Muslim-background believers enjoy beef and lamb.

13. Kenneth J. Thompson, "Allah in Bible Translations," in *International Journal of Frontier Missions*, 23:4 Winter 2006, p. 173.

14. *Kitab al-Moqadis* is the Arabic name and Muslim designation for the Bible; it literally means "the Holy Book."

15. Bhutto's paraphrase of what some call "the Messianic secret" has come through a translator from a South Asian language. In English, the verse actually has the evil spirit saying, "What do you want with us, Jesus of Nazareth? Have you come to destroy us? I know who you are—the Holy One of God!" To which, Jesus replies, "Be quiet!" (and says) sternly: "Come out of him!" After which, "The evil spirit shook the man violently and came out of him with a shriek." Mark 1:23-25.

Chapter 8: The Persian Room

1. Nadia's experiences with *Nar-Anon* reveal one of the many unexpected ways God was drawing Iranians to himself. Though the founder of *Alcoholics Anonymous* (parent of *Narcotics Anonymous*) Bill Wilson did experience a spiritual conversion associated with the Christian influence of the evangelical Oxford Group, he subsequently strayed from Christianity to a more generic "spirituality." Nonetheless, in Nadia's case the Twelve Steps led her to Jesus. See "Bill W." in

Wikipedia. Cited on the Internet 2 September 2013 at: http://en.wikipedia.org/wiki/Bill_W.

   2.   Mark Bradley, *Iran: Open Hearts in a Closed Land* (Colorado Springs: Authentic, 2007), p. 80.

   3.   Ibid., pp. 83-84. See also Hamid Enayat *Modern Islamic Political Thought* (Austin: University of Texas Press, 1982), pp. 182-183 quoted in Sasan Tavassoli's *Christian Encounters with Iran, Engaging Muslim Thinkers After the Revolution* (London: I.B. Tauris, 2011), p. 21. Enayat makes a point that "Husayn's martyrdom makes sense on two levels: first, in terms of soteriology not dissimilar from the one invoked in the case of Christ's crucifixion: just as Christ sacrificed himself on the altar of the cross to redeem humanity, so did Husayn allow himself to be killed on the plains of Karbala to purify the Muslim community of sins; and second, as an active factor vindicating the Shi'i cause, contributing to its ultimate triumph."

   4.   Tavassoli, pp. 10-47.

   5.   Bradley, *Iran: Open Hearts*, p. 9.

   6.   Ibid., pp. 69-70.

   7.   Ibid., p. 66.

   8.   Barrett, *World Christian Encyclopedia, Second Edition,* Vol. 1, p. 381.

   9.   Biographical information on Seth Yeghnazar is excerpted from the website: www.farsicrc.com. Cited on the Internet February 28, 2013.

   10.   Some of the information about the life of the Yeghnazars and Haik Hovsepian Mehr was provided by Iranian informants living in exile.

   11.   Mark Bradley, *Iran and Christianity, Historical Identity and Present Relevance* (London: Continuum Religious Studies, 2008), pp. 170-174.

   12.   "Mehdi Dibaj," in *Wikipedia*, Cited on the Internet 3 May 2013 at en.wikipedia.org/wiki/Mehdi_Dibaj.

   13.   Joseph Hovsepian and Andre Hovsepian, *A Cry From Iran: the untold story of Iranian Christian martyrs* (Santa Ana, CA: Open Doors International, 2007).

   14.   Bradley, p. 173.

   15.   *A Cry from Iran.* Dibaj's testimony at Hovsepian's funeral can be viewed on the film *A Cry From Iran: the untold story of Iranian Christian martyrs.*

16. Bradley, p. 173.

17. Revelation 12:11b.

18. Bradley, *Christianity in Iran*, p. 178. After this report came out, the International Antioch Ministries website was taken down and the organization renamed. The broadcast and ministry, however, continues.

19. Ibid., pp. 56-59. On March 15, 1951, Mossadeq led the nationalization of Iran's oil industry. Following the coup, in 1954, Mohammad Shah signed a new deal with Western oil cartels giving them effective control and 50 percent of the profits from Iran's oil fields.

20. Bradley, *Iran: Open Hearts*, pp. 65-66.

21. See "Demographics of Iran" in *Wikipedia*. Cited on the Internet 3 September 2013 at: http://en.wikipedia.org/wiki/Demographics_of_Iran#Population

22. See www.imf.org/external/pubs/ft/fandd/1999/06/carringt.htm#chart, cited 1 April 2013.

23. "Iranians Love the U.S.A.," in *Iran*, Issue 7, Summer 2013, p. 13.

24. Ibid., p. 14, citing Sara E. Quay and Amy M. Damico, eds., *September 11 in Popular Culture: A Guide* (Westport, CT: Greenwood Publishing Group, 2010).

25. Ibid., p. 15, citing Azadeh Moaveni's "Stars and Stripes in Their Eyes," in *Washington Post* online, June 1, 2008. Accessed on the Internet 21 September 2013 at: http://www.washingtonpost.com/wp-dyn/content/article/2008/05/30/AR2008053002567.html.

26. See "Crime in Iran," in *Wikipedia*, 3 April 2013 at http://en.wikipedia.org/wiki/Crime_in_Iran.

27. "Iran's rial drops 10 percent as EU bans oil imports," in *Al Arabiya*. Reuters. 23 January 2012, cited in "Sanctions Against Iran," in *Wikipedia*, cited 3 April 2013 at: http://en.wikipedia.org/wiki/Sanctions_against_Iran.

28. Julian Borger; Saeed Kamali Dehghan, "Iran unable to get life-saving drugs due to international sanctions," in *The Guardian*, 13 January 2013, cited in "Sanctions Against Iran," in *Wikipedia*, cited 3 April 2013 at: http://en.wikipedia.org/wiki/Sanctions_against_Iran. Borger and Dehghan identified 85,000 cancer patients, 40,000 hemophiliacs, and 23,000 HIV/AIDS patients among those negatively affected by the sanctions.

29. Adapted from an article by Hugh Chisholm, ed., *Encyclopedia Britannica*, 11th ed., Cambridge University Press (1911). Cited on the Internet at: www.en.wikipedia.org/wiki/Henry_Martyn#cite_note-EB1911-6 15 April 2013.

30. Bradley, *Iran: Open Hearts*, p. 89.

31. *Iran*, Summer 2013, p. 12.

32. In his book, *Iran and Christianity*, Mark Bradley writes, "If the figures from the survey carried out by Mohabbat TV were translated nationally, it would mean that 8 million people are interested in Christianity and nearly 3 million would actually want to become Christian." See *Iran and Christianity*, p. 187, note 2.

Chapter 9: The Turkestan Room

1. "Timur," in *Wikipedia*. Quoting Matthew White: Atrocitology: Humanity's 100 Deadliest Achievements, Canangate Books, 2011, section "Timur". Cited 1 May 2013 at: en.Wikipedia.org/wiki/Timur.

2. "Timur," in *Wikipedia*. Ibid.

3. http://en.wikipedia.org/wiki/World_War_II_casualties_of_the_Soviet_Union.

4. See "Battle of Talas" in *Wikipedia*. Cited on the Internet 31 August 2013 at: http://en.wikipedia.org/wiki/Battle_of_Talas.

5. Sophia's name, which translates "the Wisdom of the Ancient Word," bears this legacy.

6. K.S. Latourette, *A History of the Expansion of Christianity, Vol. VI "The Great Century, A.D. 1800 - A.D. 1914"* (London: Eyre & Spottiswoode, 1947), p. 53.

7. In the post-Communist era, Central Asia's leaders have been: 1) Azerbaijan: father and son presidents Heydar and Ilham Aliyev (1993-present); 2. Kazakhstan: Nazarbayev (1990-present); 3. Kyrgyzstan: a series of presidents and coups; 4. Turkmenistan: Niyazov was president for life (1990-2006); 5. Uzbekistan: Karimov (1990-present).

8. There were Turkic movements to Christ prior to Islam, but these were not among Muslim Turks. Both Nestorian and Orthodox Christian missionaries made inroads into Turkic peoples, such as the shamanist Naiman and Keiret tribes. The last of these Christian tribes were eliminated, however, during the reign of Tamerlane. See Samuel Moffett, *A History of Christianity in Asia, Vol. 1*, pp. 400-401.

9. "History of Germans in Russia, Ukraine and the Soviet Union," in *Wikipedia*. Cited 10 June 2013 at: http://en.wikipedia.org/wiki/History_of_Germans_in_Russia_Ukraine_and_the_Soviet_Union.

11. "Koryo-saram" in *Wikipedia*. Cited 11 June 2013 at en.wikipedia.org/wiki/Koryo-saram

10. "History of Germans in Russia, Ukraine and the Soviet Union," in *Wikipedia*. Cited 10 June 2013 at: http://en.wikipedia.org/wiki/History_of_Germans_in_Russia_Ukraine_and_the_Soviet_Union.

12. Rudyard Kipling coined "The Great Game" as the name for the contest between Russia and Britain in 19th-century Central Asia in his novel *Kim*. For a grand history of this period, see Peter Hopkirk's *The Great Game: The Struggle for Empire in Central Asia* (New York: Kodansha International, 1990).

Chapter 10: The West Africa Room

1. A frequent Muslim charge against Trinitarian Christians was that they worshiped three gods.

2. The 20th century West African nation of Ghana took its name from this ancient, and unrelated empire.

3. al Bakri in Nehemiah Levitzion and John Hopkins eds., *Corpus of Early Arabic Sources for West Africa* (Princeton: Marcus Wiener Press, 2000), p. 81, quoted in "Ghana Empire," in *Wikipedia* cited on the Internet 21 June 2013 at en.wikipedia.org/wiki/Ghana_Empre#cite_note-2.

4. Stride, G.T. & C. Ifeka, *Peoples and Empires of West Africa: West Africa in History 1000-1800.* (Edinburgh: Nelson), 1971. Cited in *Wikipedia* 8 July 2013 at: http://en.wikipedia.org/wiki/Mali_empire#cite_note-peoplesand-28.

5. "The Trans-Atlantic Slave Trade Database" cited on the Internet 21 June 2013 at www.slavevoyages.org/tast/index.faces and "Atlantic Slave Trade" *Wikipedia*, cited on the Internet 21 June 2013 at en.wikipedia.org/wiki/Atlantic_slave_trade#African_kingdoms_of_the_era.

6. Abolition was attained in large part to evangelical British and American abolitionists such as William Wilberforce.

7. Leopold ended up acquiring the Belgian Congo. The remarkable story of this great European land grab is well told in Thomas Pakenham's *The Scramble for Africa: The White Man's Conquest of the Dark Continent from 1876 to 1912* (New York: Random House, 1992).

8. A theory first proposed in 1993 by economists Richard Autry in *Sustaining Development in Mineral Econoies: The Resource Curse Thesis* (London: Routledge). For a discussion of the subject see: "Resource Curse" in *Wikipedia* cited 24 June 2013 at en.wikipedia/wiki/Resource_curse.

9. Bill Law, "Meeting the hard man of Liberia," 4 November 2006, cited on the Internet 24 June 2013 at news.bbc.co.uk/2/hi/programmes/from_our_own_correspondent/6113682.stm.

10. Alex Perry, "Global Justice: A Step Forward with the Conviction of Charles Taylor and Blood Diamonds," in *Time* magazine 26 April 2012. Cited 24 June 2013 at: world.time.com/2012/04/26/global-justice-a-step-forward-with-the-conviction-of-charles-taylor-and-blood-diamonds/.

11. The First Liberian Civil War was from 1989-1996 and the Second Liberian Civil War from 1999-2003. See "First Liberian Civil War" in *Wikipedia* cited 23 June 2013 at: en.wikipedia.org/wiki/First_Liberian_Civil_War#Impact.

12. The insanity was horrifically captured in the award-winning film by Sorious Samura, "Cry Freetown." Cited on the Internet 23 June 2013 at: www.youtube.com/watch?v=8WHl2UmJXYU.

13. The popular 2006 movie *Blood Diamond* provides one of the few Western glimpses into the turmoil and violence in Sierra Leone during those chaotic years.

14. At its greatest expanse, some time before 5000 B.C., the lake may have covered 150,000 square miles. See Michael T. Coe and Jonathan A. Foley, "Human and natural impacts on water resources of the Lake Chad Basin" in *Journal of Geophysical Research* 106 (D4): 3349-3356. Cited on the Internet 5 July 2013 at: https://en.wikipedia.org/wiki/Lake_Chad#CITEREFCoeFoley2001.

15. For a firsthand account of the contest between Christian belligerents in the South and these Islamic groups in the north, see Eliza Griswold's *The Tenth Parallel: Dispatches from the Fault Line between Christianity and Islam* (New York: Farrar, Straus and Giroux, 2010.)

16. For further study of Boko Haram, visit http://www.bbc.co.uk/news/world/africa/.

17. Guy Faulconbridge and Michael Holden, "British police ponder conspiracy after soldier murder," *Reuters U.S. Edition 23 May 2013*. Cited on the Internet 1 July 2013 at: http://www.reuters.com/article/2013/05/23/us-britain-killing-cameron-idUSBRE94L0WU20130523.

18. One of West Africa's more famous Muslim converts, Harvard professor Lamin Sanneh, has made this point a centerpiece of his testimony. See Lamin Sanneh, *Translating the Message: The Missionary Impact on Culture (American Society of Missiology)* Second Revised and Expanded Edition (Maryknoll: Orbis Books), 2009.

19. Tomi Oladipo, "Nigeria's growing 'prosperity' churches" *BBC News Africa*. Cited on the Internet 25 June 2013 at: www.bbc. co.uk/news/world-africa-14713151.

20. It is worth noting that, separation of religion and state, has allowed Muslim converts in this Room to be more welcomed into churches than in some other Rooms in the House of Islam.

21. Mogens Stensbaek Mogensen, *Contextual Communication of the Gospel to Pastoral Fulbe in Northern Nigeria*. A dissertation presented to the School of World Missions, Fuller Theological Seminary, January 2000.

Chapter 11: The Western South Asia Room

1. "Durand Line" in *Wikipedia* cited on the Internet 16 August 2013 at: http://en.wikipedia.org/wiki/Durand_Line.

2. Dominique LaPierre and Larry Collins, *Freedom at Midnight* (New Delhi: Vikas Publishing, 1997).

3. See LaPiere and Collins' chapter "The Greatest Migration in History," in *Freedom*, pp. 489-530.

4. "Narendra Modi's presence in social media soars 126% over six months: Blogworks report," in *The Economic Times*, 5 September 2013. Cited on the Internet 5 September 2013 at http:// economictimes.indiatimes.com/tech/internet/narendra-modis-presence-in-social-media-soars-126-over-six-months-blogworks-report/articleshow/22329287.cms.

5. See Matthew 13:33 where Jesus compares the kingdom of heaven to leaven or yeast in a lump of dough.

6. The Muslim movements to Christ in Western South Asia have been among the most difficult to assess, due to the extreme violence in the region. Christian missionaries who serve in the Room are divided as to the plausibility of such movements. The reader will have to decide for himself whether or not these movements exist.

7. *Hazrat*, meaning "His Presence" or "His Eminence" is a common Islamic term for Jesus and the prophets.

8. Nik Ripken, *The Insanity of God: A True Story of Faith Resurrected* (Nashville: B&H Publishing Group, 2012).

Chapter 12: The Arab Room

1. Chitra Kalyani, "Gospel joins *ansheed* (Islamic chanting) at Sufi Fest," Daily News Egypt, 17 August 2011. The Hymn "Amazing Grace" was written by John Newton (1779) and is in the public domain.

2. Philip Hitti, *History of the Arabs, 10ᵗʰ edition* (London: MacMillan Education Ltd., 14ᵗʰ reprint, 1991), p. 41.

3. Ibid., p. 4.

4. "List of languages by number of native speaker," cited on the Internet at *Wikipedia* 5 August 2013 at http://en.wikipedia/wiki/List_of_languages_by_number_of_native_speakers.

5. "Literacy and Adult Education in the Arab World," *UNESCO-Beirut Regional Report 2003*, cited on the Internet 5 August 2013 at: http://www.unesco.org/education/uie/pdf/country/arab_world.pdf., p. 11.

6. While Christians believe that the Bible can and should be translated into local languages, Muslims believe that the Qur'an is untranslatable and only accurate in the Arabic language. All translations of the Qur'an, therefore, are regarded as paraphrases, and are not readily accessible.

7. "The Arab American Institute | Arab Americans," AAIUSA. org. Archived from the original on 3 April 2010. Retrieved 2010-03-10 cited 5 August 2013 from *Wikipedia* at: http://en.wikipedia.org/wiki/Arab_people#Christianity.

8. Neighboring Abu Dhabi, for example, sits on a further 10 percent of the world's known oil reserves. See "Independent Statistics & Analysis" on the U.S. Energy Information Administration website. Cited on the Internet 26 August 2013 at: http://www.eia.gov/countries/index.cfm?view=reserves#allcountries.

9. See the discussion of "The Resource Curse" in chapter 10.

10. For an overview of the topic, see "Arab Spring: An interactive timeline of Middle East protests" on the website *theguardian.com*. Cited on the Internet 26 August 2013 at: http://www.theguardian.com/world/interactive/2011/mar/22/middle-east-protest-interactive-timeline.

11. Wyre Davies, "Tunisia one year on: New trends of self-immolations" on BBC-Africa cited on the Internet 5 August 2013 at http://www.bbc.co.uk/news/world-africa-16526462. 2012-01-12

12. Brian J. Grim, "Arab Spring Adds to Global Restrictions on Religion," in the *Pew Forum* study published June 2013. Cited on the Internet 26 August 2013 at: http://www.pewforum.org/2013/06/20/arab-spring-restrictions-on-religion-findings/.

13. Mindy Belz, "2008 Daniel of the Year," *World Magazine* Dec. 13, 2008). Cited on the Internet 7 August 2013 at: http://www.worldmag.com/2008/12/broadcast_news.

14. Raymond Ibrahim, "Islam's Public Enemy #1," in *National Review Online.* Cited on the Internet 7 August 2013 at www.NationalReview.com/articles/223965/islams-public-enemy-1/raymond-ibrahim.

15. As told to the author by an Egyptian Christian in August 2011.

16. Belz, *World Magazine,* "2008 Daniel."

17. Rachid is a popular Muslim-background Arab evangelist. See http://www.youtube.com/playlist?list=PL2B7DB420961DE413.

Chapter 13: Looking Back

1. The practice of shunning (a form of social execution common among the Puritans) those whose lives and thoughts strayed from acceptable norms of faith was echoed again and again in the interviews that arose from the nine Rooms in the House of Islam. In the more draconian responses of physical abuse, arrests, torture and execution, one has only to look at the Catholic Inquisitions of the Middle Ages to find parallel abuses of religious power.

Chapter 14: How & Why

1. In recent years, Christians have developed new and vital prayer resources for reaching Muslims, such as the *30 Days of Prayer for the Muslim World* and other prayer guides that have united the hearts of Christians with Muslim peoples who formerly were alien to them. See Paul Filidis, ed. *30 Days of Prayer for the Muslim World.* On the Internet at: www.30-days.net.

2. Bible storying is a means of communicating biblical truths with oral and non-literate learners. Rather than reading the Bible, these Bible story-ers relate the great themes of the Bible by telling the stories adapted from the Bible.

3. Such as *Any-3: Anyone, Anywhere, Any Time* and *The Camel: How Muslims Are Coming to Faith in Christ!* (both available on the Internet at www.ChurchPlantingMovements.com/bookstore cited on the Internet 11 July 2013,) and Muslim-worldview-sensitive Discovery Bible Study

outreach as described in Jerry Trousdale's *Miraculous Movements: How Hundreds of Thousands of Muslims Are Falling in Love with Jesus* (Nashville: Thomas Nelson, 2012).

4.   "I tell you the truth, anyone who will not receive the kingdom of God like a little child will never enter it." Luke 18:17

5.   It would have been logical and natural for the early church leaders to require the God-ordained-religious practices of Judaism to be mandatory for new Gentile believers, particularly such fundamental Jewish practices as circumcision, but they did not—and these early church leaders were Jews. We should keep this biblical milestone of the first Jerusalem Council in mind as we seek to communicate the gospel with Muslims.

6.   See Matthew 5:38-48.

7.   David Levering Lewis, *God's Crucible*, p. 76.

8.   Ibid., p. 78.

9.   Ibid., p. 81.

10.   Bernard Lewis, *Race and Slavery in the Middle East, An Historical Enquiry* (New York: Oxford University Press, 1990), p. 8.

Chapter 15: Our Response

1.   Arnold Toynbee made the point in his chapter on "Islam's Place in History," that "Muhammad yielded, in the thirteenth year of his ministry, to the temptation which, according to the Gospels, was resisted by Jesus at the beginning of His." It was in his 13th year, when Muhammad retreated to the city of Yathrib (Medina), that he transitioned from being a failed religious prophet to a successful political and military leader. Arnold Toynbee, *A Study of History, Reconsiderations, Vol. 12* (New York: Oxford University Press, 1964), p. 461.

2.   Stay abreast of best practices for reaching Muslims at the website www.WindintheHouse.org.

glossary

Ahl Al-Bayt - literally, in Arabic, "the family of the house;" it refers to Shi'ite Muslims, i.e. those who believe the leadership of the Muslim community should have remained with the family of the Prophet Muhammad, i.e. with his son-in-law, Ali.

Allah - the only word for God in Arabic, used in that language by Christians and Muslims alike. It refers to the creator of all things who revealed himself to Abraham, Moses and subsequent biblical figures.

ayatollah - literally "a sign of Allah." It refers to Islamic experts and leaders particularly in the Shi'ite tradition of Islam as found in Iran.

azan - from the Arabic adan, or time of prayer.

Dar al-Islam - literally, in Arabic, "the House of Islam," referring to all those who are Muslims.

Dar al-Harb - literally, in Arabic, "the House of War," referring to those lands and peoples where Islam is not yet dominant.

Druze - an 11th century offshoot of Islam regarded as heretical by orthodox Muslims. Numbering one to three million, most Druze today live in Syria, Israel and Jordan.

fatwa - formal legal opinion decreed by a mufti.

ghazi - a warrior; specifically one who has fought against the infidel, faced death and lived. Highly regarded veteran, revered as a living martyr.

Hadith - the sayings and traditions from the life of the Prophet Muhammad.

hafez - literally, in Arabic, "keeper. A hafez is one who has memorized (i.e. kept in his heart) the Qur'an.

hajj - the pilgrimage to Mecca, required of Muslims at least once in their lifetime.

Hazrat - of Arabic derivation literally meaning "Presence." Hazrat is a term of respect, such as the equivalent "Your eminence" or "Your honor" in English.

imam - literally, in Arabic, "the one in front." It refers to the the preacher and leader of prayers in the mosque.

Injil - the Gospels, or more generally the New Testament, but especially the books about Jesus.

Isa - the Arabic name for Jesus. Also spelled 'Isa and Aisa.

Isai - a follower of Jesus. Literally "one who belongs to Jesus."

jamaat - in Arabic, literally "a group or gathering". It can refer to a religious gathering such as a church or a community of believers of any type.

jihad - literally "struggle" in Arabic. It often refers to the struggle to advance Islam.

jihadi - one who conducts jihad. See also mujahid or mujahedeen (plural).

kafir - in Islam, a designation for an unbeliever, generally not a Christian or Jew, but a pagan. However, in general use it may refer derogatorily to anyone who is not an orthodox Muslim.

Kalam - literally, in Arabic, "word." It is used to refer to the Bible in parts of the Muslim world.

Khoda - a term of Persian Zoroastrian origin used to refer to God by Christians and Muslims alike in much of the Turkish, Persian and South Asian parts of the world.

Kitab al-Moqadis - in Arabic, literally the "Holy Book," a term used by Arabs and Christians to refer to the Bible.

madrasa - an Islamic school where the Qur'an and Hadith are taught. Other subjects may also be taught, but not necessarily.

masjid/mesjid - a word of Arabic derivation for the mosque. It means gathering or community.

al-Masih - literally "the Messiah." A title used in the Qur'an for Jesus.

mawlana - literally, "our master," refers generally to a religious scholar and authority, especially in South Asia.

mazar - a Sufi shrine, often a place where a Sufi preacher or saint from the past is buried. It becomes a place of veneration for Sufi pilgrims.

minaret - literally, in Arabic, "a lighthouse." It refers to the tall towers of the mosque from which the muezzin issues the call to prayer.

muezzin - one of makes the call to prayer (see "azan").

mujahid (plural mujahedeen) - an Islamic warrior engaged in jihad.

mufti - Islamic scholar and leader capable of adjudicating for the community and decreeing fatwas or formal legal opinions

mullah/mulvi - an Islamic scholar, particularly in Central Asia and Western South Asia

namaz - a term referring to one of the five daily Islamic prayers

pak - true or good, a term commonly used in South Asia.

pir - a title of Persian derivation referring to a living saint in the Sufi tradition.

rab - an Arabic word meaning "lord."

sahih - literally, in Arabic, "authentic" or "right and proper."

saidna - literally "our master." A term of respect used in much of the Muslim world for Jesus.

sardar - in Western South Asia a village chief.

salafi - literally "ancestors." A fundamentalist reform movement within Islam.

salam aleikum - literally "peace be upon you (pl.)". A common greeting in the Muslim world.

salat - prayer, generally refers to one of the five daily Muslim prayers, but can simply mean "prayer."

shahada - the Muslim confession: "There is no god but Allah, and Muhammad is his prophet." All Muslims make this confession.

shalwar kameez - loose-fitting clothing commonly worn in Western South Asia.

sharia - literally, in Arabic, "way," generally used to designate Islamic law, or the Islamic way of doing things.

sheikh - an honorific title in Arabic meaning "elder."

Shi'a - literally "partisans of Ali." Refers to the 10% of Muslims, most of whom are in Iran, who split with Sunni Muslims over the leadership role of Ali, the martyred son-in-law and cousin of the Prophet Muhammad.

Sufi - a major mystical stream within Islam aimed at experiencing Allah through mystical communion. Regarded as marginal or unorthodox by Sunni Muslim conservatives.

Sunni - literally "straight." Refers to the 90% of Muslims who adhere to the straight or orthodox teachings of Islam.

tablighi - a band of Islamic preachers who travel from place to place encouraging and exhorting the faithful.

ulama - the community of Islamic scholars. Singular - alim, an Islamic
scholar.

Wahhabi - a fundamentalist reform movement within Islam originating
in the 18th century in what is today Saudi Arabia.

bibliography

Part One: The Hinges of History

Barrett, David., ed. *World Christian Encyclopedia, Second Edition, Two Volumes*. New York: Oxford Press, 2002.

George, Timothy. *Is the Father of Jesus the God of Muhammad?* Grand Rapids: Zondervan, 2002.

Greenham, Ant. *Muslim Conversions to Christ, An Investigation of Palestinian Converts Living in the Holy Land*. Pasadena, CA: WCIU Press, 2004.

Greenlee, David, ed. *Longing for Community: Church, Umma or Somewhere in Between*. Pasadena: WCIU Press, 2013.

Hinnebesch, J.F. "William of Tripoli," in *New Catholic Encyclopedia, 2nd edition, Vol. 14*. Detroit: Gale, 2003.

Humphreys, R. Stephen. *Islamic History: A Framework for Inquiry*. London: Princeton University Press, 1991.

Jenkins, Philip. *The Lost History of Christianity, The Thousand-Year Golden Age of the Church in the Middle East, Africa and Asia—and How It Died*. New York: Harper One, 2008.

Latourette, Kenneth Scott. *A History of the Expansion of Christianity, Seven Volumes*. London: Eyre & Spottiswoode, 1939.

Moreau, Scott. *Contextualization in World Missions, Mapping and Assessing Evangelical Models*. Grand Rapids: Kregel Publications, 2012.

O'Kane, M. "Raymond of Peñafort" in *The Catholic Encyclopedia*. New York: Robert Appleton Company, 1911. Accessed on the Internet 28 November 2012 at: http://www.newadvent.org/cathen/12671c.htm.

O'Meara, Thomas F. "The Theology and Times of William of Tripoli, O.P.: A Different View of Islam" in *Theological Studies*, Vol. 69, No. 1.

Parshall, Phil. "Danger! New Directions in Contextualization" in *Evangelical Missions Quarterly*, October 1998. Cited on the Internet 7 August 2013 at: http://www.emisdirect.com/emq/issue-230/1243.

Pew Forum on Religion & Public Life. *The Future of the Global Muslim Population, Projections for 2010-2030*. Washington, D.C.: Pew Research Center, 2011.

Schmidlin, Joseph. *Catholic Mission History*. Techny, IL: Mission Press S.V.D., 1933.

Travis, John. "The C1-C6 Spectrum" in *Evangelical Missions Quarterly*, October 1998. Cited on the Internet 7 August 2013 at: http://www.emisdirect.com/emq/issue-230/2488.

Volf, Miroslav. *Allah, A Christian Response*. New York: HarperCollins, 2011.

Vose, Robin. *Dominicans, Muslims and Jews in the Medieval Crown of Aragon*. New York: Cambridge University Press, 2009.

Woodberry, Dudley, Shubin, Russell G., and G. Marks. "Why Muslims Follow Jesus" in *Christianity Today*, October 2011. Cited on the Internet at 7 August 2013 at: http://www.christianitytoday.com/ct/2007/october/42.80.html.

Part Two: The House of Islam

Chapter 4: The Indo-Malaysian Room

Cooley, Frank. *Indonesia: Church and Society.* New York: Friendship Press, 1968.

_____. New York: National Council of Churches, 1982.

Dixon, Roger L. "The Major Model of Muslim Ministry" in *Missiology: An International Review*, Vol. XXX, No. 4. October 2002.

Geertz, Clifford. *The Religion of Java.* Chicago: University of Chicago Press, 1976.

Hefner, Robert W. *Conversion to Christianity: Historical and Anthropological Perspectives on a Great Transformation*. Berkeley: University of California Press, 1993.

Partonadi, Sutarman. *Sadrach's Community and its Contextual Roots, A Nineteenth Century Javanese Expression of Christianity.* Amsterdam: Rodopi, 1990.

Rutgers, Jacqueline C. *Islam en Christendom*. The Hague: Boekhandel van den Zendingsstudie Raad, 1912.

Shipman, Mike. *Any-3: Anyone, Anywhere, Any Time*. Richmond, VA: WIGTake Resources, 2012.

Willis, Avery T. *Indonesian Revival: Why Two Million Came to Christ*. Pasadena: William Carey Library, 1977.

Chapter 5: The East Africa Room

Baker, Heidi and Rolland. *Learning to Love: Passion, Compassion and the Essence of the Gospel*. Minneapolis: Chosen, 2013.

Balisky, Paul. "Dictionary of African Christian Biography, Shaikh Zakaryas 1845 to 1920 Independent Prophet Ethiopia." Accessed on the Internet 8 August 2013 at www.dacb.org/stories/ethiopia/zakaryas2.html.

Isichei, Elizabeth. *A History of Christianity in Africa, From Antiquity to the Present*. Grand Rapids, MI: William B. Eerdmans, 1995.

Moorehead, Alan. *The Blue Nile*. New York, NY: Harper & Row, 1962.

Ripken, Nik. *The Insanity of God: A True Story of Faith Resurrected*. Nashville: B&H Publishing, 2013.

Yesehaq, Archbishop. *The Ethiopian Tewahedo Church, An Integrally African Church*. Nashville, TN: James C. Winston Publishing Co., 1997.

Chapter 6: The North Africa Room

Brett, Michael and Fentress, Elizabeth. *The Berbers*. Oxford: Blackwell Publishers, 1996.

Daniel, Robin. *This Holy Seed: Faith, Hope and Love in the Early Churches of North Africa*. Chester, UK: Tamarisk Publications, 1993.

Davis Robert C. *Christian Slaves, Muslim Masters, White Slavery in the Mediterranean, the Barbary Coast, and Italy, 1500-1800*. New York: Palgrave MacMillan, 2003.

Direche-Slimani, Karima. *Chretiens De Kabylie, 1873-1954, une action missionnaire dans l'Algerie coloniale*. A dissertation published by EDIF 2000, 2004.

Slack, James and Shehane, Robert, eds. "Public Edition of the Church Planting Movement Assessment of an Indigenous People Group on the Mediterranean Rim." Richmond, VA: Global Research Department of the International Mission Board, SBC, 2003.

Chapter 7: The Eastern South Asia Room

Bass, Gary J. *The Blood Telegram: Nixon, Kissinger, and a Forgotten Genocide*. New York: Alfred A. Knopf, 2013.

Bose, Sarmila. *Dead Reckoning: Memories of the 1971 Bangladesh War.* New York: Columbia University Press, 2011.

Carey, S. Pearce. *William Carey, The Father of Modern Missions.* London: The Wakeman Trust, 1923.

Greeson, Kevin. *The Camel, How Muslims Are Coming to Faith in Christ! Revised Edition,* Richmond, VA: WIGTake Resources, 2007.

Novak, James K. *Bangladesh: Reflections on the Water.* Bloomington: Indiana University Press, 1993.

Chapter 8: The Persian Room

Bradley, Mark. *Iran and Christianity, Historical Identity and Present Relevance.* London: Continuum International Publishing Group, 2008.

Buck, Christopher. "The Universality of the Church in the East" in *Journal of the Assyrian Academic Society,* X, 1, 1996.

Bulliet, Richard. *Conversion to Islam in the Medieval Period: An Essay in Quantitative History,* 1979.

Carrington, William J. and Detragiache, Enrica. "How Extensive Is the Brain Drain?" Accessed on the Internet 1 April 2013 at: www. imf.org/external/pubs/ft/fandd/1999/06/carringt.htm#chart.

Chisholm, Hugh, ed. *Encyclopedia Britannica, 11th ed.,* New York: Cambridge University Press, 1911.

Jenkins, Philip. *Jesus Wars, How Four Patriarchs, Three Queens, and Two Emperors Decided What Christians Would Believe for the Next 1,500 Years.* New York: Harper Collins, 2010.

Moffett, Samuel. *A History of Christianity in Asia, Volume 1: Beginnings to 1500.* Maryknoll, NY: Orbis Press, 1998.

Pew Forum. "Mapping the Global Muslim Population," Accessed from the Internet 29 April 2013 at www.pewforum.org/Muslim/ Mapping-the-Global-Muslim-Population(6).aspx.

Tavassoli, Sasan. *Christian Encounters with Iran, Engaging Muslim Thinkers After the Revolution.* London: I.B. Tauris and Co., Ltd., 2011.

"United Presbyterian Church in the U.S.A. Commission on Ecumenical Mission and Relations." Accessed on the Internt 16 March 2012 at: http://www.history.pcusa.org/collections/findingaids/ fa.cfm?record_id=91.

Chapter 9: The Turkestan Room

Benningsen, Alexander and Wimbush, S. Enders. *Muslims of the Soviet Empire: A Guide.* Bloomington: Indiana University Press, 1986.

Dalrymple, William. *From the Holy Mountain, A Journey in the Shadow of*

Byzantium. New Delhi, India: Penguin Books, 2004.

Groussett, Rene. *The Empire of the Steppes: A History of Central Asia.* Translated by Naomi Walford. Rutgers, NJ: The State University of New Jersey, 2002.

Hopkirk, Peter. *The Great Game: The Struggle for Empire in Central Asia.* New York: Kodansha International, 1990.

Hostler, Charles Warren. *The Turks of Central Asia.* Westport, CT: Praeger Publishers, 1993.

Kinross, Lord. *The Ottoman Centuries, The Rise and Fall of the Turkish Empire.* New York, NY: Morrow Quill Paperbacks, 1979.

Kipling, Rudyard. *Kim.* London: MacMillan and Co., Ltd., 1901.

White, Matthew. *Atrocitology: Humanity's 100 Deadliest Achievements.* Edinburgh: Canangate Books, 2011.

Chapter 10: The West Africa Room

Autry, Richard. *Sustaining Development in Mineral Economies: The Resource Curse Thesis.* London: Routledge, 1993.

Faulconbridge, Guy and Holden, Michael. "British police ponder conspiracy after soldier murder," *Reuters U.S. Edition 23 May 2013.* Accessed on the Internet 1 July 2013 at: http://www.reuters.com/article/2013/05/23/us-britain-killing-cameron-idUSBRE94L0WU20130523.

Griswold, Eliza. *The Tenth Parallel: Dispatches from the Fault Line Between Christianity and Islam.* New York: Farrar, Straus and Giroux, 2010.

Law, Bill. "Meeting the hard man of Liberia" in *BBC News-Africa, 4 November 2006.* Accessed on the Internet 24 June 2013 at: news.bbc.co.uk/2/hi/programmes/from_our_own_correspondent/6113682.stm.

Levitzion, Nehemiah and Hopkins, John, eds. *Corpus of Early Arabic Sources for West Africa.* Princeton: Marcus Wiener Press, 2000.

Mogensen, Mogens Stensbaek. *Contextual Communication of the Gospel to Pastoral Fulbe in Northern Nigeria.* A Dissertation presented to the School of World Missions, Fuller Theological Seminary, January 2000.

Oladipo, Tomi. "Nigeria's growing 'prosperity' churches" in *BBC News-Africa.* Accessed on the Internet 25 June 2013 at: www.bbc.co.uk/news/world-africa-14713151.

Pakenham, Thomas. *The Scramble for Africa: White Man's Conquest of the Dark Continent, 1876-1912.* New York: Avon Books, 1991.

Perry, Alex. "Global Justice: A Step Forward with the Conviction of Charles Taylor and Blood Diamonds" in *Time* magazine, 26 April 2012. Accessed on the Internet 24 June 2013 at: world. time.com/2012/04/26/global-justice-a-step-forward-with-the-conviction-of-charles-taylor-and-blood-diamonds/.

Samura, Sorious. "Cry Freetown." Accessed on the Internet 23 June 2013 at: www.youtube.com/watch?v=8WHl2UmJXYU.

Sanneh, Lamin. *Translating the Message: The Missionary Impact on Culture. American Society of Missiology, Second Revised and Expanded Edition*. Maryknoll, NY: Orbis Books, 2009.

Stride, G.T. and Ifeka, C., eds. *Peoples and Empires of West Africa: West Africa in History 1000-1800*. Edinburgh: Nelson, 1971.

"The Trans-Atlantic Slave Trade Database." Accessed from the Internet 21 June 2013 at: www.slavevoyages.org/tast/index.faces.

Trousdale, Jerry. *Miraculous Movements: How Hundreds of Thousands of Muslims Are Falling in Love With Jesus*. Nashville, TN: Thomas Nelson, 2012.

Chapter 11: The Western South Asia Room
Coll, Steve. *Ghost Wars, The Secret History of the CIA, Afghanistan and Bin Laden, From the Soviet Invasion to September 10, 2001*. London: Penguin Books, 2004.

Dehart, Joel. *The Upper Hand, God's Sovereignty in Afghan Captivity.* Self-published, 1994.

Hosseini, Khaled. *The Kite Runner.* New York, NY: Riverhead Books, 2004.

_____. *A Thousand Splendid Suns*. New York, NY: Riverhead Books, 2007.

LaPierre, Dominique and Collins, Larry. *Freedom at Midnight*. New Delhi: Vikas Publishing, 1997.

Rashid, Ahmed. *Descent into Chaos: The U.S. and the Disaster in Pakistan, Afghanistan, and Central Asia*. New York: Penguin Group, 2009.

Ripken, Nik. *The Insanity of God: A True Story of Faith Resurrected*. Nashville: B&H Publishing, 2013.

Salzman, Philip Carl. *Black Tents of Baluchistan*. Washington: Smithsonian Institution Press, 2000.

Chapter 12: The Arab Room
"Arab Americans" at *The Arab American Institute*. Accessed on the Internet 5 August 2013 at: www.AAIUSA.org.

Belz, Mindy. "2008 Daniel of the Year" in *World Magazine, Dec. 13, 2008*. Accessed from the Internet 7 August 2013 at: http://www.worldmag.com/2008/12/broadcast_news.

Chandler, Paul-Gordon. *Pilgrims of Christ on the Muslim Road: Exploring a New Path Between Faiths*. Plymouth, U.K.: Cowley Publications, 2007.

Cragg, Kenneth. *The Arab Christian, A History in the Middle East*. Louisville, KY: Westminster/John Knox Press, 1991.

Davies, Wyre. "Tunisia one year on: New trends of self-immolations" on *BBC World-Africa* cited on the Internet 5 August 2013 at http://www.bbc.co.uk/news/world-africa-16526462. 2012-01-12.

Hitti, Philip. *History of the Arabs, 10th edition*. London: MacMillan Education Ltd., 14th reprint, 1991.

Ibrahim, Raymond. "Islam's Public Enemy # 1" in *National Review Online*. Accessed from the Internet 7 August 2013 at www.NationalReview.com/articles/223965/islams-public-enemy-1/raymond-ibrahim.

Jenkins, Philip. *The Lost History of Christianity: The Thousand-Year Golden Age of the Church in the Middle East, Africa, and Asia -- and How It Died*. New York: HarperCollins, 2008.

Kalyani, Chitra. "Gospel joins *ansheed* (Islamic chanting) at Sufi Fest," Daily News Egypt, 17 August 2011.

"Literacy and Adult Education in the Arab World" *UNESCO-Beirut Regional Report 2003*. Accessed from the Internet 5 August 2013 at: http://www.unesco.org/education/uie/pdf/country/arab_world.pdf., p. 11.

Yapp, M.E. *The Making of the Modern Near East, 1792-1923*. New York: Longman House, 1987.

_____ *the Near East Since the First World War*. New York: Longman House, 1991.

Part Three: In the House of War

Abdelhady, Dalia. *The Lebanese Diaspora, The Arab Immigrant Experience in Montreal, New York, and Paris*. New York: New York University Press, 2011.

Haddad, Yvonne Yazbeck. *The Muslims of America*. New York: Oxford University Press, 1991.

Jenkins, Philip. *God's Continent, Christianity, Islam, and Europe's Religious Crisis*. New York, NY: Oxford University Press, 2007.

Additional Reading on Islam

Ali, Abdullah Yusuf. *The Holy Qur'an, English Translation of the Meanings of the Qur'an with Notes.* Indianapolis, IN: H&C International, 1992.

Brown, Jonathan A.C. *Hadith, Muhammad's Legacy in the Medieval and Modern World.* Oxford, UK: OneWorld Publications, 2009.

Farah, Caesar E. *Islam, Fifth Edition.* Hauppauge, NY: Barron's Educational Series, 1994.

George, Timothy. *Is the Father of Jesus the God of Muhammad?* Grand Rapids, MI: Zondervan, 2002.

Glasse, Cyril. *The Concise Encyclopedia of Islam.* San Francisco: HarperCollins, 1989.

Goddard, Hugh. *A History of Christian-Muslim Relations.* Chicago, IL: New Amsterdam Books, 2000.

Grim, Brian, ed. *The Future of the Global Muslim Population, Projections for 2010-2030.* Washington, D.C.: Pew Research Center, 2011.

Humphreys, R. Stephen. *Islamic History, A Framework for Inquiry, revised edition.* Cairo, EG: AUC Press, 1992.

Lings, Martin. *Muhammed, His Life Based on the Earliest Sources.* Rochester, VT: Inner Traditions, 2006.

Lippman, Thomas W. *Understanding Islam, An Introduction to the Muslim World, Revised Edition.* New York: Mentor Book, 1990.

Moffett, Samuel H. *A History of Christianity in Asia, Vol. 1: Beginnings to 1500.* Maryknoll, NY: Orbis Books, 1998.

_____. *A History of Christianity in Asia, Vol. 2: 1500 - 1900.* Maryknoll, NY: Orbis Books, 2005.

Netton, Ian Richard. *A Popular Dictionary of Islam.* London: Curzon Press, 1992.

Rahman, Fazlur. *Islam, Second Edition.* Chicago: University of Chicago Press, 1979.

Sivan, Emmanuel. *Radical Islam, Medieval Theology and Modern Politics.* Binghamton, NY: Yale University Press, 1985.

Weekes, Richard V. ed. *Muslim Peoples, A World Ethnographic Survey, 2 Volumes, Second Edition.* Westport, CT: Greenwood Press, 1984.

On Ministry to Muslims

Brown, Brian Arthur. *Noah's Other Son, Bridging the Gap Between the Bible and the Qur'an.* New York: Continuum, 2007.

El Schafi, Abd. *Behind the Veil, Unmasking Islam.* No publication information, 1996.

Garrison, David. *The Camel Rider's Journal*. Arkadelphia, AR: WIGTake Resources, 2009.

Greeson, Kevin. *The Camel, How Muslims Are Coming to Faith in Christ!* Revised Edition. Monument, CO: WIGTake Resources, 2011.

Jabbour, Nabeel T. *The Crescent Through the Eyes of the Cross, Insights from an Arab Christian*. Colorado Springs, CO: NavPress, 2008.

_____. *Unshackled & Growing, Muslims and Christians on the Journey to Freedom*. Colorado Springs, CO: Dawsonmedia, 2006.

Kronk, Rick. *Dreams and Visions, Muslims' Miraculous Journeys to Jesus*. Pescara, Italy: Destiny Image Europe, Ltd., 2010.

Livingstone, Greg. *Planting Churches in Muslim Cities*. Grand Rapids, MI: Baker Books, 1993.

McCurry, Don. *Healing the Broken Family of Abraham: New Life for Muslims*. Colorado Springs, CO: Ministry to Muslims, 2001.

Medearis, Carl. *Muslims, Christians, and Jesus, Gaining Understanding and Building Relationships*. Bloomington, MN: Bethany House Publishers, 2008.

Martin, E.J., ed. *Where There Was No Church, Postcards from Followers of Jesus in the Muslim World*. San Francisco, CA: Learning Together Press, 2010.

Musk, Bill. *The Unseen Face of Islam, Sharing the Gospel with Ordinary Muslims*. Monrovia, CA: MARC, 1989.

_____. *Touching the Soul of Islam, Sharing the Gospel in Muslim Cultures*. Monrovia, CA: MARC, 1995.

Parshall, Phil. *Muslim Evangelism, Contemporary Approaches to Contextualization, second edition*. Colorado Springs, CO: 2003.

Register, Ray. *Back to Jerusalem, Church Planting Movements in the Holy Land*. Enumclaw, WA: Winepress Publishing, 2000.

Swartley, Keith E., ed. *Encountering the World of Islam*. Littleton, CO: Biblica, 2005.

Tanagho, Samy. *Glad News! God Loves You My Muslim Friend*. Littleton, CO: Biblica, 2004.

Woodberry, J. Dudley. *From Seed to Fruit, Global Trends, Fruitful Practices, and Emerging Issues Among Muslims*. Pasadena, CA: William Carey Library, 2008.

_____, ed., *Muslims & Christians on the Emmaus Road*. Monrovia: MARC, 1989.

Muslim-Christian Polemics, Apologetics, Relations

Chandler, Paul-Gordon. *Pilgrims of Christ on the Muslim Road, Exploring a New Path Between Two Faiths*. Lanham, MD: Cowley Publications, 2007.

Darwish, Nonie. *Cruel and Usual Punishment, The terrifying global implications of Islamic Law*. Nashville: Thomas Nelson, 2008.

Fletcher, Richard. *The Cross and the Crescent, The Dramatic Story of the Earliest Encounters Between Christians and Muslims*. London, UK: Penguin Books, 2005.

Geisler, Norman L. and Saleeb, Abdul. *Answering Islam, The Crescent in Light of the Cross*. Grand Rapids, MI: Baker Books, 2002.

Griswold, Eliza. *The Tenth Parallel, Dispatches From the Fault Line Between Christianity and Islam*. New York, NY: Farrar, Straus & Giroux, 2010.

Jamieson, Alan G. *Faith and Sword, A Short History of Christian-Muslim Conflicts*. London: Reaktion Books, 2006.

Khalidi, Tarif, ed. *The Muslim Jesus, Sayings and Stories in Islamic Literature*. Cambridge, MA: Harvard Univ. Press, 2001.

Lewis, David Levering Lewis. *God's Crucible, Islam and the Making of Europe, 570-1215*. New York: Norton, 2008.

Lingel, Joshua, Morton, Jeff, and Nikides, Bill, eds. *Chrislam, How Missionaries are Promoting an Islamized Gospel*. Garden Grove, CA: i2 Ministries, 2011.

Parrinder, Geoffrey. *Jesus in the Qur'an* reprinted. Oxford, UK: OneWorld Publications, 1996.

Spencer, Robert. *Islam Unveiled, Disturbing Questions About the World's Fastest-Growing Faith*. New York, NY: Encounter Books, 2002.

Warraq, Ibn. *Why I Am Not a Muslim*. Amherst, NY: Prometheus Books, 1995.

illustration sources

Chapter 1: Something is Happening

John Tzimisces, ca. 925-976 (public domain). Painting by Klavdly Lebedev (c. 1880). Cited on the Internet 28 September 2013 at: http://en.wikipedia.org/wiki/File:Lebedev_Svyatoslavs_meeting_with_Emperor_John.jpg.

Roger II, (Creative Commons Attribution). Author: Matthias Süssen; Uploaded 21 May 2007 as "Roger II, wird von Christus gekrönt, Mosaik in La Martorana." Cited on the Internet 29 September 2013 at: http://en.wikipedia.org/wiki/File:Martorana_RogerII2008.jpg.

St. Francis of Assisi (public domain). Painting by José de Ribera (c. 1642). Cited on the Internet 29 September 2013 at: http://en.wikipedia.org/wiki/File:Saint_Francis_of_Assisi_by_Jusepe_de_Ribera.jpg.

St. Dominic (public domain). Painting by Fra Angelico, 1437. Cited on the Internet 29 September 2013 at: http://en.wikipedia.org/wiki/File:The_Perugia_Altarpiece,_Side_Panel_Depicting_St._Dominic.jpg.

Raymond of Peñafort (public domain, permission: PD-ART0. Painting by Tommaso da Modena (1352). Cited on the Internet 29 September 2013 at: http://en.wikipedia.org/wiki/File:Raymon_de_Peñaforte.jpg.

Ramon Llull (public domain US-PD). Source: Scientific Identity, (26 March 1315. Cited on the Internet 29 September 2013 at: http://en.wikipedia.org/wiki/File:Ramon_Llull.jpg.

Charles Lavigerie (public domain, PD-US). Source: NYPL; author: Albert Capelle, Paris; dated 1882. Cited on the Internet 29 September 2013 at: http://en.wikipedia.org/wiki/File:Charles_Lavigerie.jpg.

Chapter 4: The Indo-Malaysia Room

Sadrach Radin Surapranata - Cited on the Internet website: "Guru Sadrach" by Pendopo Deso. Cited the Internet on 25 September 2013 at: http://karangyoso.blogspot.com/2008/12/kyai-sadrach.html.

Sadrach's Trinity Mesjid - Posted on the Internet website "Guru Sadrach" by Pendopo Deso. Cited on the Internet 25 September 2013 at: http://www.blogger.com/profile/00848009008984057574.

Dutch East India Company Logo (public domain) Posted on the Internet by Golradir at: http://en.wikipedia.org/wiki/File:VOC.svg.

President Sukarno (public domain) Posted on the Internet by Government of Indonesia at: http://en.wikipedia.org/wiki/File: Presiden_Sukarno.jpg.

President Suharto (public domain) Posted on the Internet by State Secretariat of the Republic of Indonesia at: http://en.wikipedia.org/ wiki/File:President_Suharto,_1993.jpg.

Any-3 Book Used by permission of WIGTake Resources. Available on the Internet at: www.ChurchPlantingMovements.com/bookstore.

Chapter 5: The East Africa Room

San Tribesman (creative commons attribution) Posted on the Internet by the author Ian Beatty. Cited on the Internet 25 September 2013 at: http://en.wikipedia.org/wiki/File:San_tribesman.jpg.

Ivory Trade (public domain) Posted on the Internet by Frank G. and Frances Carpenter. Cited on the Internet 25 September 2013 at: http://en.wikipedia.org/wiki/File:Ivory_trade.jpg.

Fort Jesus; Description: Hrvatski: Vlasnistvo (Wikimedia Commons; Creative Commons Attribution-Share Alike 3.0 Unported license) Uploaded by Zeljko 11 August 2007. Cited on the Internet 26 August 2013 at: http://en.wikipedia.org/wiki/File:Fort_JesusMombasa.jpg.

Open Qur'an (creative commons attribution). Posted on the Internet by el7bara. Cited on the Internet 25 September 2013 at: http://commons. wikimedia.org/wiki/File:Opened_Qur%27an.jpg.

Chapter 6: The North Africa Room

Good Shepherd - Author's photo of a painting by Del Parson (b. 1948).

Barbarossa (public domain) Lithograph by Charles Motte (1785-1836). Source unknown. Cited on the Internet 25 September 2013 at: http://en.wikipedia.org/wiki/File:Arudsch-barbarossa.jpg.

Berber Mosaic (creative commons) Posted by on the Internet by Dzilinker. Cited on the Internet 25 September 2013 at: http:// en.wikipedia.org/wiki/File:Berbers_Mosaic.jpg.

St. Augustine (public domain). Painting by Carlo Crivelli (1487/88?). Cited on the Internet 25 September 2013 at: http://en.wikipedia.org/wiki/File:Carlo_Crivelli_-_St._Augustine_ -_Google_Art_Project.jpg.

Chapter 7: The Eastern South Asia Room

William Carey (public domain). William Carey: The Shoemaker Who Became the Founder of Modern Missions. Author unknown. Cited on the Internet 26 September 2013 at: http://en.wikipedia.org/ wiki/File:CareyEngraving.jpg.

West and East Pakistan (public domain). Cited on the Internet 26 September 2013 at: http://commons.wikimedia.org/wiki/File:Partition_ of_India.PNG.

W. and E. Pakistan (1947-1971) (public domain). Adapted from a map authored by Green Giant. Cited on the Internet 26 September 2013 at: http://commons.wikimedia.org/wiki/File:Historical_Pakistan.gif.

Tablighi Jamaat; Description: Malaysia Jamaat Tablighee Ijtima' (Wikimedia Commons) Author: Aswami Yusuf 8 September 2009. Original uploader was Muhammad Hamza. Cited on the Internet 26 September 2013 at: http://en.wikipedia.org/wiki/File:2009_Malaysian_Tablighi_Ijtema.jpg.

A Crowded Room; Description: Tablighi Jamaat (Wikimedia Commons) Uploaded by Muntasirmamunimran 24 January 2010 as "Biswa Ijtema Dhaka Bangladesh" by Cited on the Internet 26 September 2013 at: http://upload.wikimedia.org/wikipedia/commons/8/81/Biswa_ Ijtema_Dhaka_Bangladesh.jpg.

Chapter 8: The Persian Room

Armenian Cross (Wikimedia Commons). Uploaded by Vigen Hakhverdyan as "Kachqar, Armenia". Cited on the Internet 26 September 2013 at: http://en.wikipedia.org/wiki/File:Khachqar10.jpg.

Haik Hovsepian Mehr. Cited on the Internet 26 September 2013 at: http://www.elam.com/articles/Remember-Their-Sacrifice/.

Mehdi Dibaj. Cited on the Internet 26 September 2013. at: http:// www.elam.com/articles/Remember-Their-Sacrifice/.

Henry Martyn (Wikimedia Commons). From "A memoir of the Rev. Henry Martyn"; Sargent, John; London : Printed for R. B. Seeley and W. Burnside : and sold by L. and G. Seeley; 1837. Cited on the Internet 26 September 2013 at: http://en.wikipedia.org/wiki/ File:Henry_Martyn.jpg.

Chapter 9: The Turkestan Room

Tamerlane (public domain). Author: Nezivesten. Source: Pugachenkova GA, LI Rempel History of Arts of Uzbekistan from the earliest times to the middle of the XIX century. M., 1965. Cited on the Internet 26 September 2013 at: http://en.wikipedia.org/wiki/File:Tamerlan.jpg.

Suleiman the Magnificent (public domain). Painting by Hans Eworth (1520-1574?). Cited on the Internet 26 September 2013 at: http://en.wikipedia.org/wiki/File:Hans_Eworth_Osmanischer_Wurdentrager_zu_Pferd.jpg.

Joseph Stalin (public domain). Source: U.S. Signal Corps photo. Cited on the Internet 26 September 2013 at: http://en.wikipedia.org/wiki/File:CroppedStalin1943.jpg.

Catherine the Great (public domain). Painting "Portrait of Catherine II of Russia (1729-1796)" by Johann Baptist von Lampi the Elder (1751-1830). Cited on the Internet at: http://en.wikipedia.org/wiki/File:Johann-Baptist_Lampi_d._Ä._007.jpg.

Gur-e Emir Tomb (Creative Commons Attribution).Uploaded by Faqsci 15 April 2012. Cited on the Internet at: http://commons.wikimedia.org/wiki/File:Gur-e_Amir_-_Inside_views_995_Tombs.jpg.

Chapter 10: The West Africa Room

Human Trafficking; Description: Am I Not A Man? (public domain). Source: British Abolition Movement, 1795. Cited on the Internet 26 September 2013 at: http://en.wikipedia.org/wiki/File:BLAKE10.jpg.

Samuel Doe (public domain). Uploaded by Frank Hall 18 August 1982. Cited on the Internet 26 September 2013 at: http://en.wikipedia.org/wiki/File:Samuel_Kanyon_Doe.jpg.

Ahmed Tejan Kabbah (public domain). Uploaded by Kari Barber, VOA 18 September 2007. Cited on the Internet 26 September 2013 at: http://en.wikipedia.org/wiki/File:Ahmed_Tejan_Kabbah.jpg.

Marabout holy man (public domain). Uploaded by Peter Kremer 26 January 2007. Cited on the Internet 26 September 2013 at: http://en.wikipedia.org/wiki/File:Kuntamarabut.jpg.

Chapter 11: The Western South Asia Room

Mortimer Durand, 1903 (public domain). Permission PD-US. Cited on the Internet 27 September 2013 at: http://en.wikipedia.org/wiki/File:Mortimer_Durand.jpg.

Choudary Ali (1895-1951) (public domain). Permission PD-

Pakistan. Source: Rahmat Ali, a biography, by K.K. Aziz. Cited on the Internet 27 September 2013 at: http://en.wikipedia.org/wiki/ File:Chrahmat.jpg.

Narendra Modi (Creative Commons Attribution). Cited on the Internet 27 September 2013 at: http://en.wikipedia.org/wiki/ File:Narendra_Damodardas_Modi.jpg.

Chapter 12: The Arab Room

Al-Azhar Mosque (public domain). Uploaded by Tentoila June 2006. Cited on the Internet 27 September 2013 at: http://en.wikipedia.org/ wiki/File:Al-Azhar_(inside)_2006.jpg.

Hagar and Ishmael (public domain). Painting by Grigoriy Ugryumov, 1785. Cited on the Internet 17 September 2013 at: http:// en.wikipedia.org/wiki/File:Hagar_and_Ishmael_in_desert_(Grigoriy_ Ugryumov).jpg.

Vasco da Gama (c.1469-1524), (public domain). Portrait of Vasco da Gama c. 1565. Cited on the Internet 27 September 2013 at: http:// en.wikipedia.org/wiki/File:Vasco_da_Gama_(Livro_de_Lisuarte_de_ Abreu).jpg.

Mohamed Bouazizi (public domain). Cited on the Internet 27 September 2013 at: http://en.wikipedia.org/wiki/File:Mohamed_ Bouazizi.jpg.

Father Botros Zakaria. Cited on the Internet 27 September 2013 at: https://www.facebook.com/photo.php?fbid=121620193403&set=a .436063683403.238209.121618628403&type=1&theater.

index